DATE DUE

~~6 '97~~			
~~AG 5 '99~~			
~~OC 26 '99~~			

DEMCO 38-296

Obsession and Culture

Obsession and Culture

A Study of Sexual Obsession in Modern Fiction

Andrew Brink

Madison • Teaneck
Fairleigh Dickinson University Press
London: Associated University Presses

:d University Presses
440 Forsgate Drive
Cranbury, NJ 08512

Associated University Presses
16 Barter St.
London WC1A 2AH, England

Associated University Presses
P.O. Box 338, Port Credit
Mississauga, Ontario
Canada L5G 4L8

Library of Congress Cataloging-in-Publication Data

Brink, Andrew.
    Obsession and culture : a study of sexual obsession in modern
fiction / Andrew Brink.
        p.   cm.
    Includes bibliographical references and index
    ISBN 0-8386-3596-2 (alk. paper)
    1. English fiction—20th century—History and criticism.
2. Obsessive-compulsive disorder in literature.   3. American
fiction—20th century—History and criticism.   4. Hesse, Hermann,
1877–1962—Criticism and interpretaion.   5. Fiction—Men authors—
History and criticism.   6.Man-woman relationships in literature.
7. Sex addiction in literature.   8. Men in literature.   I. Title.
PR888.O28B75   1996
823'.9109353—dc20   95-30472
                                                                          CIP

PRINTED IN THE UNITED STATES OF AMERICA

Contents

Acknowledgments

For their generous assistance I want to thank members of the Toronto Literature and Psychoanalysis Group where some of this material was presented. Drs. Stephen Liebow, Ronald Ruskin, and Mary Stewart commented helpfully on the Introduction. Professor R. Brian Parker, Trinity College, University of Toronto, commented valuably on three chapters. I am grateful to Dr. Anthony Storr who read the book in its entirety and made valuable suggestions and to David Holbrook who urged me to draw more explicitly the moral meaning of this study.

Former McMaster University students Judy Eaton and George Johnson greatly assisted with the fantasy analysis technique and with proofreading. Helen Brink gave unfailing support in clarifying concepts and in putting them into readable prose. Kris Wilson-Yang produced the text, commented helpfully, and made the tables more usable; she also prepared the index.

Permission to quote copyright material has been granted by: A. P. Watt Ltd. for H. G. Wells's *Experiment in Autobiography, Ann Veronica* and *The New Machiavelli;* Random House and Smith/Skolnik for Vladimir Nabokov's *Speak, Memory* and *Lolita;* Random House and Hamish Hamilton Ltd., for John Updike's *Midpoint and Other Poems, Self-Consciousness* and *Couples.*

Obsession and Culture

1

Introduction: The Obsessive Imagination in Writers

> All obsessions are dangerous.
> —A. S. Byatt, *Possession*

I

OBSESSION is a term in broad popular use whose value in studying culture has been underestimated. Although often used loosely to describe strong sexual wishes, it has not been recognized as a term with serious critical potential. For it to become so, the meaning of obsession needs to be defined in a way consistent with psychodynamic understanding. Only when this has been done will applications to the reading of literary texts show its power and pervasiveness as a term descriptive of a cultural dynamic, perhaps the basic cultural dynamic necessary to comprehend the chronic male drivenness that is so much a part of our times. These studies of the novel mainly concern Don Juanism, a type of obsessional behavior only passingly referred to in psychiatry textbooks under "sexual disorders." To make the case that obsessional Don Juanism is a major consideration in studying the novel as a purveyor of group fantasy, it is necessary to survey psychodynamic theories of obsessions beginning with Freud. My concern is not with the complexities of obsessive-compulsive behavior as a whole, but with the pressured male sexuality known as Don Juanism that appears to be a leading thematic concern with the twentieth century's most influential novelists.

The question of creativity and the obsessional character first came to my attention in chapter 8 of Anthony Storr's *The Dynamics of Creation* (London: Secker and Warburg, 1972), a statement that can be elaborated but not improved. Storr shows how the obsessional artist wishes to control his interpersonal environment, yet strives against the rigidity that stifles creative urges. His defensive rituals serve a positive function in preparing for creativity and in the creative act itself. The freedom to create is the artist's rite of safe access to emotional conflict, feelings so powerful that they must be approached by cautious indirection. The obsessive artist's rituals make available the themes and preoccupations of his inner world as expressive processes take over from fear. The wish for order becomes form in the novel, while its content is typically bipolar, channeling both love and punitive wishes toward objects of attachment. With remarkable frequency the Don Juanian quest drives the modern novel, which in turn illuminates our deepest wishes, avoidances, and tentative resolutions of conflict.

In selecting the five novelists—H. G. Wells, Hermann Hesse, Vladimir Nabokov, John Fowles, and John Updike—I bring together a group of influential writers from Europe, Britain, and America, spanning most of this century, whose work involves male-initiated obsessive-compulsive sexual behavior. While each writer is studied for himself, I hope that by bringing them together the diverse nature, yet unity, of obsessional themes will be appreciated. The selection of texts by these writers highlights fantasies of sexual pursuit and capture of young women by amorous yet hostile males. While their obsessions are "literary," they are also familiar from everyday media accounts of bizarre and often criminal sexual violence. In other words, the "fictions" I have chosen are directly relevant to understanding the fantasies that activate some of the most worrysome antisocial behavior. Other writers could have been chosen to make the same case: that literature is tied in with destructive individual and group fantasies whose meaning must be understood in the evolution of morality. Literary creativity is a good outcome of obsessional energy, and its presence in culture sometimes allows us to see deeply into ourselves. However, cultural studies lack the developmental and psychodynamic concepts necessary to make sense of what creative writers give us. In an era when proponents of critical theory strive for linguistic sophistication rather than trying to ferret out what an author is actually saying about what he feels, when authors are asked to disappear into their texts as "author functions," it seems worthwhile to show that there are rich veins of psychosocial meaning yet to be explored. If readers of novels are willing to equip themselves with psychodynamic concepts, they will find rewarding deposits of shared relational concerns. Sexual adventuring is surely a question of the day about which the most informed debate is needed. By bringing together the essential new insights about sexual obsessions, a fresh view is gained of the most puzzling features of these novelists' work and light is thrown on social problems that too often elude understanding.

It need hardly be repeated that we live in an era of severe destabilization of the traditional connectedness of persons in families. Separation and divorce statistics remind us that monogamous union and maintenance of family coherence are on trial. Novelists tap into latent awareness of the direction of social change, their novels often being early warning systems in distressed areas of human relations. Fiction gives an enjoyable but safe way of considering the outcomes of choices powered by sexuality. Following the consequences of desires acted on is the novel's proper work, and we look to the novel for disclosures of how to experience similar tensions and conflicts in our own lives. Male sexual pluralism, as it destabilizes the family and complicates child rearing by both parents, is a question so pervasive that it could be studied in several ways. Through the novel it is possible to study fantasy as localized by the author in his fictions and as latent in the minds of his readers. Writers are hypersensitive to shifts in the relational status quo mainly because of their own off-center needs and desires, which makes of them speculators about sexual change and sometimes even propagandists for it, along with being diagnosticians of social malaise. These studies therefore combine the psychobiography of authors with fantasy analysis of their texts to show how new awareness arises.

These are not therefore primarily literary studies but an attempt to bring into sharper focus those obsession-driven forces that continue to change our social, relational, and child-rearing expectations. I am trying to show the destabilizing forces that have transformed marriage and the family in an individualistic, pluralistic society. We seem to have agreed to a temporariness of relationship that radically alters traditional marital patterns and family cohesion over the generations. Reinvented at an alarming rate throughout this century, male-female relationships have never been more problematic. Novelists bring us closer to the living dynamics of these changes, but dynamics need the illumination offered by psychosocial studies whose purposes seem superficially different from those of art. If the present study seems critical of novelists' failures to recognize their own motives in promoting alternative forms of sexual relationship, it is not out of disrespect for their gifts of communication. While appreciating imaginative power, it is not necessary to accept it purely on the novelist's own terms.

By using standards of mental health and behavior other than those framed within the novel, it becomes possible to illuminate the relational struggles that concern us most. I therefore ask questions of the novelist's own childhood and relational experience that usually are seen as irrelevant to reading fiction. This task is especially difficult with living authors, and I have been careful not to go outside the information about themselves they have allowed into print. Speculation about the psychosocial meaning of autobiographical material could be expected when novelists considered its release. It not only takes courage to write novels embodying fantasy that is bound to be attributed to the author's own life, but also special courage to supply memoirs that stimulate speculation. Psychobiography reveals possible reasons why authors are susceptible to the fantasies governing their fictions; when gender confusion and relational breakdown are written about, we are bound to ask why this particular author should formulate experience in this way. By reconstructing the author in his work (however speculatively), fantasy becomes open and discussable in a way it cannot be if the text is declared sovereign. The chief risk of psychobiography is unwarranted speculation, especially about mothering; readers are left to judge the appropriateness of my comments in light of the theories presented.

Authors cannot be held solely responsible for the fantasy they purvey; they are agents, or delegates, of wishes latent in society as well as being self-interested. If we become moralistic with writers, then we also have to ask why it was we wanted to read those particular novels. Obviously we too were interested in the fantasy, little though we might wish to see it in action. The best theory of the so-called originality of writers who stir things up (perhaps transgressing moral values) is that of Paul Streitz in "Art and Psychohistory." Based on the psychohistorian Lloyd de Mause's theory of "psychoclass," holding that each generation has its own group fantasies mediated especially by its artists, Streitz writes that "The artist is only a cultural hero because he publicly confronts what is previously an unexpressed mass problem for the group."[1]

With child-rearing practices in flux, rapid change outmodes the former generation's solution to its anxieties so a new and seemingly "revolutionary" one has to be invented that may or may not give comfort to adolescents and young adults about to become parents themselves. According to Streitz, an artist speaking for a new "psychoclass" tries to solve emotional problems central to the group because they are the problems he (or she) personally faces. Thus the new work addresses a previously taboo subject and its expression, and the new art helps individuals to work out their anxieties without providing didactic answers. Fantasy and imagination play a large part in reaching the anxious inner states that need acknowledgment and pacification.

It is debatable which writers and artists best capture the anxieties and fantasies of any age group; no doubt clusters of writers, musicians, graphic artists, and others perform this function for sometimes unclearly defined or overlapping psychoclasses. Nonetheless, I believe that each writer studied here has special claim to defining an emergent "obsessional consciousness," a group hypervalence giving permission to think in terms of male pluralism, while counting its costs in the relationships fictionally portrayed. These studies are only examples of a vast phenomenon of culture emergent since at least the Renaissance. The writers are chosen for addressing taboo subjects with the highest artistry, promiscuity (or at least serial monogamy), pedophilia, and bisexuality being prominent among the distressing subjects for which they find fantasy embodiments. We cannot learn more than a modicum about what predisposed writers to obsessional ideation, let alone discover the extent of their imaginative representation of it. What writer wants to "tell all," not to mention become a subject of a test such as the Leyton Obsessional Inventory, which uses sixty-nine questions to assess subjective obsessional traits and symptoms? We must work less specifically than this. If we feel that these writers sometimes heighten anxiety rather than settling it, applications of psychodynamic theory may explain the unease. The age of being outraged at challenges to morality is over and a new one of trying to understand motives and meanings is opening. The novelist provides an invaluable source of concentrated relational material letting us in by "fiction" on the feelings and attitudes we recognize to be our own, however little we may like them when judged by other standards. As each of these novelists opens to view a little more male obsessional behavior, we are enabled to judge by the best psychological standards available the destructiveness of particular behavior. To writers themselves—whose address to interpersonal questions is sharpened by the "confessional" mode in which they often write—we may express gratitude for their courageous disclosures.

II

A background for Don Juanism can be sketched. Psychology and psychiatry agree on the main features of obsessions, with psychoanalysis tending to see fantasy as prefiguring obsessional ideation and compulsive behavior. An obsession is an intrusive recurring mental event—a thought, an idea, a feeling, or sensation, while compulsion is a consciously repeated behavior such as counting or checking, being attracted to or avoiding something or someone. The obsessive mental intrusion arouses anxiety against which counter measures must be taken, that is: "Last time I drove my car I'm sure I hit a child: I'll have to check with the police" or "I can't get that pretty little girl/beautiful boy out of my mind; I'll follow him/her home from school and offer some candy— but that would be criminal!" Because the obsessive feels strongly aggressive in a way he has been brought up to believe is unacceptable, countermeasures are taken not only against the urge to act, but also against the thought itself. The defenses of isolation, undoing, and reaction formation are invoked to make the feelings disappear or to convert them into morally acceptable forms. A struggle of conscience or outright denial may occur with the most ego-alien obsessions. As the irrationality of an obsessive thought is realized, a wish to transform it from ego-dystonic into something more acceptable may occur. Rather than stereotyped rigidity and wish for total control, the creative writer finds release through fantasy in metaphor and narrative. As Storr observes, rituals release unconscious conflicts that become available for symbolic expression and restructuring. When personality becomes more supple than rigid, increasingly daring play with fantasy is possible. The texture of the created product is enriched. Beyond this, a moral wish for repair of the effects of destructive wishes may also emerge, counteracting the spillage of hostile feelings. Play promotes some mental representation of the predisposing trauma and, providing the trauma is not too severe, its articulation to the person's attachment system can be improved. Of course the more successful the mental representation an artist achieves, the more he is able to tolerate, enriching the texture of his products. Such persons, able to make creative use of adverse early experiences, may be called "open obsessionals," in contrast the closed type of obsessional personality that channels anxiety into rigid and controlling relational styles. The fantasy in fiction no doubt assists the "open obsessional" author to reorganize repressed experiences of his or her own—an assumption of these studies.

Because anxiety and guilt are so strong in obsessive states, the urge to confess feelings and to compensate for or "repair" real or imagined damage to women can be very strong. The urge to confess reparatively may lead to writing or otherwise expressively symbolizing inner conflict. As direct repair of obscure relational feelings is impossible, obsessionals of the "open" type tend to create imagery around their fantasies from upwellings whose source may at first seem obscure. Fantasies will be discussed as pleasurable reparative creations of the psyche, assuming they are also compromise solutions to guilt over conflicted aggressive feelings toward early attachment objects, especially the mother. Mental representations of ego conflicts in fantasy can greatly assist in reorganizing feelings about the meaning of life—especially with the help of analysis. Analyzed or not, obsessive fantasies are maleable, adaptable, and workable at will on the conscious level by shaping them into literary fictions. An internal psychic process is initiated around obsessional fantasies by which ego-alien feelings are accepted and to some extent controlled, while being transformed into a language of anxiety and esthetic resolution understandable by a whole psychoclass. Private conflict thus becomes public understanding, potentially useful to a culture-at-large otherwise baffled about the meaning of its troubles. For this to happen, the craft of fictionalizing must be of a high order, so that particular feelings about relationships are heightened by formal containment. We seem better able deal with raw feelings when they are thus distanced in "as if" situations and formally embodied by the writer's skills.

Sigmund Freud gave the concept of obsession a specific psychological meaning in his paper "Further Remarks on the Neuropsychoses of Defence" (1896b), written while the seduction theory was being reconsidered. Freud commented to Fliess in October 1895: "Hysteria is the consequence of a presexual sexual scare. Obsessional neurosis is the consequence of a presexual sexual pleasure which later transforms itself into self-reproach."[2] Self-reproaches return from repression as unshakable obsessions covering defensively for guilt and remorse; as hysteria and obsessions are said to have similar sources, we must assume that Freud meant that many or most obsessions are products of pleasurable parental sexual stimulation. Freud hit on a great truth, which prudence caused him to retract, a point that, to Freud's displeasure, his follower Sandor Ferenczi developed. While Freud described a pathology that may arise from the Oedipus complex based on the male child's erotic fantasies about his mother, Ferenczi stressed direct sexual trauma as the leading pathogenic agent. Formulated most fully in his last clinical paper "Confusion of Tongues Between Adults and Children" (1932), Ferenczi held that obsessive love when forced on a child has much the same pathogenic consequence as lack of love—a split in the personality. The parent as aggressor is internalized in the ego and will seriously deflect the child's development. This remarkable insight prefigured revisionist psychodynamic theory, from Ian Suttie and Ronald Fairbairn onward to the recent work of John Bowlby and Alice Miller, in which actual developmental failures (rather than fantasies solely produced by the child) are seen as the source of psychopathology. Ferenzci saw that unwanted adult eroticism can deeply traumatize very young children, a view that appears in his account of obsessions: "The obsessional neurosis constitutes a relapse of the mental life to that stage of child development characterized ... by there being as yet no inhibiting, postponing, reflecting thought-activity interposed between wishing and acting, the wish-fulfilment movement following spontaneously and unhesitating on the wishing—an averting movement away from something disagreeable, or an approach towards something agreeable. A part of the mental life, more or less removed from consciousness, thus remains with the obsessional patient ... on this level in consequence of an arrest in development (fixation) and makes wishing equivalent to acting because ... this repressed portion of the mental life was not able to learn the difference between the two activities."[3] Although it is not spelled out here, trauma is implicit, as is the bipolarity of splitting between disagreeable and pleasurable affects.

For the clearest phenomenology of obsessions, we must return to Freud. Strongly sadistic wishes, partially converted by reaction formation into the moral opposites of love and concern, are present in obsessions. For example, sadism may appear like that in Freud's "Rat Man," Ernest Lanzer, a twenty-nine-year-old lawyer, in whom all analyzed feelings of love and hate were directed to the patient's father. It is well to ask why Freud chose not to say more about the Rat Man's mothering as a probable contribution to his obsessional disorder, but this material was not reported.[4] That Freud had difficulty with feelings about his own mother helps explain why he resorted to mythologically based theories, such as Oedipal fantasy, rather than look at the actual circumstances of being mothered. As Freud did not share Ferenczi's passionate wish to cure patients of the effects of early trauma, his emphasis is more on their etiology. Obsessions are seen as thinking disorders, with the inspired term *deliria* offered to typify the extreme absorption and constraint, the almost trancelike condition that occurs when obsessions gather. As will appear, literary fantasy can produce a sort of esthetic delirium making forbidden wishes pleasurable in fictional narratives.

Freud described obsessional phenomena several times but never with his initial boldness about causality in childhood instinctual overstimulation. Some of his most insightful remarks concern obsessions on religion, with ritual seen as fending off fears of mortality. This appears in "Obsessive Actions and Religious Practices" (1907), while in "Inhibitions, Symptoms and Anxiety" (1926), he saw obsessional ceremonies as a way to overcome regressive temptations toward masturbation and to transcend Oedipal castration fears. Allied to such ordinary events as going to sleep, washing, dressing, and so forth, obsessions become incapacitating if conflicts over "looking" and "knowing" are severe. To prevent return of repressed feelings, especially those with hostile content, thought is made omnipotent and a supermorality develops—the basis of reparative urges, it might be added. The obsessional defense against depression has an obvious civilizing influence, but it is notoriously unstable with the "return of the repressed" conflict a certainty sometime during life. Conscientiousness, readiness to feel shame and even self-mistrust are socially valuable, and even endearing features of the defense, but they bring only pseudohealth.

Freud's most useful contribution to a theory of obsessionality is his bipolar model of the split, ambivalent ego. There is no better structural rule of thumb than this model, and it has considerable utility in describing the symbolizations found in literature. In "Notes Upon a Case of Obsessional Neurosis" (1909), Freud remarked that the true significance of compulsive acts in obsessional neurosis is "in their being a representation of a conflict between two opposing impulses of approximately equal strength: and hitherto I have invariably found that this opposition has been one between love and hate." Explaining further, Freud wrote:

> The necessary condition for the occurrence of such a strange state of affairs in a person's erotic life appears to be that at a very early age, somewhere in the prehistoric period of his infancy, the two opposites should have been split apart and one of them, usually the hatred, have been repressed.[5]

This explanation gives a picture of alternating feelings (possibly oscillating or reverberating) directed toward the same ostensible love object: the incompletely relinquished mother-lover girlfriend or wife, the girlfriend's mother, and so forth. She is wanted, even cherished, but pushed away, praised (sometimes excessively), and blamed (often unfairly) for real and imagined faults. In severe obsessions, she is first idealized but ultimately denigrated only to be replaced with a new idealized love object whose fate is to go through the same cycle of punitive pseudoattachment. Ironically, the popular term *madonna/whore complex* typecasts women rather than describing the split male ego. Women, of course, are subject to much the same defensive dynamic, but it is with the ambivalent fantasies of male writers we are concerned here. The cultural message given by the creative members of a psychoclass to their troubled contemporaries is that women are objects of love-hate.

The relational background of the bipolar, ambivalent ego is better described by Jung than by Freud. Less conceptually rigorous, Jung has the advantage of putting clearly, in human terms such as a novelist might use, the mother-son relationship most often associated with the obsessional personality in males. In "Marriage as a Psychological Relationship" (1925), Jung writes:

> Take the case of a mother who deliberately keeps herself unconscious so as not to disturb the pretense of a "satisfactory" marriage. Unconsciously she will bind her son to her, more or less as a substitute for a husband. The son, if not forced directly into homosexuality, is compelled to modify his choice in a way that is contrary to his true nature. He may, for instance marry a girl who is obviously inferior to his mother and therefore unable to compete with her; or he will fall for a woman of a tyrannical and overbearing disposition, who may perhaps succeed in tearing him away from his mother.[6]

But Jung also seems to have pulled back from, or at least softened, the theory of mother-inflicted sexual trauma on sons, when in "Aion: Phenomenology of the Self" (1951), he sees the son's attraction to the mother, "the star-crowned woman whom the dragon pursues," as beguilingly mythic.[7]

More direct than either Freud or Jung is the novelist D. H. Lawrence in "Fantasia of the Unconscious" written in 1921. Like Jung, Lawrence struggled with a powerful mother whose guiding will for her son is chronicled in the masterful *Sons and Lovers* (1913). In Lawrence's later riposte to psychoanalysis, he hits on the characteristic interaction leading to the male obsessional personality, although choosing not to use any such technical label:

At the very crucial moment when she should be coming to a state of pure equilibrium and rest with her husband, she turns rabidly against rest or peace or equilibrium or husband in any shape or form, and demands more love, more love, a new sort of lover, one who will "understand" her. And as often as not she turns to her son. . . . Seeking, seeking the fulfilment in the deep passional self; diseased with self-consciousness and sex in the head, foiled by the very loving weakness of the husband who has not the courage to withdraw into his own stillness and singleness, and put the wife under the spell of his fulfilled decision; the unhappy women beats about for her insatiable satisfaction, seeking whom she may devour. And usually, she turns to her child. Here she provokes what she wants. Here, in her own son who belongs to her, she seems to find the last perfect response for which she is craving. He is a medium to her, she provokes from him her own answer. So she throws herself into a last great love for her son, a final and fatal devotion, that which would have been the richness and strength of her husband and is poison to the boy. . . . If you want to see the real desirable wife-spirit, look at a mother with her boy of eighteen. How she serves him, how she stimulates him, how her true female self is his, is wife-submissive to him as never, never it could be to a husband. This is the quiescent, flowering love of a mature woman. It is the very flower of a woman's love: sexually asking nothing, asking nothing of the beloved, save that he shall be himself, and that for his living he shall accept the gift of her love. This is the perfect flower of married love, which a husband should put in his cap as he goes forward into the future in his supreme activity. For the husband, it is a great pledge, and a blossom. For the son also it seems wonderful. The woman now feels for the first time as a true wife might feel. And her feeling is towards her son.

Or, instead of mother and son, read father and daughter.

And then what? The son gets on swimmingly for a time, till he is faced with the actual fact of sex necessity. He gleefully inherits his adolescence and the world at large, without an obstacle in his way, mother-supported, mother-loved. Everything comes to him in glamour, he feels he sees wondrous much, understands a whole heaven, mother-stimulated. Think of the power which a mature woman thus infuses into her boy. He flares up like a flame in oxygen. No wonder they say geniuses mostly have great mothers. They mostly have sad fates.

And then?—and then, with this glamorous youth? What is he actually to do with his sensual, sexual self? Bury it? Or make an effort with a stranger? For he is taught, even by his mother, that his manhood must not forego sex. Yet he is linked up in ideal love already, the best he will ever know.[8]

Portrayed with incomparable force of feeling in *Sons and Lovers*, Paul Morel's struggle to free himself of his mother's dominating ministrations catches exactly the theoretical point made by Freud and Jung. We do not need to debate Lawrence's indebtness to them to say simply that nowhere in literature is split love-hate of women so compellingly studied as in Paul's attempted love for Miriam and then Clara set against the eroticized claims of his mother. Paul's drunken, irresponsible father is a miner associated with pits and darkness, while his mother, of a better class, is associated with flowers and light. The powerful unconscious fantasy of a mother-son attraction that runs through *Sons and Lovers* itself emerges into the clear light of day and of understanding in Paul's anguish as his mother slips away in her final illness. Her mercy killing, Paul administering a drug to control pain, leaves him distraught to the point of suicide—as clear a revelation of the destructive power of ambivalence as may be found in fiction. His capacity for charm and cruelty as a lover, on-again, his off-again fluctuations of feeling, the sheer violence of inner conflict as it damages the uncomprehending Miriam, come together as a demonstration of what psychoanalysis would see as a leading cause of human unhappiness.

From experimental psychology and biological psychiatry to psychodynamic theory there is emerging agreement about childhood traumas being the most probable origin of later obsessions. A recent textbook in psychiatry suggests that brain trauma in traumatic births is implicated in later obsessions.[9] An experimental psychologist Daniel Wegner writes: "Many of the thoughts that people wish to suppress seem to be echoes, mental rehearsals of earlier events."[10] Wegner gives examples of rape and incest, but of course lesser and earlier traumas may also be involved in producing obsessions and compulsions. Chronic repetitions of post-traumatic feelings and thoughts are said to be the result of an incomplete emotional reaction to the trauma, which indeed may occur in a minute but last a lifetime. When traumas occur early, especially at the hands of a loved and trusted attachment figure, it is especially difficult to disentangle later obsessional reworkings of the feelings. They may repeat endlessly and uselessly without the sufferer knowing their origins. The desire to suppress a feeling or thought is enough to set going "indulgence cycles" that more or less automate unwanted thoughts and impulses.[11] The psychologist H. R. Beech proposes a two-part formation of obsessions: "a predisposition to states of pathological arousal and some mechanism by which such a state leads to morbid thoughts and aberrant behaviour."[12] Beech anticipates attachment theory when he writes of "exaggerated arousals" followed by further arousals that prevent decrements; with an insufficient recovery period, or tendency to slow recuperation, the organism cannot avoid habituation. Thus learning theory makes its contribution but without saying how the system might clear itself of the unpleasant effects programmed into it. Wegner, however, writes that early trauma may start in motion a natural process of self-healing, of self-correction. "The trauma will not be overcome until the emotion is fully expressed, and rethinking it is required. . . . If obsession is a way of getting ourselves used to a trauma, then we should probably allow ourselves to do it," Wegner writes.[13] It is best for the obsessional emotion, or cluster of emotions, to enter the stream of consciousness as close as possible to its original form rather than remain a hidden usurper and deflector of energies. Of course with fantasy hiding the original unpleasant emotion, the fantasy requires decoding. This places the critic of fiction in an unusual position—having to appreciate the elaboration of fantasy as art while realizing that the most powerfully authentic fantasies are disguises for deeper unwanted emotions of early childhood, in all probability the author's own unprocessed intrapsychic conflict.

We are only at the beginning of adequate studies of traumatic parenting (especially impingement by mothers) and of attempts within criticism of the arts to understand and repair malformed assumptive models of interpersonal reality. Scientific work on obsessions is just one part of a much larger enquiry into the sources of emotional and relational maladaptedness. Criticism of the arts as social indicators will be much improved when the range and varying etiologies of obsessional phenomena are better appreciated. Scepticism about psychobiographical formulations is bound to continue until full studies of creative persons' attachments in early childhood are possible. The need for caution in developing psychobiographies of creative people is well stated by William McKinley Runyan in *Life Histories and Psychobiography, Explorations in Theory and Method.* As theory and application tend to develop together, it is well to keep in mind the criteria of trustworthy experimental method. For psychobiography to find its way forward, it is especially important to keep in touch with developments in attachment theory, as Runyan recognizes.[14]

The theory of attachment and loss proposed by John Bowlby and elaborated by Mary Ainsworth, Mary Main, and others will go far to dispel doubts about the lasting effects of early parenting, especially mothering. By observing infant and childhood attachment behavior with the mother, the development of defensive strategies to protect against losses or impingements can be predicted. This could be a boon for psychobiographers who usually have to work retrospectively by conjecture. They will more confidently be able to work back to the adaptational precursors of later psychological conflicts that appear coded into the products of creativity. The artist is likely to be one of those persons described by Bowlby as "anxiously attached" to mother and other caregivers. A review of the most recent research is in order.

Attachment theorists describe three major attachment styles at twelve to eighteen months that predict later child and adult behavior: Secure (B), Anxious Avoidant (A), and Anxious Resistant (C). Infants in the secure group are at ease with the primary caregiver, usually the mother, able to express feelings directly, and, confident of parental help, they take initiatives. Infants in the avoidant group are distant, avoiding intimacy with the mother, and are likely to be compulsively compliant with her wishes. By contrast, infants in the resistant group are markedly ambivalent, alternating angry, pouty behavior with winning helplessness to manipulate the mother. Their dominant strategy at preschool age is coercive, a coping mechanism that is likely to lead to a preoccupied, entangled relationship with one, or both, parents into adulthood. There is a further Disorganized/Disoriented (D) category in which relational strategies with mother or caregiver, are confused and fearful. In the B condition, mothering has been sensitive, direct, and consistent whereas in the A condition, mothering has been distant, interrupted (loss), or perhaps intrusive. In the C condition, mothering has been unpredictable, successively over-stimulating, understimulating, and withdrawn. In the D condition, there is likely to have been outright abuse.

Whereas the adult form of secure attachment in infancy is autonomy of personality (freedom to think and feel accurately about early attachments), that of the avoidant is dismissive of attachment, deactivating the frustrated attachment system to force feelings inward. Suppression of feelings results in reliance on cognition rather than on feelings to get along in relationships. In the avoidant strategy, feeling is thus impoverished, dismissed into an inner world of thwarted attachments and angry resentment at unfulfilled needs. As noted, the resistant or ambivalent mode of attachment leaves a personality confused and preoccupied by past family relationships or experiences. These persons may be passive and vague, fearful and overwhelmed, or angry and conflicted, given to emotional displays and not effectively analytical about them. As the resistant child has both sought and fended off maternal attachment, the emotionally tangled adult is caught in contradictory feelings that take on obsessive bipolarity. In strongly motivated persons, this can lead to pressured drivenness that is difficult to resolve into calmer effectiveness.

The creative personality, called obsessional by Storr, and which I call the "open obsessional," does not completely answer to any of the newer attachment categories arising from the studies of John Bowlby, Mary Ainsworth, or Mary Main. The male open obsessional personality cannot have been securely attached to his mother, but neither was he fully avoidant or resistant to her. She was both the source of excitement and of possible psychological capture. This mother may have had a wonderful gift of imaginative stimulation to offer, but there were also unaccountable absences and humiliations.

Some hybrid form of attachment classification is needed for these troubled but enriched personalities that become the sort of creative writers under study here. The obsessional has strongly avoidant features in that he holds feelings about attachment experience self-protectively within the imagination, and his openness to them is an achievement at which he has worked. At worst, avoidant persons are escapist, obsessing over fantasies that they dare not communicate and must rationalize because they are perverse or perhaps dangerous. (John Fowles's Clegg in *The Collector* is one of these.) More constructively, the open obsessional eases his pain by recognizing it to be his own and in need of symbolic expression rather than translation into actions hurtful to others. Avoided feelings from earliest attachment experiences are thus accepted somewhat; but a resistant, ambivalent tendency is also noticeable. This obsessively bi-polar fluctuation between acceptance and rejection of attachment readily codes itself into language describing feelings about having been anxiously attached. There is a strong urge to rework these incompatible feelings into a manageable pattern as in an esthetically pleasing composition.

Attachment terminology is difficult and still much in flux, but the best account of this hybrid attachment style is being developed by the American psychologist Patricia Crittenden, who first described the A/C classification in 1988. According to Crittenden, the A/C (Avoidant/Resistant or Dependent types in Ainsworth's and Main's scheme of personality organization, which Crittenden alternatively terms Defended/Coercive) is needed to fill out the anxious attachment modes of infant and childhood adaptation that leaves adults preoccupied with feelings associated with their earliest maternal attachments. Such personalities fluctuate between A and C states, unable to integrate avoidance of attachment with entangled feelings about it. Adopted as defensive strategies against overwhelming affect, avoidance and resistance do not easily coalesce. Crittenden writes:

> Life is a constant process of swinging between sets of unmet expectations that require access to the missing, defended-against information for resolution. Thus, the A/C exists in a near constant state of tension caused by the collision of two separate world views and associated patterns of behaviour that are not integrated. Each clash, however, provides a new opportunity for the mind to access and hold concurrently both views and, possibly, to use each source of information to correct and modify the other, thus, achieving an integration. (Private communication)

Distress is bound to be great, yet creatively mediated outcomes are possible for those A/Cs gifted with literary or artistic talent. Based on Crittenden's A/C finding, there are both imaginative and behavioral aspects for the creative artist but the imaginative predominate. Typically the creative artist's personality is A/c, with avoidance dominant over the more ambivalent resistant tendency, which in itself carries a bipolar, sometimes obsessional feature. The uppercase *A* (Avoidant) betokens inner imaginative conservation and reworking of dismissed attachment feelings, while the lowercase *c* (Resistant or Coercive) betokens oscillating positive and negative feelings about early experiences with parents. Because these feelings lead behaviorally to unsatisfactory ways of relating, they beg for change. For the artist or writer change is attempted by displaced symbolic reenactments of ambivalent feelings, including obsessive-compulsive sexuality. The reconciliation and integration of ambivalent feelings imperfectly sought in daily life are more amenable to symbolic handling.

Crittenden comments that this dynamic state of mind is more capable of enriching reality than is that of the securely attached person, and that the A/Cs are continually challenged to "re-envision or re-model reality." This explanation gives a new precision to the obsessional bipolar dynamic proposed by Freud and other psychoanalytic theorists. She is further led to argue for a Dismissing/Preoccupied adult attachment classification stemming from the A/C personality organization of infancy and childhood, an important advance for studies such as this one, which nonetheless retains the term *obsessional* because of its longer currency and combined technical and popular meanings.[15]

Links between attachment theory and recent work by Nancy

Andreasen and Kay Redfield Jamison on manic-depressive disorder and creativity are needed. The biochemistry of mood change in relation to affect regulation in attachment experience is just beginning to be explored by attachment theorists. Jamison's thesis that a disproportionate number of writers and artists are depressive, or manic-depressive (often with obsessive features), needs review in light of findings that failures of infant and child attachment precede dysfunctional, chemically mediated mood swings, especially in the C (Resistant) group. Jamison, like Andreasen before her, takes little account of the powerfully mood-forming early infant-mother experiences that attachment theorists study. Jamison is a genetic determinist, for whom the manic-depressive artist is only minimally subject to environmental influences, acting under "sealed orders."[16] Although attachment theorists have not yet ventured into the area of creativity and cultural studies, their arguments are likely to be more persuasive in the long run than those of psychiatrists limited by the dogmas of genetic and neurochemical determinism.

Meanwhile promising studies in the phenomenology and etiology of obsessions in the arts can be found. Three examples can be mentioned. In *On Obsession* (1948), Erwin Straus commented on the eighteenth-century writer Jonathan Swift's scatological obsessions as seen in his poems and in *Gulliver's Travels*. Straus finds obsessions, whose origin is in early childhood, typically distorting adult sexuality.[17] Martha Wolfenstein's "The Image of the Lost Parent" (1973) plausibly attributes much obsessive imagery in the paintings of the surrealist René Magritte to seeing the partly clad body of his mother who committed suicide by drowning when Magritte, her son, was thirteen.[18] According to Lenore C. Terr in "Childhood Trauma and the Creative Product" (1987), Magritte's pictures repeatedly dwell on moments of panic re-inacting the original trauma of seeing his mother's body. She writes of the artistic product reflecting trauma in two ways: "in the literal re-creation of the artist's experience, and in the establishment of a tone of trauma—of helplessness, confinement and panic."[19] To the study of Magritte she adds the psychological profiles of Poe, Wharton, Hitchcock, and Bergman whose powerful imagery reflects various sorts of childhood trauma. When it comes to outright fear and panic, we all belong to the susceptible psychoclass, and Terr rightly points out the "contagion" that spreads from the brilliantly expressive imagery of these artists. Other studies could be cited, but these are enough to show the promise of a psychobiographical method whose reliability can be improved.

III

Let us take bearings on the emergence of obsessional phenomena in seventeenth-century England and Europe. Lloyd de Mause's psychogenic theory of history attributes sexual discontents in the Renaissance to an "ambivalent" mode of child rearing. That is, parents tended neither to reject nor to fully care for children, leaving them anxious and prone to depression. Typically depressed by irrational guilt, the ambivalently raised male has an insatiable need for love, status, and sex, along with enormous superego demands.[20] Of course, such a mode of child rearing can persist in a culture much beyond the period of emergence when it produces its first conspicuous psychoclass. An explanation for the emergence of an obsessional psychoclass might be found in a shift from agrarian to urban life in which fathers are separated from the family unit by work, leaving infant and child care mainly to women. Such a theory is beyond the scope of this study, with the following remarks restricted to a brief phenomenology of obsessions in the arts during the Renaissance and seventeenth century. Driven and agonistic (given to confessional agonizing over psychological conflict), modern man harks back to some notable forebearers.

Described as a classical Oedipal situation by the psychoanalyst Ernest Jones (1949) and others, Shakespeare's Hamlet shows a prototypical obsessional character posed with the problem of doing justice after a crime. Torn by contrary feelings about his usurping uncle, murdered father, and complicitous mother, Hamlet agonizes over his course of action. Lengthy deliberation and delayed action show the obsessional mind at work. Matricidal feelings, together with cruel ambivalence toward his lover Ophelia, prefigure the troubled sexuality we find in the fictions to be studied. It is perhaps significant that obsessions should so powerfully declare themselves on the Elizabethan stage. The earliest English psychological use of the term *obsession* occurs in Ben Jonson's play *Volpone* (1605), and it has to do with a character being possessed by Satan.

Obsessive Satanism emerges with much greater force in John Milton's biblical epic *Paradise Lost* (1667). Milton's portrayal of vulnerable Adam and Eve in Paradise under attack by wily Satan answers almost exactly to the LaPlanche and Pontalis summary of Freud on obsessional neurosis. As Satan closes in on his victims, he exhibits inner conflict "through symptoms which are described as compulsive-obsessive ideas, compulsions towards undesirable acts, struggles against these thoughts and tendencies, exorcistic rituals etc.—and through a mode of thinking which is characterized in particular by rumination, doubt and scruples and which leads to inhibitions of thought and actions."[21] Like Hamlet, Satan is most self-punitively tortured in thinking about women whom he both loves and hates. It is Eve he erotically beguiles, leaving her to bring about Adam's fall. He is a seducer who craves forbidden knowledge and thus can be assimilated both to Don Juan and to Faust.

Obsessive eroticism is found in much English Renaissance poetry, including Shakespeare's *Sonnets* (1609), with their bisexual ambiguity, and in John Donne's *Songs and Sonnets* (1633), many of which brilliantly argue for male promiscuity with women. The principal contemporary psychologist of driven, ambivalent sexuality is Robert Burton, whose *Anatomy of Melancholy* (1621f) reviews erotic pathology in "Symptoms of Love." Obsessionalism is eroticized, as Burton saw "for love is a perpetual flux, angor animi (mental anguish); a warfare, militat omnis amans (every lover is in the wars); a grievous wound is love still, and a lover's heart is Cupid's quiver, a consuming fire."[22] These sentiments might well be the complaint of Don Juan, who emerged in Spain slightly later.

Obsessional phenomena as they appeared in myth and literature before there was a psychology to explain them can be mentioned briefly. These examples show some prototypical versions of male obsessional distress—expanded on later in discussions of the novels. Eros, son of Aphrodite and Hermes, was called a "wild boy," a sort of sexual outlaw whose uncontrolled passion disturbed the order of ancient Greek society. Eros was sometimes said to have a brother called Anteros, an antithetical figure who opposed love. Thus from early mythology Western civilization has recognized split and polarized love. Highly elaborated oppositional accounts of love and sex are found in Greek and Roman mythology before the advent of Christian morality with its emphasis on carnal sin and long before the attempts of Freud and his followers put matters in psychological developmental terms.

Reformers of sexual morality, with its heritage of repressive Pauline doctrine, looked to the Greeks for freeing precedents. The banner of Eros was carried in the twentieth-century rebellion against the sexual strictures of both Roman Catholic and Protestant churches. Eros might be termed the pagan patron-god of a pseudoreligion of erotic love that has come to characterize Western society. Prophets of a freer sexuality than that allowed by their Christian upbringing turned to "Nature," as understood by Darwinians, and to Eros, along with exemplars of erotic freedoms in Eastern religions. The highly influential *Love's Coming of Age* (1896), by Edward Carpenter, shows these liberationist features in arguing for freer sexual expression in both heterosexual and homosexual modes. From the turn of the century, Havelock Ellis's *Studies in the Psychology of Sex* had an emancipating influence on those who felt restricted by the doctrine of conventional marriage and procreation. Increasingly, fiction joined the campaign for freer sexuality, that of D. H. Lawrence and H. G. Wells being in the forefront, whereas Bertrand Russell used his brilliance as an essayist to purvey a new morality outside the Christian sanctions that he militantly opposed. In *Marriage and Morals* (1929) Russell argued for occasional adultery in marriage, addressing once again the problem of jealousy as Carpenter had done in *Love's Coming of Age*.

A full account of the momentous shift in moral standards during the twentieth century would have to consider the changing status of women and the upheavals of two world wars. Will it be possible for social historians to study on the small scale the shifts in family and individual morality, articulating them to large-scale political events? The study of obsessional themes in literature indicates why it is necessary to try. In the novels studied, typically there is a male obsessional hero bent on sexual conquest of some sort. Whether or not difficulties with his own parenting are developed by the novelist, he feels moral conflict over his wishes to pursue and dominate women. Richard Remington in Wells's *The New Machiavelli*, Harry Haller in Hermann Hesse's *Steppenwolf*, Humbert Humbert in Vladimir Nabokov's *Lolita*, Ferdinand Clegg in John Fowles's *The Collector*, and John Updike's Piet Hanema in *Couples*, all testify to a Don Juan fantasy in a post-Freudian setting.

The Don Juan legend, mainly descriptive and moral, is worthy of consideration as evidence of the troubling cultural pervasiveness of male promiscuity—the kind of driven sexuality attributable to maternal overstimulation. Don Juan's heroic phase is surely over, having spent its main force between the dramatic rebellion of Milton's Satan, the romantic exploits of Lord Byron's questing hero and G. B. Shaw's clever reversal of Don Juan's pursuit of women in *Man and Superman*. For Shaw in 1903, woman was the pursuer and effectively so. More recent Don Juans, notably those of the novelists J. P. Donleavy and Milan Kundera, lack the heroic powers of their predecessors, perhaps in response to the Women's Movement that had already declared itself in Shaw's time. Wildly outrageous in behavior, Donleavy's Sebastian Dangerfield in *The Ginger Man* (1955) is almost a self-parody. The womanizing Tomas in Kundera's *The Unbearable Lightness of Being* (1984) is to be taken more seriously, yet he is a figure of pathos. Psychoanalysis may have had a hand in the demotion of Don Juan as hero; in studies by Otto Rank, an early follower of Freud, he became a candidate for the couch.

Rank does little with the origin of Don Juan in Tirso de Molina's *El Burlador da Savilla* (1630), turning directly to Mozart's *Don Giovanni*, which he saw performed at the Vienna opera in 1921. Mozart's enigmatic opera has taxed the best critical minds, and not everyone will agree that its secrets yield entirely to psychoanalysis. Nonetheless Rank identified anxiety about the mother and birth as central to Mozart's construction of the myth. He more than hints at the mother-son tensions identified by Dorothy Dinnerstein and others as being at the basis of Western sexual discontents. According to Rank, aggressive male sexuality is an emotionally loaded attempt to return to the mother, overcoming a "birth trauma." Anxiety about women—both idealizing and denigrating them—arises from the male's inability to return to the mother who gave him life and from whom he was painfully separated. Rank thought that society evolved into a patriarchy because of painful memories of the birth trauma. Mothers are loved and feared, with fear displaced onto fathers, leaving ambivalence toward the mother pervading relations with women and all of male-created culture. Rank saw the Don Juan legend as central to the Western psyche because it sums up the real meaning of Oedipal anxiety: Don Juan's seduction of many women issues from the son's inability to resolve his love and hate for his mother. This reminds us of Freud's basic schematizing of the obsessional defense as a pulsating opposition between love and hate of the same object. Don Juan's deception of men to get at women betokens his rivalry with the father. Rank speculated on causality, writing: "As a prototype of the etiological motivation, one would cite the poem of Byron (1819–24), who had the hero grow up under the influence of an overly affectionate mother and an unfaithful, plainly 'donjuanesque' father, about whose escapades the mother kept a 'catalogue.'"[23]

In the view of David Winter (editor of Rank's *Don Juan* legend), Don Juan's peculiar combination of frustration and pleasure stems from "a special kind of ambivalence, or alternating behavior, in the mother; she mixes both rejection or frustration with affection or pleasure in such a way that the child cannot separate them. . . . In short, the child cannot develop a consistent and un-ambivalent attitude toward the mother, nor later toward women in general." As Winter continues, this ambivalence, newly an-nounced by Molina, must trace to some decisive change in child rearing in sixteenth-century Spain, and probably in all of Europe since the legend so readily entered the collective imagination. Winter points out that Don Juan's womanizing and bragging inso-lence is really a drive for power over both men and women.[24] The Don is a "ladies' man," an agonistic overcontrolled son who works out his psychological destiny through seductive exploitations of women as lover-victims. His literary legacy is greater, and often more subtle, than has been appreciated.

IV

With the revival of Jocasta Mothering, Freud's rejected trauma theory of hysteria and obsessions was also revived. Observation and research took the question of how obsessions develop beyond harsh toilet training and, as Freud later saw it, influence of the death instinct, into styles of mothering and parenting. Rather than impersonal processes, the influence of actual attachments began to be considered, with Ernest Jones in 1923 echoing Freud on the bad effects of toilet training and on the internalizing of love and hate but adding:

> This curious phenomenon becomes more intelligible when we re-member that the hate, according to my view, is first developed towards the imago of all later love objects, the mother herself; thus the capacity to love is impeded or paralysed at its very inception. It is only to be expected that any one whose love towards the mother has from the beginning alternated with hate should show the same alternation to-ward all secondary love-objects.[25]

This remarkable statement sets a course for all later investigation of misaligned mother-son attachments, Jones noting that the inci-dence of obsessional neuroses is higher in men than in women and that the boy's hatred of his mother at the anal stage compli-cates Oedipal developments in a way unlike that which occurs with girls. Returning to Freud's earliest view of 1896, that seduction of children by older persons, with pleasure out-balancing pain, led to later obsessional defense against recollecting pain, Jones cen-ters the trauma theory on mothering. Working with the actual case histories of many children, Anna Freud followed Jones, writing in *The Ego and the Mechanisms of Defence* (1937) that:

> in obsessional neurosis, as in hysteria, hatred of the mother and penis-envy are in the first instance repressed. Subsequently the ego secures itself against their return by means of reaction formations.[26]

Sandor Rado is among later psychoanalytic thinkers who see obsessional behavior as object relational, as interpersonal in origin. Rado pictured a mother-child battle over authority and autonomy in which bowel training is only one aspect of strife. "The future obsessive patient's emphatic obedience and stubborn defiance, far from being limited to his bowel responses as a child, are spread over his entire behaviour," Rado wrote.[27] Enraged defiance and guilty fear alternate maladaptively in this defense, the child's assertion of self impaired by a still more basic need for the security of being loved and cared for by the mother. If her control is experienced as excessive, and self-assertive countermeasures are taken, guilt will be felt: the more suppressed rage, the more free-floating guilt. Submission and rebellion become polarized and intrapsychic self-punitive possibilities may find their way into fantasized control of women, as appears in the fictions considered.

In "Infantile Neurosis as a False Self Organization" (1971), Masud Khan put the matter strongly by speaking of the child's "dread of annihilation" driving them into a "compliant false-self organization."[28] Khan later elaborated this in "The Concept of Cumulative Trauma," an important paper that extends Winnicott's idea of the false self and supports a plausible etiology for the pathology of obsessions. Khan reflects on the ways in which the mother's role as "protective shield" for the developing child breaks down; impingements cause "premature and selective ego-development," while collusion with the mother inhibits a "coherent ego." Indeed, repeated seemingly insignificant impingements can culminatively produce obsessive fending-off. "This in turn leads to a dissociation through which an archaic dependency bond is exploited on the one hand and a precipitate independence is asserted on the other."[29] Khan's special contribution is in seeing this as a process, not a once-and-for-all trauma. He sees that "later pathogenic interplay between mother and child aims to correct the earlier distortions through impingements." But, Khan adds, "That these attempts at recovery only complicate the pathology is an irony of human experience."[30] His summary statement should be kept in mind while thinking of cultural materials containing covert hostility to woman:

> One treacherous aspect of cumulative trauma is that it operates and builds up silently throughout childhood right up to adolescence. It is only in recent years that we have learned to evaluate as pathogenic a certain precocious development in children. Such precocity had previously been celebrated as giftedness or strong ego-emergence or a happy independence in the child. We are also inclined to view with much more caution and reserve, if not suspicion, a mother's boasts of a specially close rapport and understanding between herself and her child.[31]

Various detailed scenarios have been suggested as precursors of obsessional states, for instance that of Henry P. Laughlin (1967) in which learned rage and rectitude between mother and infant-child are the most telling terms: rage at impingement met by maternal rectitude. For Laughlin interlocking predisposing factors for obsessional neuroses are: (1) parental insecurity (2) rejection of child, which the parent conceals with a façade of caring (the child senses rejection and loses trust in the mother) (3) parental overambitiousness for the child's success and maturity (4) early overindulgence . . . inconsistently followed by later demands for responsibility and maturity (5) obsessive traits in the parents (6) parental, social, and/or religious condemnation of negative feelings (7) rejection . . . of spontaneous affection from the child, lack of spontaneity of any kind (8) overdeveloped conscience (9) unresolved defiance-submission conflict (10) blocked primordial infant rage, from whatever source.[32]

Discussion of the narcissistic elements in obsessions is found in *The Restoration of the Self* (1977) by the self-psychologist Heinz Kohut. Kohut's emphasis on empathic listening to what persons have to say about inner states is important for the present discussion. It reveals an inherent urge to emerge from imprisoning narcissism into the freer use of symbols to disclose feelings that have built up around the failure of basic mother-infant interaction. This urge may be experienced as obsessions, which are likely to be circular unless their real meaning is grasped. The creative person is one who has sufficiently overcome exhibitionism, grandiosity, and perfectionism to express the relational themes central to his being.

Kohut describes two versions of the narcissistically injured male: one in which self-pathology, "the diseased unmirrored self—is covered over by promiscuous and sadistic behaviour toward women and the equally frequent instances in which the defensive cover consists of fantasies." In both types "sadism towards women is motivated by the need to force the mirroring object's response," that is, to communicate with the mother about the source of psychological pain. Sadistic fantasies and Don Juan promiscuity are variants of "narcissistic rage wherein the dominant propelling motivation is less the revenge motif and more the wish to increase self-esteem," Kohut wrote.[33] Failures of empathic mothering are said to have been more severe in promiscuous males than in those who merely fantasize destructively towards women, but both are worrisome features of the contemporary male who does not feel secure in his gender. Kohut agrees with those theorists who find failure of fathering a major consideration in the outcome of sadistic fantasies or promiscuity in men.

Kohut writes generally, without suggesting a need for more systematic measures of failures of parental attunement. This work is being done by the more empirically oriented attachment theorists who correlate dismissal of attachment in later years (defensive deactivation of the attachment system) with certain types of parenting. As this work is new, it is too soon to expect full confirmation of Kohut's clinical experience of narcissistic and obsessional persons. Kohut's insights are also well aligned with Fairbairn's object relational theory of the obsessional defense as an internalization in the ego of both exciting and rejecting by the mother. Narcissistic identification with the mother's exciting aspect is coupled with the need to control more or less aggressively her threatening aspect. Again, a set of psychoanalytic concepts begs to be integrated into a more comprehensive theory of imagination and creativity. The writer's psyche becomes the locus of a struggle for self-esteem against the limiting factors of his early attachment experience. The more we can learn about the particulars of this—both in actual parenting and societal functions—the better able will we be to understand the meaning of fantasy bodied forth in his fiction. The writer's imaginative means of escaping the prison of his narcissism is a leading consideration in the studies that follow.

No attempt should be made here to offer a full sociological account of why adequate fathering declined during the formation period of the authors studied. Various suggestions have been made, and they are worthy of mention. It is enough here to note that the long erosion of effective fathering led to family conditions in which the incidence of domination of children by mothers became socially significant. As early as 1949, G. Legman wrote in *Love and Death: A Study in Censorship:*

> With the return of the mother as the dominant parent, certain other reversals must follow: Oedipus disappears, the father he was competing with now becomes a punching-bag and clown. Electra comes sullenly on stage, the same father—and, with him, all men—now utterly forbidden by her mother's new found strength.[34]

This state of affairs is very different from that against which feminists have inveighed as "patriarchy." Hated patriarchy may have its roots in the anxieties of men demoted from true fathering. The male psychoclass whose imaginative fortunes we are following is postpatriarchal; anxious and driven in their maleness they may be, but they are not new patriarchs founding new dynasties in which women are subordinate to their men. This psychoclass, typified by the sons of Jocasta mothers, finds its roles as husbands and fathers to be perilous. Driven heterosexuals, these men are sometimes Don Juans who like women less than they profess to do but must prove themselves by pursuit and control.

V

A far-reaching revision of Freud's Oedipal theory was proposed in 1968 by Matthew Besdine in *The Jocasta Complex, Mothering and Genius,* a rereading of the myth to emphasize the mother's sexual wishes rather than the son's, which are not denied. Besdine studies the effects of the mother's controlling attachment to her son in a series of psychobiographies of Michelangelo, Christopher Marlowe, Goethe, Heinrich Heine, Honoré de Balzac, Marcel Proust, Fyodor Dostoievsky, Jean-Paul Sartre, and others. While these psychobiographical sketches are incomplete, they do bring some common factors into sharp focus: genius is a function of the kind and intensity of mothering; the social benefits of creative art are bought at a high price in feelings of ambiguity about sexual orientation. The exclusive favor of sons by their mothers that leads to a sense of special creative powers Besdine likens to the gardener's technique of "debudding" to promote exceptionally vigorous growth. His conclusion gives a new paradigm with which to work, provocative and overly generalized although it may be:

> The concurrence of homosexual trends and genius and an examination of the lives of homosexuals and geniuses appears to demonstrate

Jocasta mothering as a common factor in both. Reducing the quantity and the intensity of mothering to the level of deprivation and affect hunger in the infant appears to have deadly effects, while increasing the quantity and intensity of Jocasta mothering seems to accelerate growth. The whole development of infant and child seems to be decisively affected by increasing or decreasing the intensity and quantity of mothering.[35]

There is much to criticize in the assumptions and methodology of Besdine's work, and attributions of homosexuality to creative people are always difficult to justify, let alone in the small compass of Besdine's papers. The year 1968 was a watershed when homosexuality as a "Sexual Deviation" in the category "Sociopathic Personality Disturbances" gave way in DSM-III, the *Diagnostic and Statistical Manual* published by the American Psychiatric Association, to homosexuality as no longer a personality disturbance. This change was surely among the most remarkable alterations of status ever effected in the history of psychiatry, and it was bound to affect the somewhat pejorative tone of Besdine's thoughts about male homosexuality. The studies on which he based his theory of Jocasta Mothering, such as that of Irving Bieber *et al., Homosexuality: A Psychoanalytic Study of Male Homosexuals* (1962), came in for reconsideration. What for Besdine is a clear-cut cause-and-effect relationship—the Biebers' restrictive, even stifling, "over-intense mother and unsatisfactory father relationship"—is not so clear at all for later theorists. Richard C. Friedman, for instance, notes a study of 1973 that appears to say something different about the quality of homosexuals' experience of being mothered.

Unlike Bieber's study, Saghir and Robins's sample did not on the whole describe mothers as being seductive and close binding. Rather they were described as involved, interested, and consciously supportive. The mothers did, however, tend to regard rough-and-tumble play negatively and to engage in feminine activities with their sons. The prehomosexual boys far more frequently than the preheterosexual boys viewed their mothers as suitable role models.[36]

The gains of intensive mothering are not just a quibble, and it is evident looking back on Besdine's assertions that much more detailed consideration of mothering style was needed to characterize Jocasta Mothering in a psychobiographically useful way. Further, Besdine's examples are no more than selectively reconstructed vignettes, often incomplete for want of historical evidence about exactly what parenting had meant. The omission of sociocultural features in the history of childhood is a major weakness of such attempts to rethink Freud's Oedipus complex, itself never more than shakily founded in anthropological and cross-cultural studies.

On the other hand, there is something memorable about the tag "Jocasta Mothering," as long as it is understood that the Greek myth is itself ambiguous, and that applications in later settings can only be suggestive, never definitive. As Besdine wrote:

> The lonely, emotionally starved widow, Jocasta, played as significant a role in the inexorable unfolding of the Greek tragedy as did her unfortunate son. Her love for the new stranger, her son, played the contrapuntal theme to the loss of her husband and child. From Jocasta's point of view, the entire legend of Oedipus can be interpreted in a different light and new conclusions drawn from it.[37]

Besdine alters the perspective of the Oedipus myth to that of mother Jocasta who unwittingly married her son and bore him four children before committing suicide in disgrace. Convinced that his firstborn would slay him, King Laius had Oedipus exposed to die, an example of de Mause's earliest category in the history of childhood, the infanticidal. Thus rejective parenting combines with later sexual entrapment of son by mother, after he had been saved, adopted, and raised by Queen Periboea of Corinth. She too, Besdine explains, was driven by deprivation and affect hunger, implying that she overindulged her adopted only son. Thus female maternal and sexual wishes take on centrality in a theory calculated to replace Freud's male-oriented Oedipus complex that too neatly exonerated parents. Did Besdine need to recast myth to state his meaning clearly? The formulation turns out to be virtually that of Freud describing the internalized love-hate of the obsessional defense, and it strongly reinforces trauma theory:

> The Jocasta mother unconsciously seeks solace and comfort for herself in the love of her child. She draws her young son to her in despair and misery because of deep human and biological needs, but shocked by her own strong feelings for the boy and by his response, she also pushes him away. This trauma of closeness and distance, attraction and repulsion, increases guilt in the boy child. It overstimulates his sexuality, so that he longs and lusts too strongly for his mother. When she punishes him by pushing him away, she confirms his feelings of guilt and creates a sense of rejection.[38]

Identification is finally not with the father, who may be absent or simply produce a feeling of guilt and inadequacy, but with the mother, an identification so taboo that in the extreme case the boy rebounds into desire for men as sexual companions. The complicated masochism and wish to expiate for sin found in such men form the dynamics Besdine finds in much art, his main example being that of Michelangelo who idealized male youth as in the striking sculpture of David. The artist becomes the hero, projecting his desires on such a heroic scale as to quell all doubts and guilt. Interestingly, Besdine's focus on homoeroticism fails to account, except by implication, for the Don Juan mode of obsessionalism notable in the fiction studied here. Many of the writers he names, such as Kafka and Poe, had complicated or even bizarre relations with women, often more than one woman, around which their fictions revolve. Besdine, of course, recognizes this without having a sufficiently refined theory to account for it. He simply explains that while some Jocasta-reared sons are attracted to women, these women are seen as unapproachable madonnas or exploitable whores, and that intimacy is possible only if there is an "escape clause," as when the woman is already married, from outside the culture or class, and so forth.[39] In a later paper, Besdine wrote more pessimistically that Jocasta-reared children's character structure with its unresolved Oedipal feelings, leads to lack of love, strong ambivalence in human relations, a paranoid streak, and an inability to accommodate to authority. Underlying guilt and masochism unfit them for any more than the most tenuous of relationships, with their accommodation to society only as violent outsiders.[40] The creative artist is obviously in a more productive relation to society, but he too may repeatedly attack it until either prevailing moral standards shift in his favor or his attacks are dismissed as inconsequential.

Whatever the inadequacies of Besdine's pioneering studies, the role of psychosexual overstimulation in the developmental process is brought to the fore. Freud is quoted as saying, "A man who has been the indisputable favourite of his mother keeps for life the feeling of a conqueror, that confidence of success that often induces real success," a remark to which Besdine gave a sinister coloration without speculating on why Freud had seen fit to replace the trauma theory with that of fantasy.[41] The revisionist study of Freud himself had hardly begun, so the full psychological meaning of Freud's "discovery" of the Oedipal Complex from his own early life (as examined by Henri Ellenberger's study of Freud's "creative illness") does not inform Besdine's work.[42] Indeed, the entire emerging theory of attachment and loss as predisposing conditions for creativity goes unmentioned—some degree of early maternal loss also seeming a necessary component of 'reparative' creative work. It is curious that while Jocasta Mothering has seized the attention of further theorists (especially women analysts) Besdine's first contribution is seldom, if ever, mentioned.

The psychology of perverse mothering is being seriously looked at by women analysts. A mystique of mothering goodness has hitherto prevented the kind of investigation offered by Estela V. Welldon in *Mother, Madonna, Whore: The Idealization and Denigration of Motherhood* (1988). With increased work on gender identity, we see more clearly the perturbations of mothering that result in anxious, angry boys. Sexually overstimulating mothers have themselves been maltreated by their mothers and they in turn by their mothers. As Welldon writes, "Again and again, the mother's mental health emerges as crucial for the development of her offspring."[43] Exerting power and control, the mother causes her child to withdraw from the threat to his or her identity; the result is splitting of the "denigrated, bad self," well known in analytic theory. Welldon's distinction is in insisting on the possibility of motherhood as a perversion.

> I suggest that motherhood is sometimes chosen for unconscious perverse reasons. The woman would know that in achieving motherhood she is automatically achieving the role of master, in complete control of another being who has to submit . . . not only emotionally, but also biologically to the mother's demands, however inappropriate they may be.[44]

Using the concept of Jocasta Mothering, and expanding Besdine's work (though never mentioning it), Welldon argues that when a mother's emotional sustainment from external sources fails her, she falls back on "inappropriate and perverse behaviour" with her infant:

> Simultaneously, and paradoxically, she experiences her perverse behaviour as the only power available to her through her exclusive emotional and physical authority over her baby.[45]

This remark is in line with Dorothy Dinnerstein's important thesis as we see. Welldon writes, "Our whole culture supports the idea that mothers have complete domination over their babies; thus we encourage the very ideas the perverse mother exploits."[46] The problem of "blaming mother" for the ills of her children is in part overcome by studying the total configuration of the mother's emotional supports and showing where they fail, especially when she is let down by a partner.

An urgent plea for reconsidering child rearing exclusively by mothers is found in Christiane Olivier's *Jocasta's Children: The Imprint of the Mother* (1989). Again it seems that the writer has in mind Dorothy Dinnerstein's remarkable *The Mermaid and the Minotaur* (1976) and, it might seem, Besdine's work too, although they are never mentioned. A French feminist and psychoanalyst, Olivier wishes to understand the dynamics of male attempts to dominate women. Impatient with Freud's reductive view of women, impatient also with Lacan's partiality to the idealized father, Olivier rethinks the Oedipus myth in terms of Jocasta's role. As she writes:

> The woman has unconscious difficulties about giving up the only male she has ever been able to keep by her; she whose father let her down and whose husband is more often away than at home.[47]

The boy then must "make his escape from the Oedipal stage *against* his mother, who does not want him to go away and leave her." In Olivier's term, this starts a "war" of the sexes, between the mother holding on and the son asserting his freedom from an attachment he can never really break. "Pinioned in the maternal love-trap," the little boy has a harder time growing up than has his sister, as evidenced by the higher incidence in boys of bed wetting, soiling, and so forth:

> It looks as if the famous "trap" so often alluded to by men must be the trap of a symbiosis with the mother that is seen as "imprisoning." Symbiosis, psychosis? At all events, a "prison" that sets off panic in the man at the thought of any symbiosis with any other woman. Never again to be caught up in the same place, in the same desire as the woman: this is the main driving force of the man's misogyny. Holding the woman away from him, keeping her confined to areas designed for her alone (family, schooling, home) is the primary objective of the masculine campaign.
>
> Setting up at all points a barrier, whether physical or social, between him and her, standing out against her desire in any and every way, keeping his distance by any and every means will be the man's greatest obsession. Even his sexual behaviour will be affected: he will be that much more sparing of the gestures and words that might recall something of his symbiotic lovingness with the mother.[48]

The more intense and prolonged the mother's insistence on holding her son to her, the more violent (although possibly suppressed) will be his rebellious feelings. It might be added that mothers are left to dominate male children because their husbands are in flight from their own mothers' domination—a self-perpetuating system more or less misogynistic according to circumstances. In a memorable phrase Olivier writes, "Misogyny is a crop sown by one woman and reaped by another."[49] As a cultural aside she states that men conspire "to remove all traces of [women's] desire; . . . to kill her in fantasy."[50] If this statement seems excessive, we have only to consider in detail the lethal fantasies that abound in the novels to be discussed. There is little doubt that these are secondary to practices in that phase of the history of childhood when the extended family dispersed, and mothers became the dominant parent. To follow Olivier's thesis, men dominate in order not to be dominated by the women they love yet fear, evidence for which abounds in the interwar fiction of a sick society in the West. The book ends with the Dinnersteinian thesis clearly enunciated:

> What a strange society it is which, using the excuse that it is raising the level of material comfort via the father's salary, steps up psychic disturbance by way of an exclusively feminine upbringing and education. Not only do we have the absent father; we also have the permanently present mother.

> How can I not say that the main outcomes of the contemporary family are misogyny in men, and guilt in women?[51]

So strikingly original is Dorothy Dinnerstein's *The Mermaid and the Minotaur: Sexual Arrangements and Human Malaise* that it has been slow to win the position of centrality it deserves in gender studies. Dinnerstein looks at nothing less than survival of the species in terms of the imbalance of parenting in the nuclear family that has come to characterize modern society. Female domination of children must give way to shared parenting if we are not to continue reaping the malign rewards of hatred and aggression that unbalanced mothering too readily produces; perhaps, she thinks, it is already too late for fundamental change:

> Our sexual arrangements, I argue, are used to keep unresolved a core ambivalence that centers upon our species' most characteristic, vital, and dangerous gift: our gift for enterprise, for self-creation.[52]

Since "a deep strain between men and women has been permeating our species' life as far back in time as the myth and ritual permits us to trace human feeling," we might ask what chance there is now to extricate ourselves from patterns of mistrust and hatred.[53] If the very texture of "normal" society is set by neurotic child rearing, then what are the chances that true insight and alteration of course can be effected? *The Mermaid and the Minotaur* sets out to describe a "massive communal self-deception" that female-dominated child rearing is the best possible and that the destructive results simply have to be accepted. We are on a suicidal course, she says—speaking while the "cold war" still threatened "mutually assured destruction" in a nuclear "exchange," and as feminism was empowering women to protest war. There is only one option: "melt down" (another nuclearism) the patterns of parenting that lead to the subhuman male escapism. Male aggressiveness is tagged as maladaptive in a world tooled for destruction by technology. Aggressiveness is an expression of ambivalence about women, about the mothers who first introduce male children to their physical being, including sexuality. The long dependency period, together with exclusive female caregiving, set our human course for ambivalence and destructiveness.

Dinnerstein does not review previous attempts at a psychogenesis for anger and destructiveness, including sexual rapacity in boys. She does not write about Jocasta Mothering as such, nor is there a psychogenesis suggested for obsessional states that include fantasies of control and retaliation against women. There is, however, a brilliant account of how it is that, while girls make the transition to adult sexuality through a measure of rejection of the mother and idealization of the father, boys are prevented by taboos on homoeroticism from idealizing the father, so must maintain the mother as split between good and bad aspects. This clarification of Freud's original observation is a useful redirection of theory much in keeping with revised psychodynamic theory from Ronald Fairbairn to Alice Miller.[54] Her point is that original infantile ambivalence toward the mother is perpetuated, and too readily redoubled, by the closeness of mother-son so typical of the interwar family in America. Angry feelings of restriction and control by mother are sealed off as much as possible, which results in emotional impoverishment along with dangerous acting out of aggression by men. Dinnerstein writes:

> The truth of emotional experience—their own and others'—tends on
> the whole to be more threatening to [men]. As a result their freedom

to feel emotional intimacy—with themselves and others—tends . . . to be more constricted, hemmed in by the massive denial which is necessary to keep so much truth at bay. And their physical sex pleasure—though wider-ranging than women's and much less likely to be plumb thwarted—is likelier to be impoverished by dissociation from deep personal feeling.[55]

Their deepest feelings about their mothers walled off, denied, men do not "grow up" in the way women do into sensitive, empathizing beings. This explanation goes a long way toward understanding why those male novelists with the sensitivity to do so, compulsively investigate power relationships with women, relationships of control and countercontrol. In responding to the ambivalently internalized mother by forming fictions around her surrogates, they portray in comparative safety the dangers they most fear—dangers shared in society as group fantasy, a sort of preconscious semiawareness of something wrong that can't quite be defined or corrected. Dinnerstein could be referring to the novel when she writes:

to try to grow up, we go on paying a heavy, hostile, costly magic homage to the original magic protector: not to woman herself, but to an abstraction of woman as captive goddess of a more armchair realm. Still, the attempt to grow up—however equivocally made—is in each life a step forward.[56]

Captive goddesses are exactly what we find in the obsessionally toned male novels under study; they are women in bondage to the imagination of writers speaking for the collective anxiety of not being able to accept the residue of feelings left by pathological mothering. The novel is a vehicle for disclosing, examining, and perhaps modifying prerational, preverbal feelings without immediate risk to writer or reader. It is one way the culture has found to bring awareness to unconscious sources of suffering, to self-create, or re-create in the thwarted process of growing up. The novel thus belongs to what Dinnerstein calls the "project of sexual liberty" in which women's needs along with men's have at last come to light and demand practical re-arrangements, especially in child rearing. In a society accelerated to the point of reckless change, special regulators are needed, even if they only release danger signals, as novels and films are sometimes able to do. These may be small elements in a generally grim prospect for obsessionally driven, destructive man deeply uncomfortable with his sexual arrangements. With technology out of control and hidden anxieties profilerating with population growth, what can the mere fringe of the creative arts be asked to do other than witness the malaise? Dinnerstein's brilliant psychosocial analysis enables us to ask the right questions about culture's constructive functions.

Dinnerstein brings us back to trauma theory, having argued that male aggression and domination of women is the result of instinctual overstimulation when mother is exclusively, or predominantly, the caretaker. While this explanation is not exactly what Freud meant by "seduction," it is close enough to make us wonder what corroboration for Dinnerstein's thesis there may be. Other analysts, such as Robert Stoller, suggest such terms as *symbiosis anxiety* to describe the son's stance to his mother. When theorizing about the psychogenesis of perversions, Stoller writes:

> One can wonder if at its most primitive level, perversion is that ultimate in separations, mother murder (more than, as Freud may have felt, father murder). It would be ironic if some of the forms that masculinity takes, some of its strength, insistence, fierceness—machismo—*require* anlagen of feminity; the potential to be feminine is an unacceptable temptation that must be resisted by behaviour and attitudes that society labels "masculine."[57]

A search through the psychoanalytic literature would disclose similar statements about the behavioral outcomes of unwitting or even unwilling impingements by mothers on their immature male offspring. Scattered work on maladaptive forms of maternal attachment is now beginning to be consolidated into major statements such as John Leopold Weil's *Instinctual Stimulation of Children: From Common Practice to Child Abuse* (1989). This one-hundred-case study, using material assembled over twenty-five years, redirects attention from Freud's later view of neuroticism arising from the child's self-generated fantasies back to his original view of difficulties stemming from the child's exposure to sexualized contacts with parents. Fantasy is once again seen as arising from the disturbances of parent-child interaction, a pseudoprotective device against instinctual overstimulation.

This more productive way of looking at fantasy (and dreams) is in keeping with advances in attachment theory stemming from the work of Bowlby, Ainsworth, Main, and Crittenden on forms of "anxious attachment." Although not explicitly cited, this concept is strongly present in Weil's study of instinctual overstimulation:

> The findings of the study suggest that sexualized forms of stimulation of children are associated with the predictable dream content and

symptoms which contrast with those associated with severe corporal punishment.[58]

In children "who have been exposed to visual and/or tactile erotic contacts with the adult genitalia," Weil found "a prevalence of night terrors and hysterical twilight states, disturbed thoughts, dreams, fears, and activities involving eyes, biting, cutting, and fire, as well as the emergence of sexual disturbances among children who have been exposed to such forms of stimulation."[59] These are the imaginative concomitants of anxious attachments, interior danger signals, messages of distress by which the individual communicates with himself. It is shown that suppression of episodes of sexual overstimulation increases "the likelihood for these reactions to be expressed primarily within the child's dreams, fantasies, thoughts, or symptoms."[60] Attachment behavior for involuntary "imaginative" reactions is graphically displayed in case studies. While there is nothing of the artist's shaping power or craft, the basic reaction to trauma is not dissimilar.

Weil is particularly interesting on the "driven," self-destructive quality of behavior among abused boys, with obsessive phenomena everywhere evident. He does not differentiate abuse by gender, mothers and fathers both appearing as abusers in the case histories. The psychogenesis of obsessive-compulsive symptoms is seen mainly in a Freudian framework of anal stimulation, with fantasies of death the frequent concomitant. It is possible that other sources of compulsion deserve equal attention in Weil's studies, so frequently are obsessive features noticed in the cases. Indeed most antisocial behavior exhibits obsessionality in some degree. Teenage sexual promiscuity is one outcome of childhood exposure to intolerable levels of sexual stimulation by parents,[61] while punitive rage in overstimulated children shows up in dream imagery of teeth, fire, bearing down on another person, falling, and preoccupation with death, including killing.[62] Rock-video imagery could usefully be studied in this context, as could displays of nihilist violence in pornographic "men's magazines." Obsessionally destructive fantasy material, increasingly familiar since its introduction by insurrectionist Dada and surrealist artists, is stock-in-trade in the visual and musical commerce so patronized by frustrated youth and by males of later age who have not been helped by their culture to understand the sources of their rage.

I wish to comment on just two critical discussions of Don Juan behavior, one by a humanist psychiatrist Leonard L. Glass, "Man's Man/Ladies' Man" (1984), and the other by a "recovering Casanova" Peter Trachtenberg, *The Casanova Complex: Compulsive Lovers and their Women* (1988). The unanswered questions about what "normal" male gender identity and orientation may be are clarified by these studies. The shifting norms of male behavior—including attempts to normalize Don Juanism—are evident from the novels themselves; here we find the search for criteria of judgment to yield some useful guidelines. Both commentators pull against the impetus of imaginative writers to install in culture the male sexual obsessionism that has been gathering force at least since the Renaissance. Their work is only a beginning in the response from the social sciences to a trend whose momentum may be unstoppable, if Dinnerstein is to be believed. The "Playboy ethic" may be too firmly entrenched to alter, now that revisionist morality from Wells to Updike has penetrated so far into the collective psyche. Unless they are enduring intolerable suffering, people are unlikely to change their modes of sexual pleasure seeking. These studies are, nonetheless, portents of another phase of moral revisionism whose outcome cannot be predicted.

The main difficulty with Glass's and Trachtenberg's pioneering studies is lack of integration with supporting psychoanalytic theory, especially the revival of Freud's trauma theory by Ferenczi and others. Perhaps it is too soon to expect them to connect the effects they observe in males to the "anxious attachments" of infants and children to their mothers, as described by Bowlby and his followers. Unfortunately, Bowlby's theory of attachment does not directly address the obsessional's predicament, so its self-evident relevance remains to be proven. This research is especially important as Glass proposes "a developmentally based model for the evolution of hyper-masculinity" in two modal forms: the Man's Man and the Ladies' Man. He pleads for recognition by clinicians for recognition of the men "who end up with compromised and distorted masculine identities."[63] So far this recognition appears to have been small perhaps because the dynamics of male sexual ambivalence Glass describes are hard to distinguish from the norms that have established themselves through the media, literature, and film.

Admittedly, Glass's categories are very general, inviting many variations and gradations of difference within and between them; nevertheless, they do hold up to scrutiny, helping us to see Don Juan obsessionalism in its contemporary guises. The Man's Man is decidedly macho, a jock, given to physical exploits to prove strength and endurance or, in the professional realm, to feats of power and dominance furthering their rise in a hierarchy. He is eager to exclude women and resists dependence on them, disowning the feminine component of his own personality. About the psychogenesis of this character type, Glass writes:

> Primarily, the Man's Man has experienced his mother as a disturbingly, disproportionately powerful and compelling influence, stirring the boy's anxiety about merger. Dynamically inadequate buffering by the father could have a quantitatively similar impact. Thus a boy's orientation may be determined by anxieties about closeness with mother unrelieved by a father who is typically remote, ineffective or unappealing.[64]

Most often the father is frightening and insensitive, and the boy's relationship with him is by "identification with the aggressor." Such sons relate to women only as the dominant partner in a rigid, stereotyped way that lets her know who is boss. He is typically homophobic, heavily defended against homosexual tendencies.

The Ladies' Man on the other hand, is the Don Juan or Casanova, the charmer who romances many women and has his way with them. He is cultivated, not clumsy and crude like the Man's Man. He has a repetitive compulsion to seduce women, to acquire, control and then push them away, never allowing any sustained tie. This predatory and narcissistic character pathology has a typical family origin:

> mother is usually that primitive, attractive (i.e. eroticizing) borderline level . . . , hysteroid character who is most prepared to cultivate and engage in repetitive seductions. At least one other factor appears necessary: I have found evidences of profound superego disruptions in the paternal environment of these men, ranging from a kind of ethical slipperiness to outright criminality.[65]

Glass may be the first to recognize that his profile of the Don Juan is not sharply enough differentiated to do more than give an indication of causality. As defense against homosexuality is also present in the Ladies' Man, more needs explaining like that of the Biebers' study of the CBI (Close, Binding, Intimate) factor in mothering. What actually is the connection, if any, to homoeroticism and outright homosexuality? How much is biological (genetic), how much family dynamics in predisposing a boy to becoming a Man's Man, Ladies' Man, or homosexual? Glass really didn't know, nor do we. Of one thing he was certain, that the restless, driven energy of hypermasculinity may seem attractive but on close inspection is destructive, however much a part of the prevailing culture it may be. Glass writes in a trenchant sentence:

As a permanent bastion from which the affected individual derogates women, homosexuals, other men, and the feminine aspects of himself, hypermasculinity is a clearly defensive and crippling form of character pathology.[66]

In a society profoundly puzzled and undecided on this point, its novelists clarify by using simulations the interpersonal meanings of hypermasculinity.

Peter Trachtenberg writes in a fashionable genre—the confession of somebody afflicted by a psychological disorder who has surmounted it and wishes to understand it better. *The Casanova Complex* popularizes the issues around compulsive sexuality that have long bedeviled psychoanalysis and psychiatry. This book performs a useful service in summarizing the questions we have opened here. Data is gathered from fifty womanizers and a theory synthesized:

> Among the men I interviewed I found four basic themes . . . "thrill seeking," "game playing," "escaping" and "devouring." These motivations differ: womanizing is the thrill seeker's attempt to give meaning and resonance to an arid life; for the escape artist, it is a flight from life itself, an attempt literally to "fuck my life away," as one man told me. But in all four themes, one encounters an underlying hunger and impoverishment of spirit and an unconscious view of women as faceless instruments of pleasure, ego gratification and relief. All women are interchangeable and divided into two rigid categories: those to pursue and those to run from.[67]

Typically, Trachtenberg's Casanovas—including profiles of Lord Byron, Gary Hart, Frank Sinatra, and Ernest Hemingway—seek power over women but are not so much wicked as sick. With AIDS among heterosexuals threatening easy recreational sex, their compulsiveness can no longer be overlooked. Has Trachtenberg read Glass and Besdine? It is hard to tell from this journalistic book, but his etiological findings for Don Juans and Casanovas are mainly in keeping with theirs, with one crucial difference in the emphasis on narcissism, which he feels has replaced hysteria and obsessional neurosis as the dominant disorder of our time.[68] Nonetheless, his study is full of evidence for the addictive intractability of obsessive-compulsive patterns of sexuality that the "talking cure" cannot eradicate. Countercontrol of controlling mothers is well documented. The etiology of Casanova love addiction is much as one would expect it to be, echoing D. H. Lawrence and others. Of the typical pattern of mothering he writes:

The care they gave their sons was often oppressive, characterized by nagging and overprotectiveness. Indeed, the love these men experienced in childhood was often tainted by maternal narcissism: their mothers loved them not as separate beings, but as extensions of themselves and as vehicles of their own psychic dramas. . . . And there was little consolation in the love of their fathers: they were absent, either physically or emotionally during their sons' critical years. . . . Often the father was not only inadequate but threatening, a physical and emotional terrorist. A high proportion were alcoholics, workaholics or compulsive gamblers, which made them unpredictable as well as inaccessible. . . . The mothers of Casanovas seem to have had an unusual and highly exclusive identification with their sons: they were not only their offspring, but their fulfilment, bandages for their psychic wounds and hapless stand-ins for missing husbands and their own mothers and fathers. . . . Casanovas never quite relinquish the omnipotent and grandiose self-images of infancy. . . . The love they knew as children turns out to have been painfully inconsistent. As solicitous as their mothers were of their physical well-being, they were oddly callous when it came to emotional needs. . . . The inflated self-image of the Casanova turns out to be merely that, a thin, hyperextended membrane enclosing a core of unloved, unlovable self. . . . They will continue to seek nurturance—and even a sense of personal completion—from mother substitutes long after childhood has passed. The desperation that underlies this quest is usually disguised.[69]

This profile of parenting for the Casanova/Don Juan is as complete and accurate as is likely to be found, yet much more needs to be known about the earliest attachments from infancy onward—at what point does the mother's narcissistic use of her male child become irreversible? What factors in the relationship between mother and father predict womanizing rather than homosexuality, as the profiles can be similar? What is the role of bisexuality in the Casanova complex? Developmental and gender studies will undoubtedly suggest answers, but the ferreting out will not be simple, because, as Trachtenberg points out, the Casanova complex is right in the core of our culture; it is a "culturally syntonic disorder," and, despite the anguish of marital separations, family disruptions, and the risk of AIDS, a culture is difficult to criticize, let alone significantly modify.[70] Many novelists are alert to sexual obsessionality as group hypervalence because of common child-rearing practices that they themselves have experienced. Countercontrol of controlling mothers, when widespread enough in society, leads not only to heightened sexual tension in the "war" of the sexes, but also to deep psychic distress in both men and women. This unease spurs a wish for change; one hopes it will not be a change into repressiveness but toward the sort of shared parenting Dorothy Dinnerstein sees as the only way out of the self-destructive impasse we are witnessing. As creative "open obsessionals," certain novelists, however enmeshed in the very tensions they describe, can help us to see beyond the sexual mal-adaptions that beset modern consciousness.

2

H. G. Wells: The Confessions
of a Sexual Rebel

Art is selection and so is most autobiography."
—H. G. Wells, *The New Machiavelli*

WHAT sort of confessional writer was the novelist and autobiographer H. G. Wells (1866–1946)? No longer Christian, Wells thought of himself as "an essentially religious person," but not in a way that constrained sexual behavior.[1] Wells is among the first and most influential post-Christian literary prophets of a new morality of sexual freedom. There is evidence that he saw sexuality as revelation in a new religion, as did Bertrand Russell in his love letters to Lady Ottoline Morrell (1911f) and D. H. Lawrence in *Lady Chatterley's Lover* (1928). Wells's confessions are therefore unlikely to be Augustinian in the sense of converting from a sinful way of life to one of holy obedience. When St. Augustine repented of "a wayward passion, void of understanding," flourishing outside a marriage bond, he looked for help to the higher love of God.[2] For unbelieving Wells, thoughts about God limiting human desire tended to be derisory, and his confessions are not about failures to serve such a God. They are, however, about guilt and inadequacy, about regrets, even remorse, over failed sexual relationships in a life of many loves. Wells indulged in several spectacular love affairs outside his marriage, the most notorious of which was with Amber Reeves by whom he had a daughter in 1909. In this circumstance, the prolific novelist Wells turned confessional, using fiction to reenact his amour and its ramifications. *Ann Veronica* (1909) and *The New Machiavelli* (1911), scandalous in their time but tame enough now, show Wells at his most confessional about the Amber Reeves affair. What did he try to accomplish by writing these novels? Are they insightfully self-analytic,

52

constructive, even reparative statements, helping him to change unrewarding behavior, or are they mainly advertisements for a breakaway antimorality?

Theodor Reik's remark on confession as a manifestation of guilty feelings is pertinent: "confession is conscience speaking up," partially gratifying a need for punishment. Confession makes "unconscious material into verbal presentations and verbal perceptions," allowing "self-understanding and self-acceptance," Reik writes.[3] How much unconscious material did Wells produce, how open to guilty feelings was he, and to what extent was self-understanding achieved? Given the pervasiveness of Wells's auto-biographical impulse in fiction and autobiography itself, these are revelant questions. But, it will be asked, isn't confession too solemn a theme for the exuberant Wells, whose "sexual swagger" is more often remarked on than is any penitential impulse? Braggadocio can be deceptive, signifying more anxiety than certainty. Speaking to Arnold Bennett, Wells called *Ann Veronica* "the Young Mistress' Tale," for example, showing the male author's proprietorship over his heroine.[4] It will be seen that Wells was not a confident lover but a deeply anxious one, always needing to reassure himself in morally ambiguous predicaments. He was subject to mood changes that he imperfectly understood. As J. R. Hammond writes, "The admission that despair was always near to him is a salutary reminder of the complexity of his persona; outwardly ebullient, he could be . . . intensely withdrawn and, in certain moods, profoundly pessimistic about his fellow men" and, it might be added, women.[5] A plausible reconstruction of Wells's bipolar mood shifts, especially in relation to the women he loved and left, can be made from the extensive biographical information left to us.

What follows is an interpretation based on disclosures made mainly by Wells himself. I shall reconstruct Wells's developmental course according to the theory that he was what Matthew Besdine calls a "Jocasta-reared genius" and Leonard Glass calls a "Ladies' man." Wells saw life review as an essential task, but he lacked the psychology to understand what he was saying. Freud's Oedipal theory seemed inapplicable, but Wells's disclaimer now seems too neat for belief. Wells ruled out the Oedipal theory as applying to himself by saying that what may be true of Austrian Jewish families is untrue of English in terms of stimulating infantile sexuality. By focusing strictly on sexuality in his proper nineteenth-century Viennese home, Freud is easily dismissed:

I cannot detect any mother fixation, any Oedipus complex or any of
that stuff in my make up. My mother's kisses were significant acts,
expressions not caresses. As a small boy I found no more sexual significance about my always decent and seemly mother than I did about
the chairs and sofa in our parlour.

Wells indeed denies *any* unconscious transmission from the
mother:

I believe that all the infantile sensuality of suckling and so forth on
which so much stress is laid, was never carried on into the permanent
mental fabric, was completely washed out in forgetfulness; never co-
agulated into subconscious memories; it was as though it had never
been.

He continues:

the psycho-sexual processes of the northern and western Europeans
and Americans arise *de novo* in each generation after a complete break
with and forgetfulness of the mother-babe reaction, and so are funda-
mentally different in their form and sequence.[6]

His own sexual life he claims to have been stimulated by looking
at political cartoons in Punch featuring Britannia, Erin, and Co-
lumbia, and at a Greek Venus in the Crystal Palace. Writing in
the early 1930s, Wells was not challenged on this too neat self-
exemption. But the careful reader of his autobiography discovers
that his relations with his mother were indeed manipulative and
binding to a degree he does not admit, and that if they were not
explicitly seductive they were sexually disorienting. Wells tries to
throw us off the track of what is plainly said about the place his
love-starved Jocasta mother had in his young life: the claim that
sexuality, no matter its style or intensity, should arise *de novo* is
defensive. This claim is made evident by Wells explaining in *Experiment in Autobiography:* "I write down my story and state my
present problem . . . to clear and relieve my mind." He cannot
claim a worldly detached persona, that of the scientific world-
reformer.[7] A mere "apology" for a life won't do; he must write a
"frank autobiography," which means bringing in

all the tangled motives out of which my *persona* has emerged; the
elaborate sexual complexities, the complexes of ambition and rivalry,
the hesitation and fear in my nature . . . ; and in the interests of an
impartial diagnosis I have to set aside the appeal for a favourable
verdict.[8]

The language here is both medical ("diagnosis") and legal ("verdict"), as though Wells were expecting a judgment for a relational style whose origin he did not understand. The autobiography, and certain of the novels, beg for a level of interpretation that could not be expected of Wells himself.

II

For all its failure to make vital connections, Wells's *Experiment in Autobiography* is a remarkable document, taking us lucidly into his past in lower-middle class Bromley, Kent. A family configuration will assist the discussion of Wells's parents' marital relationship:

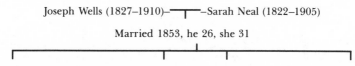

Joseph Wells (1827–1910)–⊤–Sarah Neal (1822–1905)

Married 1853, he 26, she 31

Frances ("Fanny")("Possy") b.1855   Frank b.1857   Fred b.1862   Herbert George b.1866
(died aged 9 in 1864, of appendicitis)

Wells the autobiographer is not so schematic in presenting the interplay of these persons; emphasis naturally falls first on his mother, then his father, then their life together, with sibling relationships taken as incidental to his own responses to parents. We will see that Wells felt angry rebellion toward both parents—especially toward his mother for domineering, and toward his father for absenteeism—and that this prompts him to write empathetically of both. In fact he tries "to restore my mother's picture of the world, as she saw it awaiting her, thirty years before I was born or thought of."[9] It was a conventional world picture, hierarchically arranged from God in heaven to earth with its Victorian social ranks, on down to the Satanic kingdom below. While respectability was maintained by Queen Victoria (his mother's ideal alter ego) and the upper classes, evil thoughts and deeds were explained by Satan's wiles. With a background in Ulster Protestantism, Sarah Neal's Christianity tended toward the lurid, and its moral severity inspired Wells with dread ("I feared Hell dreadfully for some time").[10] He takes several pages to attack her Christianity, explaining how he came to disbelieve in the God and Satan of her relentless teachings. Obviously an able woman, Wells's mother suffered an inferior social position from which religion, to some extent, delivered her. Hardship and personal sorrows were assuaged.

My mother in my earliest memories of her was a distressed over-worked little woman, already in her late forties. All the hope and confidence of her youth she had left behind her. As I knew her in my childhood, she was engaged in a desperate single-handed battle with our gaunt and dismal home, to keep it clean, to keep her children clean, to get them clothed and fed and taught, to keep up appearances.[11]

Joseph Wells's portrait is enquiring, realistic, and finally appreciative, although resentments are manifest. A failed professional gardener in the era of great estates, and later an unsuccessful shopkeeper, Joseph distinguished himself only as a local cricketer. He was sporty, seldom home, and a "man's man." Suffering from "a certain intractability of temper," Joseph had difficulty establishing himself in any line of work.[12] His marriage to Sarah was troubled from the start. In their biography, Norman and Jeanne Mackenzie call the marriage "no more than a lingering disaster, and the birth of children was a source of worry rather than a blessing."[13] His crockery business faltered, and Sarah was left to manage both it and the children while Joe played cricket. After breaking a leg in 1877, even the cricket was removed. As Jeanne MacKenzie writes,

> When Wells was fourteen the family broke up. His father sank into bankruptcy, his mother returned to Uppark as the housekeeper [she had previously been there as a lady's maid], and he—who had hoped to train as a pupil teacher—was sent instead to a draper in Windsor.[14]

Wells was thrown out into the world with little prospect before him, and there were many changes before finding his way as a writer. Would he have found that way had his mother not been literate? Remarkably she kept a diary of her discontents, recording grumbles about life in the basement kitchen at Atlas House, Bromley. Determined to better herself and her family, Sarah kept an account of how things were going. For example, when Joe left for Gloucester on Christmas Eve, 1862, and the children had measles, she wrote: "But what a Xmas alone with my Pets. Could I have left him as he has me?"[15] The pattern persisted after Wells's birth, when he realized what complaints against his father were being confided to the diary. Was this the origin of Wells's own confessional bent? After all, his mother had taught him to read and write, imparting the little culture she had picked up in school. Wells attributes his bookishness to a recuperation when he read voraciously after breaking a leg, aged seven to eight. His emergence into higher culture happened during the brief residence at Uppark (aged fourteen), where his mother had become housekeeper; the enrichments of this country house made it impossible to be contented as the draper's apprentice his social station dictated. Enormous energy and drive were needed to move him from complete obscurity to the international eminence he eventually enjoyed as novelist and seer.

Some hints about how Wells's native vitality was empowered can be found in the biography of infancy. Both depressive and obsessive features of personality seem to have come about in relations with his mother. Wells was born in a particularly depressing phase of Sarah's life when she was still mourning the death of nine-year-old Fanny. Fanny had been an impossibly beautiful, pious, and good child (the only girl) for whom Wells was to be the replacement. Disappointingly he was a boy: "My mother decided that I had been sent to replace Fanny and to achieve a similar edification. But . . . Fate was mocking her."[16] The Mackenzies usefully quote Sarah's diary about her relations with the new infant. Tension and frustration were in the air from the start:

> When nearly a month old she noted "Baby so cross and tiresome", and Baby very cross", and even a year later she remarks of him "never had so tiresome a baby as this one". On 28 April 1868, she recorded, "my precious baby fell out of bed and cut his eye. Oh how sad it is to be over-worried. No one to help. Joe out. Sent for doctor. Had to hold him myself while the cut was sewn up." Successive entries report her "full of anxiety and care" (on 1 May); "my precious child just running about so nicely. Quite made him baby again." "Sadly low and distracted" (on 3 May); "God help me." And on 5 May, "In sad care and sorrow about my child. Oh why did I use a nasty bottle? All my others did without it. How grieved I feel now. I wish I could recall the past. How disfigured my pretty sweet boy looks."[17]

Sarah had been too depressed to breast-feed Wells, whose incomplete attachment she laments. Wells himself wrote, "I was born blasphemous and protesting. Even at my christening, she told me, I squalled with a vehemence unprecedented in the history of the family." That he got a double message from Sarah of close bound acceptance, together with punitive control for his misbehavior, is suggested by his observation that "she was to undermine her own teaching with cod liver oil."[18] It is tempting to see the resulting ego split figured in such mythic formulations as that between the gentle Eloi and the carnivorous machine-minding Morlocks in Wells's first fiction, *The Time Machine* (1895). The Eloi are dominated by a sphinx in this story. The riddle of woman was to be deeply disturbing for Wells throughout his life.

Was this because of confused gender on Wells's part? We remember that his mother viewed him as a replacement after Fanny's death. Husband Joe had been little help in the crisis, with Sarah left "to do her weeping alone" for a child she ever after idealized. Wells thought that Fanny's ("Possy's") death broke his mother's simple faith in God's goodness, and he suffered for her religious anxieties: "She wanted me to believe in order to staunch that dark undertow of doubt."[19] But where Possy had been a prodigy of early piety, Wells was one of early impiety, no doubt rebelling against his mother's overcontrol. Further, there is evidence that Wells's mother actually wanted him to be a girl, treating him as such up to at least age three. Wells's vehement anti-Oedipal protest may have been to eradicate feelings about this, but such feelings cannot be eradicated, only integrated, which did not happen. The Mackenzies catch a glimpse of Wells as "mother's boy" a few years on:

> Physically small, never robust in health, he became the spoilt youngest son of an anxious woman, a petulant child whom his schoolmates were later quick to identify as a "mother's boy."[20]

They report his contemporary, William Baxter, saying that Wells's "gifts" and "mannerisms" drew the attention of his girl cousins; but they do not suggest cross-sexuality. Anthony West (Wells's son by Rebecca West), however, puts the matter more directly, writing that Sarah "can't be able to conceal it from him that to please her he should have been a girl." West's evidence for this is a photograph of his father, before age four, "dressed in a frock with an off-the-shoulder neckline, short puffed quarter-length skirt running to about two and a half yards on the hemline." While admitting that in 1869 such dress for boys was not unusual, West makes the point that gender formation was nonetheless complicated:

> In a family in which things were going wrong between husband and wife in such a way that the children had to be aware of it, this complicated the matter of sexual identification for obvious reasons. A small boy who was fond of his mother, and who had good reason to fear his father, was more than likely to feel that he was being disloyal to her when he put on the uniform of maleness and moved out of her world.[21]

Several outcomes of such a situation are imaginable. Among the lesser distortions of later relational style is that of becoming a hypermasculine "ladies man," the amorous male who persuades successive women of his profound and unqualified love for them when it is in fact heavily qualified with resentful misgivings. Such a male needs abundant "freedom," and cultural advance for him consists of urging society to relax its controls on love and sexuality so he can maneuver freely. (It could be argued that much liberal protest from Renaissance writers onward is about such freeing up of mores owing to competing sexual compulsions of the writers' own: Shakespeare, Donne, Milton, and even J. S. Mill, for example, each weighing the consequences of a wish for emancipated sexuality.) As a historical latecomer in this "great tradition" of emancipationists, Wells used such novels as *Ann Veronica* and *The New Machiavelli* to make his case pleasurably. A temperate polygamy, rather than outright promiscuity, was his wish, with his Don Juanism centering on the women he thought could meet his voracious needs.

There are several ways of looking at this. Wells may simply be criticized as an immoralist, as Lovat Dickson does: "What one sees in his life is the almost complete absence of any moral values," causing "a limitation in an artist," as well as in a human being.[22] Wells's seeming callousness to the consequences of his many amours is a remarkable feature of the sensibility that also sought world peace and large-scale social justice. He resembles Bertrand Russell in pleading for international morality while his private affairs were dubiously moral. He also resembles Russell in his dependency on woman as a caretaker, something not usually associated with the "lady killer" image. In the recently published third part of his autobiography, Wells wrote: "I am an insufficient and often irritable 'great man' with an infantile craving for help."[23] He often infantilized his relationship with women, using pet names and baby talk to cover anxiety about need. A theory will help to make fuller sense of this.

In "Man's Man/Ladies' Man: Motifs of Hypermasculinity," Leonard L. Glass proposes a way of seeing the Don Juan relational style. While the "man's man" ("macho" or "strong" type) repudiates oppressive relations with his mother, and therefore dissociates from women to some extent, the "ladies' man" feels "triumphant contempt" for his mother, but remains identified with her. The contempt is protective, yet it leaves the "ladies' man" capable of close rapport with women. His way with them is likely to be controlling, though seemingly suave and compliant; unlike the sometimes crude and gauche "man's man," the "ladies' man" shows "keeness in sizing up his [female] objects."[24] While the "man's man" has typically had a powerful mother and an inadequate father, the "ladies' man" has had a *seductive* mother along with a dangerous or absent father, according to Glass. "His repetitive compulsion to seduce and control his libidinal objects is matched only by his unfailing need to push them away—to avoid an authentic and sustained tie to them." Glass continues, "Consequently, the Ladies' Man is incapable of being authentically emotionally committed to a woman; although he has an impressive intuitive awareness of women's moods and longings, a narcissistic and predatory flavor pervades his relationships with them."[25] This paradigm goes a long way toward explaining the meaning of "confession" in Wells's autobiography and fiction as a means of dealing with contrary and, to some extent, hidden aspects of the self. Wells the writer was seeking to stabilize the destabilized aspects of his internalized mother—with ambiguous fictional results.

III

Wells's compulsive relations with women, both inside and outside marriage, is now well documented, most fully by himself in the long-suppressed third part of his autobiography. While the two volumes of 1943 indicate this tendency, it was not until *H. G. Wells in Love: Postscript to an Experiment in Autobiography* (1984) that his concept of the "Lover-Shadow" became known. Marriage to his cousin Isabel Wells (1891) and divorce to marry Amy Catherine Robbins ("Jane") in 1895 suggest sexual restlessness of whose full intensity Wells wrote independently of his account of intellectual and artistic development. The central feature of his emotional life is neglected in the autobiography with "Jane's" death in 1927 only mentioned (although Wells paid tribute in the introduction to *The Book of Catherine Wells* [1928], a collection of her writings.) His son, G. P. Wells, writes that Wells began his *Postscript* late in 1934, having been disillusioned in an affair with Moura Budberg, who refused to marry him.

> The shock of disillusion was followed by a deep, nearly suicidal depression. Slowly he worked himself out of it. The self analysis involved in the writing of the *Postscript*, which he then undertook, played a major part in his recovery.[26]

While Wells insisted that the *Postscript* concerned "not the main strand of my life but the sexual, domestic and intimate life sustaining it," the truth seems to be the reverse.[27] *Experiment in Autobiography* fashioned a socially acceptable persona—the progressive scientific writer, historian, and internationalist, concerned with the future of man—while the real person of motivating conflicts remained unknown. Suffering compelled Wells to expose the hidden part of his story—the emotional fevers and chills that should have caused him completely to rewrite the autobiography, once they had been acknowledged. The protective division remains, with the *Postscript* being so long posthumous as not to trouble living persons. How frank and how insightful is this exercise in understanding the inner man?

There is some uneasy self-querying, together with evidence that Wells realized the Lover-Shadow to be unreal: "elusive dream-stuff," as he calls it.[28] Yet there is an almost equal measure of rationalization when Wells attributed his wish for changed lovers to "the normally constituted brain." His psychology of attachment is inadequate.

> I think that in every human mind, possibly from an extremely early age, there exists a continually growing and continually more subtle complex of expectation and hope; an aggregation of lovely and exciting thoughts; conceptions of encounter and reactions picked up from observation, descriptions, drama; reveries of sensuous delights and ecstasies; reveries of understanding and reciprocity; which I will call the Lover-Shadow. I think it is primarily sexual and then social.[29]

This product of an imagination is "rather more male than is normal," he later admits and then pleads that, despite a "lurking infantilism," he has never allowed the Lover-Shadow to become "a sought-after saint or divinity."[30] He also admits that the "beloved person is for a time identified with the dream," making the relationship temporary, conditional, and entirely a function of male wishes.[31] The result is a sort of serial monogamy bordering on polygamy, with Wells mentioning "fear and aversion systems" in recognition of the psyche's bipolar attraction-aversion to successive Lover-Shadow figures, idealized only to be darkened by mistrust sooner or later. "She was to be a lovely, wise and generous person wholly devoted to me," he wrote not realizing that this would be called male chauvinism.[32] Indeed "Jane" enacted this role, as Wells pursued his elusive female ideal beyond her, "a Shelley-like liberalism of sexual conduct" he termed it, sometimes becoming a "crude disposition to *get* girls and women," he confesses.[33] These amours were hardly love affairs; "passades" is what he decided to call them, always disguising the amount of hostility they actually contained. It is not that Wells lacked insight into the hopelessness of pursuing perfection in a woman; at the end of the section on the Lover-Shadow he finds "chastity" and "peace of mind" appealing. But the degree of insight is not enough to check the impulse of "why not?" chase women who excite him most.

The writing is a curious tissue of insights from which he retreats into self-justification by universalizing and normalizing hypersexuality. Anxiety over maleness is pervasive, as he insists that his impulses were exclusively heterosexual.[34] In fact the section on the Lover Shadow is an unsatisfactory Jungian pastiche, reading as self-exculpation trying to pass as archetypalism. Wells is no Dante or Petrarch with their beguiling mythologies of the loved and lost ideal woman; nor has he come as far as John Fowles coyly trying in *Mantissa* (1982) to renegotiate with reality the hapless male wish for ideal sexuality. Fowles writes:

> I'm calling your disgusting, prototypal male bluff, that's what it means. And I'll tell you what a modern satyr is. He's someone who invents a woman on paper so that he can force her to say and do things no real woman in her right mind ever would.

> Who do you seriously think you're talking to? Who do you think was the Dark Lady of the *Sonnets,* for a start? You name them, I've known them. And not just Shakespeare. Milton. Rochester, Shelley. The man who wrote *The Boudoir.* Keats. H. G. Wells.[35]

Wells's separation of public persona (the crusading world citizen) from the private sexual self remains artificial with the failure to see the pseudo-reparative reaction formation at work in the autobiography. The term *Lover-Shadow* is not really examined for the ambiguity of its meaning. To be Jungian, Wells would have had to examine the dark side of the anima, which would have led him in the section on love affairs back to the feelings of oppression by his mother. He would have seen his idealizing "passades" as alternatives to his mother's anxious Christianity: a pseudo-religion of erotic love, with retributive features. As it is, an oversimplified animus figure emerges struggling to illustrate a male prowess belied by the evidence of how unsatisfactory his pursuit of ideal women really was. In this sense, the *Postscript* deconstructs itself, falling apart at the seams of Wells's rationalizations and evasions. It confesses much more than he grasps and holds together. Perhaps the fiction of the period of greatest sexual exploits contains more insight into their meaning.

IV

Wells's affair with Amber Reeves resulted in three confessional novels, *In the Days of the Comet* (1906), *Ann Veronica* (1909), and *The New Machiavelli* (1911), the latter two discussing the intricacies of the older married man falling in love with a lively girl. The situation was as the Mackenzies describe:

> When [Wells] was married to Isabel, he thought he had found his ideal type in Jane. Once he was married to Jane, he again began to feel stifled, and his infidelities became more frequent and blatant. By 1907 the unconscious pressure to escape had again built up. Rosamund Bland and the other young ladies with whom he dallied were more the object rather than the cause of his distracted behaviour.

> But the situation in 1908 was not the same as it had been in 1893. Apart from his domestic ties he was a public man with both political and literary reputations, and he could not take risks as impulsively as he had done when he was an insignificant young journalist earning a living in Grub Street.[36]

Amber was the brilliant daughter of Mr. and Mrs. Pember Reeves, New Zealanders who had come to London in the diplomatic service; successful at Cambridge and the London School of Economics, Amber exerted a fascination that Wells could not resist. Soon she was pregnant by him, but divorce was avoided and she remained his mistress. As Wells wrote, "She was overflowing with erotic adventurousness and pride," as he theorized about "free love" and thought of ways to make a triangle with Jane workable.[37] Under the illusion of a higher morality of romantic love, they eloped (briefly) to France, only to return to the inevitable complications in London among family, friends, and Fabian Socialist associates. "There was much vehement coming and going, and I made a complicated fluctuating fool of myself," Wells wrote in retrospect of relations with the girl he dubbed "Dusa," short for Medusa. The impossible relationship was dissolved when Amber married Blanco White, with Wells ending his rueful confession by calling himself "unscrupulous."

In the Days of the Comet (1906) concerns a double revolution: that of socialism against capitalism and that of sexual pluralism against monogamy. The novel's critics wondered whether Wells meant that the "great change" to socialism would necessarily bring "free love" along with it, an inference readily drawn from the novel.

As the hero Willie Leadford's mother is dying at the novel's end, a young girl Anna Reeves appears like an angel of mercy to replace the daughter who died in childhood. Anna is erotically exciting to Willie, not supplanting but supplementing Nettie over whose class-bound love he has agonized and plotted through the story. Anna is surely Wells's flame Amber Reeves, while Nettie is Isabel, the cousin he married. The novel's message of "free love" tries to justify events Wells felt himself actually to be following. To put it in cosmic terms—a comet passing close to the earth changes everything for the better—is to invoke the highest justification for changes in morality of the most subjective origin. With science fiction almost incongruous in the novel, we find in the brilliant subtext concerning Willie's relations with his mother explanation enough of Wells's theme. Willie's conflicted angry eroticism is that of the loved but oppressed mother's boy, who has seized on Nietzsche to write the adventures of an alienated sexual rebel. It is a parallel case to that developed more powerfully by Lawrence in *Sons and Lovers* (1913) a few years later; both writers searched the obsessive anxieties of an emergent group of working-class men who had been disabled for monogamy by their mothers.

"Why should one even sacrifice one's own future—because one's mother is totally destitute of imagination?" Wells writes of Willie who lives with his mother.[38] Willie is not only emotionally encumbered by his mother, but also bound by the limited religion and cultural awareness of her class. He feels "bitterness against all she held sacred," which cannot be discussed because she is so intimidated by class prohibitions. Willie feels a "scar" at having treated his mother badly as he "pushed past" her, away from being "stifled in the darkness, in a poisoned and vitiated air" (p. 33). These are strong fantasy words in a novel where the mother remains a moral reference point throughout.

Not surprisingly Wells's language describing love for Nettie is that of war, accompanied by guilt and shame. The novel is suffused with images of panicky violence and war hysteria: class war impending in Edwardian England mingles with moral war over sexual desire. A melodramatic scene, with hysterical language, develops around Willie's wish to buy a revolver to kill Nettie or Verrall, her lover. Rage mingles with impotence as he stalks them. It is as if Wells the novelist needed a miracle to deliver his hero from the extremes of adolescent emotion, with the comet a device to do so. In the utopia that follows the comet's arrival, such emotions are quieted into a rational pansexuality, or at least this is where the discussion tends. Now Nettie can have both Edward Verrall and Willie, and Wells writes in this tractlike part of the novel:

> There had been many at the season of the Change who had thought that this great enlargement of mankind would abolish personal love; but indeed it had only made it finer, fuller, more vitally necessary. (p. 186)

The scandal in Edwardian London over Amber Reeves was the basis of Wells's controversial *Ann Veronica*, quaint now in the society portrayed but in its time too close to reality for comfort. Why did Wells write this fiction so closely paralleling the adventure with Amber? Was it out of male bravado leading to guilt that had to be assuaged, and then atoned for? My view is that *Ann Veronica* is less a compensatory feminist tract in support of Amber's self-determination than it is Wells's own romantic wish fulfillment, a writing up of the affair as Wells wanted it to be, not as it turned out for him. No particular moral lesson is drawn for himself or Amber, with the relational truth not appearing until *The New Machiavelli* when it had been overlaid by other problematic sexual experiences.

Ann Veronica gives a glowingly sympathetic account of a spirited girl's attempt to free herself from male domination, from her heavy father, and men like him. She flees the respectable gentility of an upper middle-class household: Ann had lost her mother at thirteen, so father and an aunt are in charge. The irony is that, even against a background of suffragism, Ann Veronica Stanley is forced to compromise her flight into independence by going into debt to an older man, Ramage, who tries to seduce her. Unwilling to marry well-meaning Manning, Ann Veronica is swept into romance with Capes, a younger but married biology instructor. With his Darwinism Capes is in the forefront of thought, as Wells saw it; his intellectual verve and daring containing much of Wells's view of himself, with the self-portrait romanticized as Wells experienced the euphoria of being loved by the charming and brilliant Amber. But so also does the would-be seducer Ramage contain something of Wells in his early forties contemplating having to trick women he could no longer attract. Ann Veronica is never strictly Amber, but the vibrant temperament is derived from her, with the erotic adventure almost exactly paralleling that which Wells was engaged in while writing. He was prepared only to admit that the novel was "a pallid reflection of some aspects of our situation—or rather of the sentiments of our situation."[39] He was attempting, in fact, an apologia, a wonderful vision of what love brings to those willing to risk all.

The Mackenzies rightly call *Ann Veronica* "a tract masquerading as a piece of romantic fiction," making the point that the novel spoke powerfully to the young about a generation gap and the need for rebellion.[40] It was indeed rebellious sexual propaganda Wells wrote to justify actions taken for subjective reasons that are not studied in *Ann Veronica*. That novel simply constructs the situation as he most wanted it to be, making a closing sequence "a fulfilment of his own fantasies," as Jeanne Mackenzie writes in her introduction. Self-justification powerfully enters as Capes speaks for Wells's "new morality" of being able to subdue the guilt of an illicit but ecstatic relationship with a girl ten years younger than himself. Capes rehearses for Ann his story of marital discord, opining that he has been "vicious" in a former betrayal of his wife, coming to Ann as "damaged goods." This only makes Ann "love [him] more," the staging of a morality of romantic escapism in Switzerland with which the novel closes.[41]

> She lifted steadfast eyes to him. "Dare!" she said. The tears were wel-
> ling over now, but her voice was steady. "You're not a man for me—
> not one of a sex I mean. You're just a particular being with nothing
> else in the world to class with you. You are just necessary to life for
> me. I've never met any one like you. To have you is all-important.
> Nothing else weighs against it. Morals only begin when that is settled.
> I'm not a bit afraid of anything—scandal, difficulty, struggle. . . . I
> rather want them. I do want them."
> "You'll get them," he said. "This means a plunge." (p. 256)

As Wells tried to convince the reader, Capes's and Ann Veronica's escape to Switzerland was like a rebirth, a religious experience on which a whole new morality could be founded.

> Capes thought.
> "It's odd—I have no doubt in my mind that what we are doing is
> wrong," he said. "And yet I do it without compunction." "I never felt
> so absolutely right," said Ann Veronica. "You *are* female at the bot-
> tom," he admitted. "I'm not nearly so sure as you. As for me, I look
> twice at it . . . Life is two things, that's how I see it; two things mixed
> and muddled up together. Life is morality—life is adventure. Squire
> and master. Adventure rules and morality—looks up the trains in the
> Bradshaw. Morality tells you what is right, and adventure moves you.
> If morality means anything it means keeping bounds, respecting im-
> plications, respecting implicit bounds. If individuality means anything
> it means breaking bounds—adventure. Will you be moral and your

species, or immoral and yourself? We've decided to be immoral. (pp. 271–72)

Now the reader is supposed to think: anything this beautiful can't be immoral. To insure this impression, Wells steps up insistence that Ann is an "Immortal," a "goddess" to whom he is willingly a "slave": "'Your priestess,' whispers Ann Veronica softly. 'A silly little priestess who knew nothing of life at all until she came to you'" (pp. 284–85). The novel ends as a sentimental success story, examining none of the implications that had been so distressingly part of the Amber Reeves scandal. These implications are left for Wells's more searching first person confession, *The New Machiavelli*, his next novel after the lighthearted *The History of Mr. Polly* (1910).

The New Machiavelli looks at the question "Why not" [be guided strictly by the excitements of sexual desire]?[42] It surpasses the uncritical *Ann Veronica* by reconsidering the romantic urges that had led to the affair with Amber Reeves and others. A reparative intention may be claimed for this novel as it reconstructs Wells's life from childhood into his years of tortured eroticism. Not everything in the story of his persona Remington is meant to be factually accurate—Wells was never at Trinity College, Cambridge, for instance. But the novel connects personal developmental events with political and literary ambitions much as they were in Wells's actual life. It is a narrative of feeling states, with Wells trying to convey *what it felt like* to pass through the stages that carried him into Fabian politics and out again owing to overmastering sexual needs. The compulsive affair with Amber (Isabel Rivers in the story) is examined in relation to his marriage to Jane (Margaret), along with his earliest formative relations with both parents. In other words, a first person etiological point of view operates, with Wells trying to understand the linkages among various phases of his difficult life. Was he responding to the call of Freud then beginning to be heard in English intellectual circles? Without the evidence to explain so radical a departure in the novel we must simply ask how successfully Wells provided a causality for his personal narrative.

The opening section on parenting is critical in judging Wells's success in building a plausible account of the sexual style that had proved so problematic in the affair with Amber. The terms *Don Juan* (Ladies' Man), or even Lover-Shadow, are not used, as Wells has no diagnostic category for himself. Remington's condition is nonetheless accurately described:

I seemed always to be seeking something in women, in girls, and I was never clear what it was I was seeking. But never—even at my coarsest—was I moved by physical desire alone. Was I seeking help and fellowship? Was I seeking some intimacy with beauty? It was a thing too formless to state, that I seemed always desiring to attain and never attaining. Waves of gross sensuousness arose out of this preoccupation, carried me to a crisis of gratification or disappointment that was clearly not the needed thing; they passed and left my mind free again for a time to get on with the permanent pursuits of my life. And then presently this solicitude would have me again, an irrelevance as it seemed, and yet a constantly recurring demand. (p. 174)

Recollecting his youthful escapades, Remington's language is both evasive and moral: "I was no systematic libertine . . . things happened to me and desire drove me," he comments. But in speaking of using prostitutes his language is surprisingly moral: "ugly and shameful," alerting us to a strongly moral theme driving the novel's enquiry (p. 175). It is this residual moral sense that gives Wells a hold on his material, along with determination to display it as candidly as possible.

If the standard is taken as D. H. Lawrence's portrayal of Paul Morel's relations with his parents in *Sons and Lovers,* then Wells a little earlier had more than prepared the way. When the Machiavellian artifice of love and statecraft is set aside as an awkwardness in the novel (Remington's sense of exile need only be stated as such), Wells can be admired for the etiological vigor with which his novel opens. Enough is said about Remington's parenting to open the question about how a frustrated capacity for loving may lead to excessive interest in political power. If Wells lacks Lawrence's ability to feel the utter reality of working-class life, he does have the ability unforgettably to portray parents in their social setting.

As expected, portrayal of Remington's mother takes precedence. She is shown to have interfered with the child's escapist playing, rather than encourage playing to engage more realistically with the world. Mother is remembered wearing "spring-sided boots," like some anticipated storm trooper. She was always "fetching" the young Remington somewhere, doing to and not being for the child whose strong will tested her nerves. He especially had to evade her religious rule making on Sundays, playing with cannon-carrying ships, pretending they were Noah's ark. There is little pleasant in the portrait of Remington's controlling yet uncertain mother; it is affectionate but puzzled, resisting out-

right anger from the novelist, while resentment boils beneath
the surface.

> I can see her and feel her as a loving and feeling and desiring and
> muddle-headed person. There are times when I would have her alive
> again, if only that I might be kind to her for a little while and give
> her some return for the narrow intense affection, the tender desires,
> she evidently lavished so abundantly on me. But then again I ask how
> I could make that return? And I realize the futility of such dreaming.
> Her demand was rigid, and to meet it I should need to act and lie.
> So she whose blood fed me, whose body made me, lies in my mem-
> ory as I saw her last, fixed, still, infinitely intimate, infinitely remote.
> (p. 49)

Although Wells's mother lived until he was thirty-nine (1905),
Remington's mother dies of appendicitis when he is only sixteen.
It was of this disease that Wells's sister "Possy" had died making
the early termination doubly significant. Yet he could not kill off
his mother's interior presence, in part goading and persecuting
him, in part imploring him to be the perfect child she had lost.
It was an unintelligible set of instructions, with their ambiguity
governing Wells's portrait of Remington's mother. Like his own,
this mother keeps a diary in which no word of love for her husband is to be found: "I went through all her diaries, trying to
find something more than a conventional term of tenderness for
my father. But I found nothing" (p. 48).

The portrait of Remington's father as a science teacher is, of
course, fabrication; but the psychological profile is recognizably
that of feckless Joe Wells. The passage on his incompetence as a
gardener is fine domestic comedy with the distinct touch of pathos
for his father that Wells had shown in his autobiography. Descrip-
tions of Dickens-like immediacy catch Joe Wells exactly:

> "Slaves to matter! Minding inanimate things! It doesn't suit me, you
> know. I've got no hands and no patience. I've mucked about with life.
> Mucked about with life." He suddenly addressed himself to me, and
> for an instant I started like an eavesdropper discovered. "Whatever
> you do, boy, whatever you do, make a Plan. Make a good Plan and
> stick to it. Find out what life is about—*I* never have—and set yourself
> to do—whatever you ought to do. I admit it's a puzzle." (p. 30)

Controlling mother, disapproved-of, weak but lively cricketing
"man's man" father is a formula for the mystification of sexuality,
as appears in chapter 4. Wells could not decipher what was wanted

of him as a man so, having suffered confusions of gender, for which the hypermasculine role was an attempted corrective, he set about in the novel to discover "factors and early influences." Remington says, "I sought to pierce the web of appearances about me," deciding that it was not religion that upset him but sexuality.

> I was afraid to think either of sex or (what I have always found insepa-rable from a kind of sexual emotion) beauty. Even as a boy I knew the thing as a haunting and alluring mystery that I tried to keep away from. Its dim presence obsessed me none the less for all the extrava-gant decency, the stimulating silences of my upbringing. (p. 76)

As noted, pent-up adolescent desires found their object in plaster Venuses at the Crystal Palace that translated into sexual fantasies, much as Wells tells it in his autobiography. This early sexual de-flection prepares for the novel's triangular misadventure. Wells's summary of the genesis of unconscious contents ("a locked avoided chamber," still further suggesting Freudian influence) could hardly be bettered:

> The strangest thing of all my odd and solitary upbringing seems to me now that swathing up of all the splendours of the flesh, that strange combination of fanatical terrorism and shyness that fenced me about with prohibitions. It caused me to grow up, I will not say blankly ignorant, but with an ignorance blurred and dishonoured by shame, by enigmatical warnings, by cultivated aversions, an ignorance in which a fascinated curiosity and desire struggled like a thing in a net. I knew so little and felt so much. (p. 77)

The amount of concern with Edwardian political life in *The New Machiavelli* does not seem strange because of the theme of power that this novel develops. Remington tries to direct his sexual anxieties into the political control systems by which society is gov-erned, only to find that his credibility has been sacrificed by the affair with Isabel. With both free love and politics closed to them, the lovers must flee to Europe, fugitives from the mess they have made. There is nothing of *Ann Veronica*'s romantic glow (as Capes and Ann flee to Switzerland) at the end of *The New Machiavelli*. Subdued with chagrin, Remington is left with little more than the power to tell his story of collapsed ambitions. Most significant about this novel is not its evoking of no longer topical politics, but its brilliantly synoptic view of a ladies' man in crisis.

Wells relates the displacement of Margaret by Isabel with de-scriptive exactness, revealing the illusion of a pseudoreligion of love. How far Wells was aware in its narration of the illusion is debatable—he no doubt fluctuated in awareness. We must remember that the novel is not an Augustinian confession: it brings about no repentance and change, being at best exploratory. The emotional crisis Wells sets up begins, not surprisingly, with Margaret (Jane) being idealized as a saving saint of womanhood almost too good to touch: "All the time that I was seeing her as a beautiful fragile, rather ineffective girl, I was also seeing her just as consciously as a shining slender figure, a radiant reconciliation, coming into my darkling disorders of lust and impulse." He contemplates "praying to her and putting all the intricate troubles of my life at her feet" (p. 177).

He treats her as a votive object, a saint of love capable of "saving" his soul, creating a harmony out of his inner discord. But the reparative wish is a futile investment of hope in another fragile human being with needs of her own. We soon hear of dire subconscious forces, "the cavernous hidden life" in the male, which destroys all idealization and the marriage into the bargain.

> Down there things may be prowling that scarce ever peep out to consciousness except in the grey half-light of sleepless nights, passions that flash out for an instant in an angry glance and are seen no more, starved victims and beautiful dreams bricked up to die. (p. 195)

In these lurid words (reminding us more of Bunyan's *Pilgrim's Progress* than of contemporary fiction), Wells tried to find a language for the onset of punitive resentment against gentle, self-sacrificing Margaret. Indeed, Wells's wife Jane was to selflessly give him comfort and manage his household and business dealings through a series of affairs, not only with Amber, but also with Elizabeth Von Arnim, Rebecca West, Moura Budberg, Margaret Sanger, and Odette Keun to name the most prominent, until her death in 1927. Remington's charges against Margaret are never very specific, consisting mainly of contrasts between his "rough-minded" and her "tender-minded" ways: "My quality is sensuous and ruled by warm impulses; hers was discriminating and essentially inhibitory" (p. 196). He withdraws from her, engaging in "immense spiritual concealments" and "spiritual subterfuge" (p. 197).

> My idealization of Margaret had evaporated insensibly after our marriage. The shrine I had made for her in my private thoughts stood at last undisguisedly empty. (p. 207)

Wells thus writes confessionally of a divided attitude to love, coming of the structural division in himself, the "divided self" of which every psychodynamic theory from Freud to R. D. Laing says much. While Wells's formulation remained primitive, it shows him struggling toward an understanding of why marriages go wrong. Speaking of "a hidden life," he contrasts the "back self," having an unseen history of its own, with the "ostensible self," which is the public self of everyday life. Their demands are easily incompatible, as he strove to explain in 1908–9 when writing *The New Machiavelli.* Wells therefore has Remington grope for reasons for turning against Margaret, but as noted these are not very substantial—"a curious irritability towards Margaret," or "Her serene, sustained confidence in vague formulae and sentimental aspirations exasperated me," and so on (p. 283). A familiar Don Juan formula is used to say what was wrong: "My own feelings were curiously divided," on the one hand, the romantic idealization of "her purity and beauty," on the other, the fear of "servitude," feeling "caught": "it had been my own act to rivet on my shackles." (pp. 289–90). The attempt to explain this ambivalence is inadequate but in the right direction:

> I missed the chance of sisters and girl playmates, but that is not an uncommon misadventure in an age of small families; I never came to know any woman at all intimately until I was married to Margaret.

Forgetfulness of his mother seems almost deliberate as Remington sums up effects, apart from probable causes:

> From a boyish disposition to be mystical and worshipping towards women I had passed into a disregardful attitude, as though women were things inferior or irrelevant, disturbers of great affairs. (p. 299)

Women as mothers are either helpers or inhibitors of human development, and when they are called "disturbers" we infer some degree of inhibition, even trauma at the hands of such as Sarah Wells. But these remarks in the novel are chronologically distant from those of Remington's childhood in the opening chapters, with Wells conceptually innocent of any lasting effects of probable trauma. The countercontrol of women seen as "disturbers" of inner peace is spoken of without grasping its real meaning. As Wells puts it, the old problem of women was temporarily solved by "marriage and disregard," only to find the "fundamental obsession of my life returned." This obsession is the inability to take a clear view of women: "Is she to be tried and trusted or guarded and controlled, bond or free?" (p. 300). Remington's need for a glorious and vibrant new love in Isabel comes into focus as the essence of freedom—until the threat of *control by her* reemerges, necessitating countermeasures. We see incidentally the lineaments of Wells's suffragist rationale for freeing women from fear-inspired male domination, a corrective if there were to be social and political justice. We may wonder whether male feminists, such as Wells and Russell, were typically working off the cruelties they inflicted by obsessive countercontrol measures against women.

What does Wells say about Remington's atonement for wrongs done to Margaret? He writes, "I do not want to seem to confess my sins with a penitence I am very doubtful if I feel"; yet he goes on to say of himself and Isabel, "we are two bad people, we have acted badly," accepting culpability without intent of penitence. The rationale of impulsive love as its own justification resembles Lawrence's later: "I will confess that in my mind is a belief in a sort of wild rightness about any love that is fraught with beauty," said with a partial retraction in the balance of the statement (p. 316). Wells sees moral havoc in post-Victorian sexuality: "We are *forced* to be laws unto ourselves and to live experimentally," yet following the life force of impulse can easily lead to scandal of the sort that ends Remington's career. The debate in Wells's soul is reduced to starkly dramatic terms—to Isabel "as natural as a savage" while Margaret languishes uninterestingly (p. 317). He and Isabel are subject to "passion that lay like a coiled snake in the path before us," the myth of The Fall empowering Wells's editorializing on the moral dilemma of his times: "Such friendships are not uncommon nowadays—among easygoing, liberal minded people" (p. 318). The Fall is accepted, its extended moral consequences in the destinies of hurt, rejected lovers and perhaps unwanted poorly parented offspring, unexamined. Wells had a thesis to impart directly, without the wit of a Shaw. The new liberals have a hardly "easygoing" choice before them, as Wells the tractarian steps forward from his fiction. Speaking of Remington's affair with Isabel, he says:

If men and women are to go so far together, they must be free to go as far as they may want to go, without the vindictive destruction that has come upon us. On the basis of the accepted code, the jealous people are right and the liberal-minded ones are playing with fire. If people are not to love, then they must be kept apart. If they are not

to be kept apart, then we must prepare for an unprecedented tolera-
tion of lovers. (p. 320)

This heralds a massive shift of values toward the "permissive
society" that took shape in the aftermath of two world wars, coin-
ciding with the sort of scientific and technological advances Wells
wanted. Yet the psychological, social, and cultural roots of permissiveness have never been looked at together. What is the connection between the driving force of science and technology and
the sort of sexual obsession of which Wells writes? ("I became a
monomaniac to whom nothing could matter but Isabel. Every
truth had to be squared to that obsession, every duty," as he wrote
(p. 367)). The novel cannot tell us, its compass being too small for
the questions raised.

Wells the compulsive lover was notorious in his time, "a discriminating philanderer, a taster of many dishes, a charmer with few
defeats," as Juliette Huxley writes.[43] He was also a determined
destroyer of a faulty moral consensus that had been built up over
untold generations in England. Darwinism permitted the expression of more primitive urges and emotions than Victorian civilities
could easily contemplate. Wells's criticism was seized on by discon-
tented young readers looking for an alternative to stultifying sexual conventions. Yet his was a distorted prophecy, the teachings
of a ladies' man who strove as best he could in autobiography and
fiction to discover the psychogenic factors underlying his compulsions. Wishing, no doubt, to clear up the distortions, he could not
do so lacking a psychology. The documents he left help to form
the basis for such a psychology as yet fully to be formulated in
the wake of fictional "discovery."

Wells's hypersexuality is poorly understood for instance by David C. Smith, Wells's most recent biographer who writes flatly that
he "had a substantial need for sexual release." Smith adds, "His
life was in something of a turmoil," indicative of the overly admiring and complacent tone of this biography.[44] Smith likes to think
of Wells's being chased by women, not the reverse, with the idea
of need for "release" being simplistic Freudianism unbefitting a
contemporary biographer. Nor does Smith see that Wells's rejection of the historical past, his glorification of a scientific future,
and his grandiose idea of a world state are more escapist than
reconstructive of the undesirable effects of erotic drivenness.
Wells needs to be seen as a principal shaper of the emotionally
overwrought, crisis-laden atmosphere of late twentieth-century
sexual relationships. His audacious challenge to monogamy mer-

its at least an equally audacious challenge to him and his art. As Vincent Brome rightly commented, freedom of the sexes "was first made articulate by Wells, laughingly reaffirmed by Shaw, developed in lyrical unrestraint by Lawrence, and given a cynical sanction—if not smear—by Aldous Huxley."[45] Wells's womanizing was no triumph of masculinity but evidence of persisting lifelong developmental failures with his mother and father. His sexuality was distorted first in gender confusion, then in matters of over-control with insufficient maternal communication about what she expected of him and herself. It was courageous of Wells to agonize over these early influences and their effects, but such insight as he had did not seem to reduce his alternating idealization and hostility toward the women he "loved." In the end each of Wells's spectacular affairs was a futile attempt to surmount the polarities of sexual ambivalence. The shadow always fell over the lover, as Wells moved on to new conquests. Further, the touching moment of bad conscience over the fiasco with Amber Reeves that resulted in *Ann Veronica* and *The New Machiavelli* did not recur. Wells apparently convinced himself of the desirability of his style of loving, as the cultural avant-garde increasingly took it as their own. The novel of ideas, it may be concluded, is always limited by the quality of its ideas, however winningly embodied they may be.

3

Hermann Hesse and Bisexuality

Condition of Man: inconstancy, weariness, unrest.
—Blaise Pascal, *Pensées*, #127

Hᴇʀᴍᴀɴɴ Hesse is the modern novelist who most imaginatively portrays bisexual ideation, in all likelihood as a product of childhood suffering. Taken together, *Demian* (1919) and *Steppenwolf* (1927) brilliantly pose the question of male bisexual ambivalence as a form of erotic alienation and compromise formation. Whether Hesse simply learned about bisexuality and wrote about it out of interest or was compelled to do so as a mode of psychological relief, or some combination of the two, is the major question to be addressed. However it happened, the archetypal imagination was brought into play with unprecedented results in these two novels, now classics in Western fiction. The development of Hesse's imaginative power may be traced to his encounter with psychoanalysis as proposed by Freud and redirected into archetypalism by Jung and his followers.

Hesse was a naturally confessional writer assisted by psychoanalysis to realize the power of childhood experiences. He was not so much an autobiographer narrating in detail events of childhood as a self-mythologizer looking for the essence of experience. In "Life Story Briefly Told" (1925) we learn that Hesse was a rebel:

> I was the child of pious parents, whom I loved tenderly and would have loved even more tenderly if I had not very early been introduced to the Fourth Commandment. Unfortunately, commandments have always had a disastrous effect on me, however right and well meant they may be—though by nature a lamb and docile as a soap bubble.[1]

But had his parents really been so loved, or is there other evidence? In a story, "A Child's Heart," which may be taken to represent Hesse's own experience, he writes:

The adults acted as if the world were perfect and as if they themselves were demigods, we children were nothing but scum . . . Again and again, after a few days, even after a few hours, something happened that should not have been allowed, something wretched, depressing, and shaming. Again and again, in the midst of the noblest and staunchest decisions and vows, I fell abruptly, inescapably, into sin and wickedness, into ordinary bad habits. Why was it this way?[2]

Hesse the angry rebel is implicit in this passage: a child filled with guilt he did not understand.

It is easy to guess that a child made to feel so guilty and inadequate would retreat into imagination. Fortunately for Hesse, there was an alternative to Pietism in religions of the East to which his missionary family gave access. Claiming to have "practised the Western virtues of impetuosity, greed and unquenchable curiosity," Hesse nonetheless partook of Eastern religion and mythology in ways that allowed a more passive contemplative mode of life.[3] While action and contemplation are never fully reconciled in his fiction, at least recognition of a need to do so is present. This is the magician's task, the transformation of the ordinary into the wondrous, which Hesse the writer certainly could do. His guiding motif was bicultural: the god Pan, the Greek pastoral god of fertility and amorousness, and the Hindu god Shiva, the phallic destroyer who is also the penitential ascetic. The Hindu dancing god, first encountered in his grandfather's collection of exotic art, took on multiple identities: "Shiva, Vishnu . . . God, Life, Brahman, Atman, Tao, or Eternal Mother. It was father, was mother, it was woman and man, sun and moon."[4] We are thus introduced indirectly to the seemingly contradictory bipolarities that abound in Hesse's fiction. It may seem odd that the mother should figure so prominently in associations to an erotic male god; it is part of our problem to understand this better than Hesse himself was able to do.

Hesse makes clear that both the rich mythic learning and the collections of his maternal grandfather, working through his mother's personality more than through that of the remote grandfather himself, had lasting impact. In comparison, his father's Pietism (the attempt to put the spirit of Christian living above Protestant doctrine) had little to offer, unless Hesse's confessional bent in fiction may be in part attributed to the experiential emphasis of Pietism. It is important to hear Hesse at length on how the spell of his mother overshadowed paternal influence. From the maternal grandfather:

from this unfathomable one, I knew, came the secret that surrounded my mother, the secret, age-old mystery, and she too had been in India for a long time, she too could speak and sing in Malayan and Kanarese, she exchanged phrases and maxims with her aged father in strange, magical tongues. And at times she possessed, like him, the stranger's smile, the veiled smile of wisdom.

Hesse continues:

My father was different. He stood alone, belonging neither to the world of the idols and of my grandfather nor to the workaday world of the city. He stood to one side, lonely, a sufferer and a seeker, learned and kindly, without falseness and full of zeal in the service of truth, but far removed from that noble and tender but unmistakable smile— he had no trace of mystery.

The remarks on his father's limited influence are concluded:

at times I strove to emulate him, full of admiration and zeal, all too much zeal, although I knew that my roots reached deeper into my mother's soil, into the dark-eyed and mysterious. My mother was full of music, my father was not, he could not sing.[5]

As with the other writers we are studying, Hesse had both parents, but the mother was clearly dominant in his early development and thus in his imaginative life. How was it that the rebellious son Hesse always wanted to be a poet, to find the cause of human suffering not so much in politics as inside himself? What so sensitized him to suffering, especially his own: indeed, what had mothering to do with his address to Europe's wars, not so much as political eruptions as emanations of the distressed psyche? As a pacifist, reviled for his opinions during World War I, Hesse stood apart. What new expression of psychological organization did this represent, and was there adaptive utility for society in Hesse's special discoveries? By his profound revelations of inner reality, of divided self (including bisexuality) I believe that Hesse is among the most important post-Freudian/Jungian writers of fiction to redefine the problem of male aggression.

Early family dynamics help to explain why Hesse was such a rebel from orthodox Christianity and "normal" family organization, yet at the same time a religious seeker and a lover of women. Beyond the isolation that strict Pietism itself imposed were the particular dynamics of Hesse's family in which mother impressed him more deeply than father. Hermann's relations with his mother became so tense that she constantly worried about his behavior. When Hermann was born in 1877, his sister Adele was two; in 1879 and 1880 Gertrud and Paul were born but died in infancy. It would be three years before Marulla was born and another two years before Johannes's birth. This left Hermann exposed in an upset and grieving family. Probably it was then that this exceptionally gifted and energetic (hyperactive) boy, from ages one to two, became enmeshed with his mother. Anxiety about further deaths could well have made her tense with him, producing a struggle of wills for his own good. By age three, when Hermann was going to nursery school, his mother thought of his temperament as "violent," a condition that worsened with various attempts in schools and institutions to control his conflicted vitality. Worrying, obsessive, and narcissistic trends in his personality showed early and were misunderstood by his parents.

Hesse's feelings about women were pained and ambiguous throughout his life, a feature that in his fiction looks like obsessional Don Juan control (a defensive countercontrol method in the assumptive realm of interpersonal relations). Not only is control of women, as much by idealization as by outright manipulation, a feature of the fiction, but also is the bisexuality that functions as a built-in escape allowing release of emotional pressure. Multiple "loves" and ambiguity over preferred gender, make *Demian* and *Steppenwolf* problematic, as we shall see. The correlative in life was a history of tense relations with female lovers, including three marriages of which two ended in divorce. To his great credit, Hesse used his creative powers to understand the crisis-prone emotional life he led. Part of him was critical of the destructive impulses he habored. Writing about Casanova in 1925, Hesse found the famous womanizer a slight but fascinating figure. In Hesse's view Casanova lacked "the heroic quality," the "isolation and tragic loneliness without which we cannot picture genius"; yet he judges Casanova's libertinism far above that of the "Berlin Don Juans" of his own day.[6]

II

Sexual guilt is a pervasive feature of Hesse's writing. In "Life Story Briefly Told" he presents the fantasy of the guilty seducer sent to prison at age seventy only to ask for paints to "play" with imagery like a child. A beautiful landscape is created to take Hesse's mind from his imprisonment, but his captors put him on trial for "seduction by magic of a young girl," suggesting the charge brought against Harry Haller for "murdering" Hermine in *Steppenwc'f.*[7] The alacrity with which Hesse admitted to "guilt" indicates the depth and pervasiveness of bad conscience in his family and culture. The theme repeats itself in obsessional fantasies in fiction, for instance in Fowles's *The Collector* where sexuality is both secretive and punitive, and in Nabokov's *Lolita* where Humbert Humbert must explain to judge and jury his misdeeds with a female minor no matter what "enchantment" the magic of pedophilia may have engendered. Hesse is similarly an enchanter who creates painful situations while hoping to be free of them. Why was it that the prison of childhood guilt built around Hesse was so nearly impossible to escape?

When Hesse wrote of loving tenderly his pious parents, he omitted to say how much he despaired of making real contact with either. Born 2 July 1877 in Cawl, Wurttemberg, Hesse entered a world of postmissionary Protestant strictness that was embodied differently in each parent. The common factor, however, was guilt and depression that sapped the vitality Hesse so craved. The biographer Ralph Freedman describes Hermann's father Johannes as thin, ascetic, and having constant headaches, while his mother Marie's face seemed impassive and severe—a statement at odds with Hermann's own description of his mother as having "the stranger's smile, the veiled smile of wisdom." In other words there was an enticement Freedman isn't seeing, yet he does mention her "warm, lively eyes."[8] These were the eyes of mystery that drew Hermann to his mother with the promise of a quality of contact never achieved owing to her own legacy of childhood depression. Though Hesse could write appreciatively of his father, the evidence is that through much of his childhood, he was less open to contact than was his mother. Chronic ill health, the sequel of his early life as a missionary in India, dogged him during his career in religious publishing, and, when Hermann was twelve, Johannes broke down completely and was hospitalized for compulsive weeping and melancholia, a circumstance that greatly affected his son.

When Marie married Johannes, she was a thirty-one year-old widow with two sons whose missionary father Charles Isenberg she had married in India. Isenberg's early death left her at twenty-eight, "severe, middle-aged," according to Freedman.[9] This tragedy was the culmination of the almost unbearable emotional hardships of Marie's childhood and youth. Born to missionary parents in India, she enjoyed less than four years of their care before virtual abandonment. When her mother became ill, she took Marie with her when she was sent back to Europe to recuperate but left her daughter, just turning four, at a home in Basel so that she could resume missionary work in India. Remembering the scene of separation at the home for missionary children, Marie wrote:

> I can still see how I stood weeping in the courtyard and tried to hold on to my mother by force, hanging on to the edge of her shawl. I was pulled away and carried into the nursery. My entire inner life was outraged. I felt as though the whole world had conspired against me.[10]

However common such separations were for missionary children, Marie's was not well managed and in her anger she destroyed toys. Marie spent eight years in the home before being sent to a strict religious boarding school for girls. Her diaries show adolescent struggles between an increasingly alien ideal of Christian service and an eroticism to which she was introduced by a "wayward teacher Fräulein Lotte during Marie's last few years in Basel."[11] Marie rebelled against Pietistic restrictions on freedom, as she found solace in befriending outcasts at school. This led her father to remove her from the school, first to return to her foster parents in Basel and then to live with a French Calvinist family. At fifteen, she was allowed to rejoin her parents in India, and on shipboard she had a romance with a man she wanted to marry. Unfortunately her parents found him unsuitable and she was asked to submit to their wishes. In February 1858, influenced by missionary preaching, Marie experienced an illumination that changed the direction of her life back to religious service. Hesse's mother was thus a woman of energy and passion whose early life of broken attachments made her vulnerable to depressive mood changes, rebellion alternating with submission to the will of others. Freedman suggests that "the contradictions in the mother may foreshadow those in the son," a remark bearing further investigation.[12] It should also be mentioned that Hesse's mother was a writer of sorts, keeping both girlhood journals and journals of her early married life. Confiding in writing was her only form of self-analysis it seems; her son would push well beyond the limitations of this mode of self-healing confession.

Five years older than Hermann's mother and less given to self-expression, Johannes's childhood was marked by maternal loss and substitute caretaking. His father, a country doctor, had three wives. When Johannes's mother died in childbirth, he was left to be brought up by the third wife, the second also having died in childbirth after a brief marriage. If anything, Johannes's psychological overload of grief over loss was greater than Marie's. He was a difficult child—angry, defiant, and anxious—who was eventually sent away to Estonia, much as his difficult son Hermann would be sent away. It is little wonder that Johannes always had "a sad aspect," that his health was fragile and that depression should overtake him while he worked for his father-in-law's missionary magazine as editorial assistant. Johannes too had ability as a writer, but there is nothing to indicate that it touched Hesse's forming imagination. Observing his father's melancholia may, however, have awakened compassion for suffering, which Hesse the pacifist always showed. A strong male identification would always elude him, while he understood the problem of male suffering better than almost any writer of his generation.

Hesse's autobiographical writings do not hint at early bisexual interest, do not in fact mention problems of gender at all. In "Childhood of the Magician" Hesse records his feelings that a secret cultivation of the imagination acted as a protection against a society dismissive and sometimes cruel toward children. Here is the novelist's testimony to the saving power of imagination without saying precisely from what, in his experience of being parented, it was saving him. We might infer disciplinarian strictness and sexual repression; better the dancing Shiva from India than the fear of child's play in Protestant Germany. But what did this mean in actual developmental terms? Hesse was not for saying, or could not say. That normal sexuality was not explained to him appears from the split-off "little man" ("angel or demon") sequence, recounting adventures of the antiself from earliest childhood. The little man suggests a spontaneous self that had to remain secretive within the strictly regulated family—the self that only imagination could nourish and follow. Hesse does not fully spell out that it turned into a raging rebel with which no school or house of correction could deal. It is enough that he describes the little man as adolescent phallic eroticism (the advent of erections, a mystery he could not solve alone). In this narcissistic phase, guilt assailed him. Near to suicide, as he describes himself, with anxiety about human reproduction, Hesse turned to a willing neighbor Frau Anna, who initiated him into the mystery of female sexuality. He praises Frau Anna as being "natural and open, always aware, never deceitful or embarrassed," an obvious contrast to mother and perhaps sisters.[13]

There are two disadvantages in discussing bisexuality in Hesse's novels. The first, lack of sufficient psychobiography, will probably remain a barrier to discussion of his psychosocial development.

The flight into childhood imagination is indicative of something wrong, but precisely what is hard to say. That Hesse's mature fiction dwells on bisexuality is suggestive, but beyond that it is unwise to speculate. The other difficulty is with the theory of bisexuality itself, as the causes are not fully understood. However, the question whether he simply picked up a current idea or was compelled by it after reading psychoanalytic literature hoping for self-help, can be tentatively answered. Freud had insisted on innate bisexuality in *Three Essays on the Theory of Sexuality* (1905) and in other writings. Somewhat later, Jung speculated that anima and animus were present in varying combinations in both men and women. It was the Viennese psychiatrist Krafft-Ebing who in 1896 had described bisexuality as a sort of mental hermaphroditism, not far off from homosexuality. Also prior to Freud's *Three Essays* Magnus Hirschfeld and Havelock Ellis publicized the idea of innate bisexuality.[14] Thus the idea was readily available to Hesse; yet its massive acceptance into his novels speaks for a personal shock of recognition he must have felt. Whatever its origin, we cannot doubt that Hesse worked with a personal conflict in the matter of bisexuality, trying it on as a solution to the pervasive anxiety stemming from sexual repression in a maternally overstimulated but also paternally disciplined family. Much more would have to be known about Hesse's reactions to each parent for anything certain to be said about bisexuality as an outcome.

III

Demian (1919) was the unexpected product of Hesse's personal analysis with the Jungian analyst Josef B. Lang. It completely changed his mode of writing fiction from the naturalistic conventional narrative to a mythic inwardness serving the discovery of unconscious imperatives. Reflecting the shock of World War I violence, the novel asks new questions about conflicts in the male psyche—the conflicts that lead men to war. *Demian* examines with a new precision the attraction to and the repulsion from females as mothers and lovers, together with the phenomenon of male hero worship. Male erotic attraction to the same sex in its most idealized "hero"-like form makes the novel a young man's book. Yet it reads as a sophisticated analysis of ambivalence toward women and of male bisexuality, an analysis possible only for a skilled writer who has begun to understand the revelations of psychoanalysis. It was published under a self-protective pseudonym.

Hesse's analysis with Dr. Lang was necessitated by a depression that would not remit. In 1915, Hesse suffered a "crisis of nerves" brought on by the mental illness of his first wife Maria Bernoulli, an illness of his son Martin, compounded by the death of his father in March 1916. As Hesse wrote to a friend, "On the way home from my father's burial I suddenly collapsed completely. An almost unbearable headache plagues me most, otherwise only weakness, some dizziness, and feelings of anxiety."[15] Opinions differ about exactly what went wrong with Hesse: Miriam Reik thought he was "suffering from symptoms of a compulsion neurosis," while Ralph Freedman simply points out that he "felt reduced to a state of helplessness for the fourth time since adolescence: in his twenties in Basel; at thirty in 1907 when he was just moving into his house in Gaienhofen; in India when he was unable to face himself in an alien world; and now, following the death of his father."[16] His suffering was bad enough that he was hospitalized in the "Kurhaus Sonnmatt" where his "crisis of nerves" was treated with mild shock (a treatment he had earlier had during his troubled childhood), massage, and sunbathing; but the analysis was by far the most meaningful part of his cure.[17] His bereft state of double loss and anxiety over illness reconnected him with the timeless mythic elements in human experience—an enlargement beyond family distress to the great archetypes of the human family.

Lang's analytic method will never be known in full, his case notes having been destroyed except for a few entries. From these we gather that Lang thought of the psyche as a mine shaft along which the analyst hammered to free his trapped patient. Meeting his patient in the depths of the psyche was attempted, successfully as Hesse felt. Lang seems to have used a guided imagery technique to enlarge the particular suffering's frame of reference, inducing "rebirth" into larger archetypal awareness. For Hesse, whose imagination was already highly developed, the journey from spiritual death to rebirth was just right, serving the need to mourn losses and to overcome in some degree the chronic feelings of guilt from which he suffered. The analysis with Lang served Hesse well by allowing him to admit his own pathological processes, freeing their energies for a new and socially useful art of the unconscious. By thinking of himself as a "psychopath," paradoxically he was able to circumvent the worst emotional disasters of Novalis and Nietzsche, disasters of which he was mindful when entering this exciting but dangerous phase of his art.[18] His testimony to the usefulness of psychoanalysis to the creative artist is found in "Artist and Psychoanalyst" (1918), a classic of its kind.

For a writer who had so recently been seriously depressed, the essay's tone is remarkably positive and clear in its recommendations. First, the artist should never doubt the value of fantasy arising from the unconscious; it is his most useful source of inspiration, "living experience" rather than contrivance. "Sincerity towards oneself" is essential to authenticity in the new art of "truth to nature emerging behind collapsing traditions." Thus Hesse recognizes that the spiritual crisis of his era will not be met by the Christianity of the church but from within the psyche's resources themselves—these not necessarily being at odds with the essences of world religions, including Christianity. Second, and highly important in reading both *Demian* and *Steppenwolf,* is Hesse's recognition of the centrality of human development, of evolution itself:

> Going back to mother and father, peasant and nomad, ape and fish, nowhere is the origin, relatedness and hope of man so earnestly and shakingly experienced as in a serious analysis.

To this he adds:

> Neither the repression of the material which emerges from out of the unconscious, of uncontrolled ideas, dreams, playful phantasy, nor continued surrender to the shapeless eternality of the unconscious, but the loving listening to the hidden springs and only then criticism and selection from the chaos—this is the way every great artist has worked.[19]

Here in a few words is the entire program for two of the most remarkable attempts to use literature to adapt to the tragedy of split feelings and violent outcomes of formative relationships with mother and father.

Demian is a strange, almost surrealistic novel that readers often do not fully comprehend. Perhaps Hesse himself did not fully comprehend the bisexual theme that emerged when he tried to redefine human nature through discerning his own. "Few people nowadays know what man is," Hesse wrote in the prologue to this confessional novel.[20] Each man is an expression of evolution, of the collective, yet is unique, he observes. "We enjoy a common origin in our mothers; we all come from the same pit" (p. 8)—a curious image bespeaking something hellish or dirty about death and rebirth through the mother. Indeed, the novel centers on the problem of how a son should feel about his mother, at what level of idealization he should place her in a man's world of homoerotic attraction, tension, and war. The novel reaches its climax in a paroxysm of war that Hesse attributes to "the divided soul filled with the lust to rage and kill, annihilate and die so that it might be born anew" (p. 153). Emboldened by Freud, Jung (and possibly J. J. Bachofen) Hesse enters the paternal realm of war making to ask how male feelings about the mother may be implicated. There is no clear answer, but the questions of gender confusion, bisexual anxiety, and the need for violent rebirth are brilliantly displayed.

Gender anxiety appears in the youthful hero, Sinclair (consistently Hesse's persona) who tries to emerge from his constricting family by associating with the school bully, Franz Kromer. Sinclair feels superior to, even despises, his father's "ignorance":

> It was the first crack in the sacrosanct person of my father, a first incision in the pillar on which my whole childhood's life had rested but which every man must destroy before he can become his own true self. (p. 20)

Hesse writes as if enunciating Freudian Oedipal doctrine. But by going on about the insufferability of his father's religion, and about feeling alienated from the family, Hesse points to the weakness of fathering, not to its rivalrous strength. Kromer looks like a strong male, a supplement to the weak father deplored by Sinclair/Hesse. Hesse's shrewd observation on the failure of Sinclair's father has broader implications pointed out by the psychoanalyst Alexander Mitscherlich who remarks on "the disappearance of the father imago so closely associated with the roots of our civilization, and of the paternal instructive function." Mitscherlich sees the failure of German fathers to provide role models for boys (as they did in traditional farming and village life) to be a cause of both the nationalistic inflation of a "fatherland" and the hating rejection of the father with its "psychical concomitant anxiety and aggressivity."[21] He does not add that there consequently may be increased anxiety about the mother if her emotional availability is more than that of the father. The point here is that Hesse wrote in an atmosphere of World War I violence about an anxiety with respect to male potency, an anxiety that was manifesting as masculine attempts at proving virility in an orgy of killing.

Why was it that *Demian* struck such a responsive chord with the war-shocked intellectuals of its day? Surely it was because Hesse had probed behind the facade of the "good" family into the tensions and guilts that sent young men into self-destructive rebellion. Although not a combat soldier, Hesse knew the dynamic from his suicidal youth when he was branded with "moral insanity" at school.[22] To deal with adolescent male rebelliousness—and proneness to be victimized by one's overwhelming emotions at that stage of life—Hesse sets up in *Demian* a polarity of maleness for Sinclair to choose between. Manipulated and bullied by Kromer, Sinclair's protector is the idealized male, Max Demian. An Adonis-like male with remarkable powers, Demian arrives as a new boy at school. His father has died and he lives with a wealthy and beautiful mother, Frau Eva. Demian is portrayed as heterosexual as "he associated with girls and 'knew everything'" (p. 33). Demian's presence is Sinclair's only shield against recurring nightmares in which Kromer, agent of a murderous unconscious wish, threatens to kill Sinclair's father with a knife. In this crisis of male identity, Sinclair's mother treats him with "extreme indulgence," as though he is possessed with some demonic force. Neither parent has any idea of how to react to their distressed son, as indeed Hesse's own parents reacted ineptly with him.

Like Hesse idolizing his grandfather's Indian Shiva, lord of the cosmic dance, so Sinclair must find a new god. As nonattenders of church, Demian and his mother exemplify religious emancipation; much of Sinclair's anxious deliberation over Christianity is with Demian. Discovery of the god Abraxas combining good and evil opens the possibility of reconciling the godly and the satanic, the twin forces Sinclair recognizes in himself.[23] From age eighteen Sinclair is assisted by Pistorius, an eccentric organist and teacher of the occult, in forming a new religion true to the psyche. Hesse was in fact thirty-eight when he was analyzed by J. B. Lang, the model for Pistorius. The novel portrays the difficulty of separating religious quest from tormenting interpersonal and intrapsychic forces. Perhaps this is the point Hesse wished to make. For our purpose, however, it is best to stay with the emergence and development of bisexuality as the novel's main theme.

Demian is a phantasmagoria of gender ambiguity, with bisexuality being attributed to both primary and secondary attachment objects. Sinclair's recurring dream or fantasy is of his mother walking toward him "but when I entered and she was about to kiss me, it was no longer she but . . . Max Demian and my painted portrait—yet it was somehow different . . . very feminine." The portrait is a "kind of god-image or sacred mask, half-male, half-female, ageless, purposeful yet dreamy, frozen yet mysteriously alive" (p. 89; p. 78). Or, again Hesse has Sinclair speak of his mother, who lives in "our old house under the heraldic bird" symbol of possible rebirth. "I advanced to embrace my mother but she would turn out to be the large half-male, half-maternal woman who filled me with awe and for whom I had the most violent attraction" (p. 104; see also pp. 114, 123).

In the "violent attraction" to the mother we find the key to this entire fantasy complex, making sense of its disguise and revelation of sexual anxiety. Sinclair must transform Demian into a feminine being (as happens for instance on p. 49), and must convert his ideal female lover, significantly called Beatrice, into a "boyish" female (p. 75) because he cannot accept purely female intimacy. Sinclair is indeed both charmed by his mother and in flight from her; he is bisexual, neither able to fully affirm the homoeroticism implicit in Demian nor able to trust Beatrice's "holy altar" of feminity. Sinclair is perpetually caught in a compromise solution to the instinctual overstimulation by mother, as father's authority goes into decline. It is little wonder that the obsessively created ideal portrait of Beatrice should turn out to be androgynous, laden with both associations to his mother and to Demian. By a final narcissistic move the portrait becomes himself, end product of a series of split-self personifications and displacements (p. 79).

With such a set of contradictory attachments across gender boundaries, it is easy to see why the story must end in violence on the battlefield. Pent-up rage is far more prominent than the will to spiritual rebirth of which the novel repeatedly speaks. The most powerfully desired outcome is homoerotic closure with Max Demian, which occurs at the close of the narrative when he bestows a kiss on wounded Sinclair—again with the protective qualification that it has been sent by his mother Frau Eva. What other outcome is there for the artist who has created a portrait, "called it mother and knelt before it in tears; I called it devil and whore, vampire and murderer" (p. 91; see also p. 111)?[24]

When the authentic voice from the unconscious produces such images in dream and fantasy, we know that powerful idealization will be needed to make mother tolerable to consciousness. To undo the fantasized damage to mother, Sinclair turns Demian's mother Frau Eva into a Magna Mater, a goddess of transcendent feminity—a sort of Jungian anima who presides over the world of men and their misdeeds. Elevated above all ambiguity, she is the "universal mother," an icon to venerate in a new religion. Yet this idealization is the novel's least believable innovation, with the final narcissistic self-image of desired Demian (seen in a black mirror) more imaginatively convincing. Reparation to the injured (and injuring) mother is not convincingly made in *Demian,* Sinclair knowing that he will always suffer from a psychological irritant, "a crystal of glass in my heart," as he puts it (p. 148). The imagery of shattered mirrors will appear again in the reparative exercises Hesse invents for Harry Haller in *Steppenwolf*, where the same bisexual theme prevails.

Steppenwolf (1927) was written in the midst of another depressive crisis, and quite possibly it saved Hesse from the suicide his protagonist Harry Haller threatens on reaching his fiftieth birthday. Again Hesse uses a fictional persona to work out his own difficulties that, with a second failed marriage, were reaching breaking point. In 1924, he had married a young singer Ruth Wenger, but incompatibility soon declared itself; she became ill with tuberculosis at the same time the psychological and family troubles of his former wife Mia took a turn for the worse. Hesse felt trapped in a prison of his own making. While he still saw his analyst, J. B. Lang, it is by no means clear that they were doing rigorous work together. A brief analytic encounter with Carl Jung himself in 1921 had proven difficult, and Hesse wondered whether monkish asceticism might not serve just as well as psychoanalysis in controlling his compulsions. In any case, it is doubtful that Jung could have been much help in mastering impulses to sexual relationships outside marriage, his own life being complicated in this way. Jung's own summary of the encounter is less than satisfactory; speaking of *Siddhartha* and *Steppenwolf*, he said:

> They are—to a certain extent—the direct or indirect results of certain talks I had with Hesse. I'm unfortunately unable to say how much he was conscious of the hints and implications which I let him have. Unfortunately I'm not in a position to give you full information, since my knowledge is strictly professional.[25]

We may at least be sure that the encounter with Jung reinforced Hesse's conviction that the most important of life's events take place in the theater of the mind, and that if one's personal neurosis can be gone past, the mind's archetypes open the way to God. Through Jung's teaching and example he sought a transcendent vision, but what in fact did he find on further opening the channels of enquiry first discovered in *Demian*?

The message was that the old compulsive bisexual compromise was still in force and that it could be as distressing as ever. Two marriages had not brought relief but a sense of entrapment; neither the abandon of bohemian life nor the exacting investigations of psychoanalysis could give release. Some essential part of the childhood scenario had not been fully enough investigated, some source of discomfort with the mother. In *Steppenwolf* Hesse would reopen the subjective exploration but with fewer Mother Eva-like idealizations. Now that he had decided to bring life to an end by suicide, he would invest feeling about being mothered in Hermine, the pretty young woman in the bar. Hermine is mother, lover, analyst all in one; she is also a boylike girl capable of changing sex. To better understand the meaning of this defensive tactic, which reveals new elements of Hesse's deepest truth, his felt need for a therapeutic regression should be recognized. It is most eloquently spoken of in "Back to the Womb," one of the Crisis poems written just preceding *Steppenwolf:*

Back to the Womb

Sometimes from the dismal gray
A happy moment rises up to me,
As flowery as a woman's name,
Daphne, Louisa, Emily.
Sometimes from a slitted sleeve
A woman's skin flashes white,
A loving glance from puckered eyes
Sends me a message of delight.
And though I know these joys are brief,
My longing for them burns no less.
The curve of every woman's bosom
Fills me with passionate tenderness.

In short, I've turned into a child,
Secretly looking everywhere,
In all his trivial pursuits,
For a mother's breasts, a mother's hair.
Welcome, brief shifting flames of love,
I kiss your eyes, so brown, so blue,
In courtship and capricious love-play.
Woman, eternal mother, I welcome you.
To love you leads, I know, to death.
Too quickly my moth-dreams expire.
Oh, let me not die someday in darkness,
Oh, let me perish in the fire![26]

The poem's image of burning with desire is no cliché but a metaphoric truth brought out in the last lines where perishing in the fires of lust is a real possibility. But the truth of Hesse's pursuit also comes out as unfinished, or defective maternal nurture that he is trying to make good in erotic encounters. Thus Hesse's enmeshment with his mother is revealed as the starting point of ruinously obsessive-compulsive sexuality. To interpret at the most hopeful this dire poem, we might say that Hesse asks not for the fire of lustful self-destruction but for the light of self-understanding. In some measure the novel *Steppenwolf* clarifies sexual ambivalence, together with bisexual maneuvering, to get beyond the pain of having been mothered as Hesse must have been. Some of the hidden conflicted script of what actually went on with his parents is revealed in the novel's cumulative fantasy. The fantasy of sexual pluralism, brief affairs with no lasting commitment culminates in the "All the Girls are Yours" sequence of *Steppenwolf*. It is a lament for the failures of these compulsive affairs.

The novel depicts the shabby Steppenwolf, Harry Haller, ill, defeated, and in a midlife crisis, yet seeking healing forces to rescue and redirect his life. Intuition tells him that he must reconstruct his childhood of superficial bourgeois security that nonetheless led to antagonistic and rebellious feelings toward his parents. By becoming a lodger with a motherly person, Harry puts to the test his self-destructiveness, his failure to attain inner harmony. He sees his new lodgings as a "temple of order" where the contemplation of azalea and araucaria plants symbolizes perfect balance and harmony. Yet inner imbalance besets him, especially in relations with his women lovers. As the nephew reports, when Haller brings home a young woman, "an extremely violent, I may say even brutal, quarrel occurred which upset the whole house and for which Haller begged my aunt's pardon for days after."[27] No amount of art, music, intellectualizing, or Buddhist contemplation can deliver Harry from his anger at the female companions he so much needs. A depressed Don Juan, he has been through countless affairs and the disastrous marriage with Erika, only to conclude that he is diseased, isolated, and old. Every new initiative to "be loved as a whole" fails him until the imaginative reentry into the world of child's play awakens the truth about his deep ambivalence toward women. The agent of this awakening is Hermine, an anima figure, called up among the believable wonders of this extraordinary fiction. The lineaments of Hesse's own crisis after the failed marriage with Ruth strongly show through the Harry Haller persona; the novel is a confessional attempt at self-cure drawing on archetypal energies to "play" Hesse/Haller into renewed life. It is thus fully in line with analytic objectives;

but what discoveries about the main blocking agent, latent bisexuality, does it make?

Steppenwolf represents a large conceptual advance over *Demian* in that Hesse had fully recognized the cogency of the psychoanalytic doctrine of ego splitting. Harry Haller's suffering is seen metaphorically in the split between the wolf and the man within. He feels himself to be on a pilgrimage toward "ideal harmony," by becoming" a child once more" to overcome "separation" by an "expansion of the soul" (pp. 72–73). The test will be in how well Harry negotiates his encounter with Hermine, the girl in the bar who becomes his mother/analyst. By performing this test on Harry, Hesse assessed the chances for spiritual integration to overcome the narcissism and sexual compulsiveness that were wrecking his life. It was an act of courage to confront his deepest anxieties about love/hate toward women; that the outcome was to be at best ambiguous does not take away from the daring of Hesse's fictional adventuring.

Haller's fate is studied in the "Steppenwolf Treatise," a mock psychoanalytic case study of Harry's type of "schizomania," possibly suggested by Freud's study of the "Wolf Man" (1918). Had Hesse been thinking of Freud's "Wolf Man," he would have felt confirmed in his view that obsessional neurosis begins in childhood, even though he does not attribute primal scene experience to Harry, nor suggest that he might have been seduced by a sister, as happened to the "Wolf Man." Hesse might have chosen to imagine himself a developing infant in his family constellation but instead examines the phenomenology of his love-hate relations with women in the person of Hermine. This leads to a sometimes tender, sometimes furious attempt to escape the split-ego polarities that tear him, culminating in a sort of Pavlovian deconditioning experiment that takes him to the limit of endurance but without collapsing the contraries into the spiritual unity he so desires.

Harry's encounter with Hermine comes as close as the novel gets to the "transference neurosis" Harry needs if he is to move beyond his punitive obsession with women. He needs a revelation of how he really felt about his mother, not a furthering of idealization as with Frau Eva. That he "acts out" unrecognized wishes toward his mother in murdering Hermine, his angel of mercy who offers to remother him, is evidence of the active unconscious about which Hesse desperately needed to know. Only by acknowledging matricidal feelings could he hope for relief of depression. The uncovering of feelings predictably reveals once again the dynamism of bisexuality, Harry's strategy for dealing with intense erotic attraction to females prohibited by the incest barrier. It should be noted that Hermine is called not just "mother" but "sister"; Hesse had two sisters, Adele, two years older and Marulla, three years younger (pp. 125, 144).[28]

Harry's encounter with Hermine takes place at the Black Eagle, where he has resorted as his embittered Steppenwolf self. The name of the pub and Harry's self-identification are redolent of the sort of defensive hypermasculinity that one associates with the most cunning and cruel impulses on which Hitler and the Nazis played. Haller is no Jew-hating Nazi fodder, but he does exhibit something of the tension between sexual compulsiveness and fear of women that has been shown to have contributed to the rise of Nazism.[29] Hesse of course was a pacifist, which, if anything, allowed him to tap deeply into destructive fantasies left unchallenged by most artists and writers of his era. In a sense *Steppenwolf* may be seen as an early warning system for the build-up of male fears and self-destructive obsessions that contributed to Nazism, a pathology of the group mind as much as it was the outcome of economic hardship and political ambitions.

Harry complains to Hermine that he can't dance, that he is too rigid and repressed to live life to the full: the parents who had urged him to learn Latin and Greek "had never danced themselves," thus setting up the narrative for culmination at the Masked Ball, where defenses are relinquished to the reality of psychological organization around bisexuality (p. 101).[30] Harry confesses his suicidal loneliness to Hermine who chides him for running away from reality. The mother/analyst interprets his "baby" nature to him, as he cannot see it for himself. With the relationship solidified ("I dreaded her going and leaving me alone"), Harry's regressed baby self emerges (pp. 105, 102).[31] In dreaming of Goethe, the towering genius of German literature, Harry idealizes male "Immortals" of the creative arts—something predictable from the idealization of Max Demian in the former novel. In Hesse's praising of Goethe's mobility of imagination in play, it is important to notice the odd image in a "handsome leather or velvet box" Goethe shows Harry: "a diminutive effigy of a woman's leg on the dark velvet" (p. 112).[32] When Harry grasps the leg, it becomes a threatening scorpion. The severed leg is an image of female sacrifice, betokening sensual, sadistic, and punitive wishes; the box may be a coffin. It is not long in the narrative before we hear of Hermine (his "mirror" of self and "window" onto a better world) becoming "sinister" in her wish to control him. She will "play" with Harry as a "little brother" for life and death (p. 125). But she too is a split being, symbolized by two orchids, and takes on the protective aspect of boyishness, a boyhood friend Herman, which is indeed Hesse's own name shortened. Hermine's hermaphroditism thus signifies the very narcissistic wound from which Harry suffers, and so she cannot unambiguously be his healer. She is indeed a projection of his split ego, whose "love" for Harry turns her into a sacrifice for his mother's desire for too close control of her son. "You will carry out my command and—kill me," Hermine announces, a chilling wish Harry fulfills when he finds her asleep after coupling with the jazz musician Pablo in the Magic Theatre (p. 126).[33] Amidst his guilt and remorse for murdering Hermine, he recognizes that the wish for this unnatural act had been "my own"—Harry's most powerful insight (p. 244). No amount of gender switching in dancing with Hermine as Herman at the Masked Ball; no amount of Pablo's deconditioning attempts in the Magic Theatre, attempts calculated to relieve Harry of his pathology, can halt the projection of bisexual wishes. The wolf image in Harry's psyche cannot be erased, shattered, or even laughed into final submission. As Mozart, the Immortal, brings out in the last judgment, Harry must accept with humor his condition, understanding why he refuses to have Hermine brought back to life so he can marry her. The novel ends with a frank statement of the repetitiousness of Harry's obsessive ambivalence: "I would traverse not once more, but often, the hell of my inner being" (p. 248).[34] The frightened child within Harry is thus discovered and mobilized to transferential attack but not resolved into the spiritual unity for which Harry's better self longs. Hesse could not be more explicit about his meaning: where Pablo has already given Hermine a "love bite" beneath her left breast, Harry stabs with a knife. As he has earlier remarked, "In so far as a mother bore me, I am guilty," a prophecy from which no auto-analysis will finally deliver him (p. 212).

In no other novel does Hesse so decisively enter the inner world of his own being. The Magic Theatre may be seen as the narcissistic and self-negating ego undergoing transformations, with the entire novel possible to read as an intrapsychic allegory in which persecutory introjects are freed up and rearranged in a healthier way. While it is true that Harry does not disavow his promiscuous behavior, he does see that "I was a child in the stream of sex, at play in the midst of all its charm, its danger and surprise" (p. 230). He sees that the frightened child had "fled" from women and "stumbled" over them, which easily leads to "killing for love"

(p. 231). Hesse was still far from renouncing these damaging pleasures when he wrote *Steppenwolf,* and the less subtle reader may even believe that he is sponsoring them. There is no final closure in *Steppenwolf,* a tense ambiguity being its mood to the end. Lack of resolution of sexual anxiety through "humour" is predictable since Harry still talks about "the whole deadly foreboding of love, the foreboding of woman" (p. 226).

This foreboding reemerges in other novels, not so much canvassing the bisexual solution as the possibility of eliminating women altogether in male relationships. As far as appears, this is not a solution to which Hesse resorted himself, but it is a preoccupation in certain of the novels. In *Siddhartha* (1922), a saga of ascetic Buddhist pilgrimage in search of the unitive life, Hesse develops the male companionship of Govinda and Siddhartha, probing their complementary yet opposing awarenesses. This fictional strategy is also followed in *Narcissus and Goldmund* (1930) and in the remarkable *Glass Bead Game* (1943), after which Hesse was awarded the Nobel Prize for literature. The pervasive, but defended-against homoeroticism of these novels is remarkable, but it was not a satisfactory solution to Hesse's intrapsychic difficulties, any more than it was for another great writer preoccupied with bisexual fantasy—Ernest Hemingway in the unfinished novel *The Garden of Eden* (1986).[35] Bisexuality may not be such a rare occurrence in fiction as one might think and should be looked for in other instances, when dilemmas of sexual orientation in our time are being studied.

Hesse no doubt idealized fathers as cultural heroes to counterbalance the excesses of the female closeness he feared. This happens, of course, with the exemplary Immortals: Goethe and Mozart, in *Steppenwolf,* with search for the lost father perhaps more operative in other novels than is outright homoerotic desire. It has been suggested that Narcissus personifies the ideal father Hesse missed in Johannes. The sculptor Goldmund, with whom Narcissus is polarized, has Hesse's own artistic temperament and struggles with the woes of sexual pluralism. As Hesse wrote in a letter:

Like Goldmund, I have a naively sensuous relationship with women, and like Goldmund, I would love boundlessly, if only an inborn as well as acquired respect for the souls of my fellow humans (that is, women) and a culturally conditioned shame about mindless self-abandon to the senses did not hold me back.[36]

This typifies the moral Hesse who through art emerged from conflict and depression, a writer of passionately contrary impulses who became mindful of the suffering he could cause others. It is little wonder that in later life Hesse should have been treated as a guru, with correspondents all over the world seeking his guidance.

As to the ascetic solution to inner conflict, Hesse pondered it deeply in *Magister Ludi (The Glass Bead Game)*, begun in 1932 and worked over for the next decade. To examine the enclosed devotional life (in which obsessionally ritualized discipline there would be no time for sexual adventuring) Hesse invented the utopian city of Castalia where the glass bead game had attained high sophistication. But as Magister Ludi, his protagonist Joseph Knecht tires of the too abstract game by which the order maintains the ascendancy of contemplation over action in the world. He leaves Castalia to reenter the world, his only possession his flute. The curious, perhaps parodic, ending in which Knecht drowns on diving into cold water following his young student Tito, recalls Aschenbach's obsessive-compulsive pursuit of Tadzio in Thomas Mann's *Death in Venice* (1925). In a sense, Knecht also inhabits a diseased city of the mind where fantasy too easily overwhelms reality. It is quite possible that Hesse knew exactly what he was doing by ending the novel with death by drowning: a sort of negative tribute to the female element.

However, for Edmund Remys, Knecht's fatal plunge into the lake is a rejoining of the "mother world" after an unfulfilling sojourn in the "father world" of the Castalian order, with its stultifying glass bead game.[37] Such an interpretation is probably to take Hesse's reading of J. J. Bachofen's *Mother Right* (1861), a treatise on matriarchy, too seriously. If Knecht's fatal plunge is reunion with the primal mother, then mothering is death, the Dark and Terrible Mother, who may just as well as her opposite inhabit the unconscious. This is the death goddess Kali, studied by Erich Neumann, a goddess who in decadent turn-of-the-century German culture was celebrated for combining Eros with Thanatos.[38] With the unconscious thus charged with the devouring mother, Jung's prescription for individuation through reconciliation of anima and animus is unlikely to be fulfilled.

Hesse's feelings about women were far too complicated to resolve by any such single symbolic action as Remys suggests. More likely, Tito is both a narcissistic self-image of the ideal child Hesse had wished to be and the eroticized ideal male he desired but could not allow himself to pursue out of guilt. The ideal father was not to be repossessed; mother's excessive attentions could not be put fully in abeyance; Hesse found himself in an impossible position for which humor and resignation would serve him best. Knecht ends as a male sacrifice torn between opposites he cannot reconcile. At least in this novel, there is no female sacrifice, as when Hermine symbolically pays for Harry's difficulties with his mother in her bourgeois household.

For Hesse, the novelist, literary creativity as self-therapy did not retrieve the minutae of his earliest unsatisfactory attachments to parents. At the time there was, of course, no model of attachment behavior to guide him, beyond the Freudian Oedipal theory, which he knew to be incomplete. Nonetheless, intuition told him to reconstruct, if only behind a protective veil of mythology, the particular feelings of an oppressed childhood. His performance as confessional magician-writer would be open to a wide range of interpretations. Perhaps we are in a better position now to understand his literary accomplishment. Instead of uncovering the elements of a full autobiography, Hesse left culture its finest and most memorable fictional account of destructive sexual ambivalence and of the imaginative struggle to affirm life, despite the emotional subversion of his obsessions.

4

Love and Death in Vladimir Nabokov's
Lolita: A Fantasy Analysis of an Obsession

Art at its greatest is fantastically deceitful and complex.
—V. Nabokov

VLADIMIR Nabokov's *Lolita* (1955) is perhaps the quintessentially obsessive heterosexual narrative of recent times. Its pedophilic perversity spawned the term *Lolita Complex/Syndrome*: adult male obsession with preadolescent girls as sexual objects. The question is: what propelled Nabokov to write this undoubted literary masterpiece, partly a permission to fantasize sexuality with very young girls, but also a moral fable about its consequences? "Beauty plus pity—that is the closest we can get to a definition of art," Nabokov once said.[1] It may be questioned whether *Lolita*'s perverse beauty does not compromise the moral pity of this novel, a vision of pedophilic sexuality as misogyny and death.

We know from psychological studies how damaging to young girls incest in any form can be, yet its attraction remains for many men. *Lolita* was written before much study of father-daughter incest, and it is doubtful that an author would risk such a book now. Feminist studies such as Elizabeth Ward's *Father Daughter Rape* and the psychiatric work of Judith Herman, Diana Russell, and Karen Trocki in "Long Term Effects of Incestuous Abuse in Children" are rapidly changing attitudes to sexual exploitation of girls in the family.[2] Nonetheless, Nabokov's masterpiece is widely read and Stanley Kubrick's film is likely to be replaced by a newer version. Nabokov's rewriting of the age-old "Beauty and the Beast" myth remains compelling.

Authoritative though it is, Brian Boyd's literary biography *Vladimir Nabokov: The Russian Years* (1990) does not fully replace Andrew Field's *The Life and Art of Vladimir Nabokov* (1986), whose point of view is largely rejected by the new biographer. If, as Boyd says, Nabokov believed in "art for *life*'s sake," then the issues of psychopathology that Field began to address cannot be so easily relegated as Boyd attempts to do.[3] Boyd's unstinting admiration of Nabokov the writer prevents him from asking the more difficult questions about relational and sexual wishes that are needed to decide the cultural meaning of *Lolita*. By repeatedly insisting that Nabokov had an "idyllic childhood and youth," Boyd forfeits the chance to work with actual materials presented by the writer in his autobiography *Speak, Memory: An Autobiography Revisited* (1966).[4] That Boyd is innocent of psychology leaves his biography simply "literary," with Nabokov's fuller cultural implications unstudied. My study draws mainly on Nabokov's own testimony about his Russian childhood as it bears on the obsessive themes of his pedophilic fictions. A stylist who is master of indirection, Nabokov's language in fiction lends itself to fantasy analysis of emotionally charged words and images. Where he is not explicit, his rich recurring imagery is eloquent of underlying attitudes to females. The argument will adduce the evidence of fantasy to account for the uncommon power of *Lolita* as an inventing of an America where forbidden sexuality between an adult male and preadolescent girl can be imagined.

The review of Nabokov's early life suggests the origin in anxiety about incest of an obsessive pedophilic fantasy that Nabokov turned into sexual pathology in his fictional character Humbert Humbert. The fantasy Nabokov tapped is undoubtedly that of the desire many fathers feel for their sexually awakening daughters, a taboo area from which writers had kept clear until Nabokov gave it exaggerated tragicomic treatment in Humbert Humbert. As Nabokov's personal history is far from complete, speculations are bound to seem gratuitously pathologizing unless taken in the spirit of an unfinished enquiry. Despite inconclusiveness, it is worth considering psychobiographical particulars to show the propaganda for pedophilia in *Lolita* as of less universal appeal than the function of an author's struggle with himself over anxiety about incest. The novel pleads the case for "unhappy, mild, dog-eyed gentlemen, sufficiently well-integrated to control our urge in the presence of adults, but ready to give years and years of life for one chance to touch a nymphet. Emphatically, no killers are we" (p. 82). But as the story of how Humbert Humbert despoiled Lolita unfolds, clearly a sort of soul-murder is under review. Death of the spirit of youth, nullifying female life itself, is disclosed. However much Humbert comes to realize the horror of his crime of nearly incestuous sex with captive Lolita, and whatever repentent protestations of love for her he may utter, the deathly pall cannot be lifted. Humbert is a killer of sorts, having sadistically tormented a captive girl with his compulsive sexuality; compassion for Lolita comes too late (in chapter 32) when the damage cannot be undone.

By citing psychobiographical evidence in *Speak, Memory* and the fictional *Ada* and other sources, I try to show Nabokov, in nostalgia and pain, trying to reconstruct as much of his childhood experience as could be tolerated. Allusive and sometimes strangely opaque as these writings may be, they do try to recover childhood memories in a sincere and moving way. Humbert's compulsively predatory sexual actions are nowhere to be found in Nabokov's autobiography. Nabokov is not Humbert Humbert, and there is no indication that he ever molested a child or even considered doing so. Yet his preoccupation with incest (given a grotesque form in *Lolita*) indicates a possible source for the novel's power and explains the perseverence with which Nabokov pursued the theme over many years of writing.

Questions about motivation and meaning have surrounded Vladimir Nabokov's *Lolita* since first publication in 1955 by the Olympia Press in Paris, France. (The Olympia Press had specialized since the 1930s in publishing literary erotica in English for the emigré market.) Four New York publishers rejected the novel until Putnam's published it in 1958, whereupon it became a top bestseller. The reviewers mainly welcomed *Lolita,* giving the novel less disapproval than might have been expected, but there were perplexities. What, after all, was Nabokov saying about his attitude to Humbert Humbert, the novel's pedophile hero or antihero? This fiction about the erotic obsession of a man in his forties for a twelve-year-old prepubescent girl made explicit a taboo theme that had long lurked in both British and American literature and art, as we shall see. The fiction is so clever and sophisticated in its parodic ironies that literary critics have found it almost impossible to agree about just what Nabokov is saying about Humbert's illicit relationship with Dolores Haze, "Lolita," or "Lo" for short. Perhaps the answer is that Nabokov did not know just what he felt about his "hero" or about the girl, or that he felt several things about each, some of them contradictory, leaving the fiction confusing because he was confused. One thing, however, is certain: *Lolita* is an elaborate fantasy, with Humbert Humbert creating her from plain Dolores, just as Nabokov creates Humbert creating her in his erotic excitement. A new, more objective technique for analyzing how the fantasies are built up throughout the novel is needed. Fantasy analysis looks at Nabokov's eroticized wordplay for patterns of repetition and regularity in emotive words and images defining attitudes to relationships within the novel. Attitudes to women especially must be looked at in the context of fantasy language, language conveying "love" for nymphets (certain females age nine to fourteen) but hate for their mothers, and for older women in general; or, does it turn out that all females, young and old alike, are objects of hatred in this novel, with its final message about male attachment to females one of fear and avoidance that subsides into nihilistic death? Most readers nowadays agree that *Lolita* is not exactly a love story; but it may be too simple to label it alternatively a hate story, with no mitigating features. By treating the novel as a dream, or trance-fantasy, created from the constituents of Nabokov's own imagination, we may be able to clarify its meaning.

In following this procedure we shall disregard the author's insistence that psychological factors have little to do with the craft of fiction. "All my books should be stamped Freudians, Keep out," Nabokov said in 1963.[5] Nabokov insisted his novels were self-contained, aesthetically complete, admitting of no social significance—a precious view of art but one still widely held. Critics who see the psychological issues in *Lolita* tend to remark that Nabokov has so cleverly covered his tracks in spoofing Freud, and all psychoanalysis and psychiatry, that there is no use in this line of enquiry. As J. P. Shute writes, Nabokov engages in a "number of pre-emptive strategies: notably polemic, parody, and guerrilla raids into Freud's realm to mine the ground."[6] According to this way of seeing the novel, its psychological profile of Humbert Humbert is a ruse to tease and yet inform us of nothing but the futility of psychoanalysis. We are told that he has been a mental patient, having breakdowns after a divorce; the parodic foreword by John Ray, Jr., Ph.D. solemnly states that Humbert Humbert is "abnormal," that the "desperate honesty that throbs through his confession does not absolve him from sins of diabolical cunning."[7] Shrewd readers see the "diabolical cunning" to be Nabokov's own as he constructs a pseudo–case history for his fictional pedophile pervert, whose princely yet inane name is meant to repel. That there is also something winning, even lovable, about this self-confessed monster is an ambiguity in need of explanation. The confession of crime opens with a statement about "a gentle easy-going father," a hotel keeper and a "very photogenic mother" who died in a freak accident when the child was three. Brought up by his maternal aunt with whom his father is said to have had casual sexual relations (was she actually Humbert's mother?) Humbert suffered "the fatal rigidity of some of her rules," extremely fond of her though he was (p. 12). She died when he was sixteen, leaving him well liked and petted by everybody, in the care of his father who sent him away to school. This semi-orphanhood is inverted with the fatherless Lolita being brought up by her mother, who marries Humbert and soon dies leaving the child solely in his care—perhaps to become a narcissistic self-object. Among Nabokov's several digs at psychiatry is the statement that Humbert had wanted to become a psychiatrist, but "switched to English literature" since the true pursuer of nymphets needs to be both artist and melancholic madman (pp. 17, 19).[8] Humbert has a hard time convincing himself that "there was really nothing wrong in being moved to distraction by girl children," seductive nymphets nine to fourteen, "split" off from their postadolescent sisters with whom Humbert appears to be impotent (p. 20).[9] Psychiatry, which has delivered Humbert from depression, is also his oppressor that he strives by deception to outwit:

> In hospital I discovered there was an endless source of robust enjoyment in trifling with psychiatrists; cunningly leading them on; never letting them see that you know all the tricks of the trade; inventing for them elaborate dreams, pure classics in the style (which make them, the dream-extortionists, dream and wake up shrieking); teasing them with fake "primal scenes"; and never allowing them the slightest glimpse of one's real sexual predicament. By bribing a nurse I won access to some files and discovered with glee, cards calling me "potentially homosexual" and "totally impotent." (p. 34)

The sadistic, controlling intent of this statement of knowing better than the therapist is typical of obsessional patients, as Nabokov might or might not have realized. Did Nabokov himself really have "all the tricks of the trade," or is this arch rejection of the reader's access to the "real sexual predicament" only a thin parodic disguise that should not impede our enquiry?

But before proceeding to a fantasy analysis of *Lolita* let us review some more conventional aspects of the novel. The usual way to interpret a puzzling book such as *Lolita* is to look for a "tradition" in which the author worked. If precedents can be found for his thematic preoccupations with pedophilia and incest, for example, he may be absolved at least of starting something new out of an obsession of his own. We do not have to go back to the Middle

Ages with Dante's devotion to Beatrice or Petrarch's hopeless love for the child Laura to find precedents for Nabokov's themes. The morbid imagination of the American story writer and poet Edgar Allan Poe (1809–1849) is frequently cited as stimulating Nabokov's fiction of youth-inspired eroticism. Poe's poem "Annabel Lee" is about a child love and the young girl's haunting death—a clear precedent to the very name of Humbert's aching childhood love for the young Annabel who "died of typhus in Corfu" before its consummation (pp. 13–15). Lolita is her reincarnation twenty-four years later. In "To My Mother" Poe wrote a poem on his dead mother, who died when he was only two, and also on his aunt-mother-in-law who supported the curious marriage to his thirteen-year-old cousin Virginia Clemm. Virginia survived only to eighteen, dying in 1847 after which Poe did not remarry. Nabokov openly acknowledges this: "Oh Lolita you are my girl, as Vee was Poe's and Bea Dante's, and what little girl would not whirl in a circular skirt and scanties?" (p. 99). Nabokov's use of the double, in the manner of Poe and other writers, has been amply studied and does not need repeating to make the point that Nabokov's literary sophistication allows him ready camouflage whenever needed.[10]

Further, Nabokov is familiar with the work of the nineteenth-century British fantasist the Reverend Charles Dodgson (1832–1898) who, as "Lewis Carroll," wrote the children's classics *Alice in Wonderland* (1865) and *Through the Looking Glass* (1871). Based on stories Dodgson invented to entertain the child Alice Liddell, these bizarre inventions place a preadolescent girl in a topsy-turvy realm of adventure and peril. In his chapter on pedophilia, Norman Kiell makes less of the sadistic fantasies in Carroll's books than perhaps he should. In *Alice in Wonderland,* the King and Queen are sadistic parents, the Queen's typical response to any annoyance being a castrating "off with his head," as happened when a game is being played:

> Alice thought she might as well go back and see how the game was going on, as she heard the Queen's voice in the distance, screaming with passion. She had already heard her sentence three of the players to be executed for having missed their turns, and she did not like the look of things at all, as the game was in such confusion that she never knew whether it was her turn or not.[11]

The Queen whose menace is greater than the King's, is a creation of Lewis Carroll's that has analogues in the menacing mother figures of *Lolita,* as we shall see. The Queen's sadistic ferocity is of the sort seen in psychoanalytic theory as deterring the Oedipal boy from acceptance of his mother as a love object, throwing him back on narcissistic self-holding. In self-holding he may identify a sexualized female child with his own thwarted state. Both Carroll and Nabokov, one pre- and the other post-Freudian, seem to have intuited this situation, working with it imaginatively as idealization of preadolescent female love objects. The inference, for Dodgson at least, is not difficult to draw: he had a prurient side as seen in his hobby of photographing preadolescent girls, some posed, but many sleeping in innocent unawareness of the eyes of that were on them. (Death fantasies should not be missed in these quaintly erotic images.) "Naked children are so perfectly pure and lovely," Carroll wrote in *Confessions of a Caricaturist,* but such sentimentality does not make the pictures any less controlling in the fantasy life of this unmarried Oxford mathematician and cleric.[12] It should come as no surprise that Nabokov had translated *Alice* into Russian (Berlin, 1923), his first book.

Was he protecting himself when in an interview with Alfred Appel he denounced Carroll's perversion? Denying that he had taken over Carroll's idea of inventing language, Nabokov noted simply that like many children brought up speaking English, "I have been always very fond of Carroll." This sounds disingenuous, and he continues to moralize on Carroll's attraction to nymphets:

> He has a pathetic affinity with H. H. [Humbert Humbert] but some old scruple prevented me from alluding in *Lolita* to his wretched perversion and to those ambiguous photographs he took in dim rooms. He got away with it, as so many Victorians got away with pederasty and nympholepsy. His were sad scrawny little nymphets, bedraggled and half-undressed, or rather semi-undraped, as if participating in some dusty and dreadful charade.[13]

In the novel, Quilty, a perverse photographer, suggests Carroll, a suggestion Nabokov rejected; Appel did not persist in identifying the affinities, which are certainly present. Later in his *Annotated Lolita* (1970) Appel chose to annotate only "A breeze from wonderland" in part 1, chapter 29, noting that the novel contains "several references to *Alice in Wonderland.*" He does not annotate the reference in part 2, chapter 27 that identifies Lolita-like nymphets with Alice:

> I used to recollect, with anguished amusement, the times in my trustful, pre-dolorian past when I would be misled by a jewel-bright win-

dow opposite wherein my lurking eye . . . would make out from afar a half-naked nymphet stilled in the act of combing her Alice-in-Wonderland hair. (p. 240)

If it is not precisely Lolita Humbert is thinking of in his reverie of arousal, the association is so close it does not matter. This is not a "sad scrawny little nymphet" photographed in a "dim room" but a seductive young voluptuary much as Lolita is portrayed in the novel. The Americanization of culture had transformed Carroll's innocent, unknowing darlings into brashly prepubertal experimenters with a sexuality thrust on them by their sex-obsessed culture. It is thus that *Lolita* takes to its logical limit Poe's morbid obsession with child brides, and Carroll's with the hidden delights of innocence in female children. To link death with the glowing but futile child amours of Humbert is to anticipate the outcome of fantasy analysis of *Lolita*, a novel laden with the language of death. The theme of death did not get into the fiction simply by borrowing it from Poe; it has the quality of being over-determined in Nabokov's own psychology of creativity, as will be illustrated. Both of Nabokov's predecessors in the art of nympholepsy were personally involved in their fantasies, but was Nabokov also involved? While not easily established, the evidence must be considered for what it tells us about the novel's compulsive power.

When it comes to pedophile fantasy in Nabokov's accounting for his motivation in writing *Lolita*, he is a master of evasion. Answers to questions are blocked and thwarted, but there are some remarkable (perhaps unintentional) revelations of feelings about women. Explaining the genesis of his book as an "autobiographical device," following the John Ray "impersonation" with which he coyly opened Humbert Humbert's confessional case history, Nabokov remains anxious, even at the novel's close, that it have a sympathetic hearing. "On a book Entitled *Lolita*" was introduced as an afterthought into Putnam's 1958 edition, and it remains to ingratiate the author with the reader while laying down the rules for reading the novel strictly as fiction. He dates the "first little throb of *Lolita*" to 1939 or 1940, "the initial shiver" coming of a seemingly irrelevant story about a caged ape drawing in charcoal. But what was Nabokov's train of thought that had lead to an earlier fiction about a questing "Arthur" marrying a desirable nymphet's sick mother who conveniently dies, leaving him to love the nymphet, despair over her and commit suicide? The first story was read to friends, then "destroyed" according to Nabokov, but its fifty-five page typescript in Russian (under a pseudonym) unexpectedly turned up among his papers sometime before 1959, at which time he proposed publication to Putnam's, as is explained in "Author's Note Two" to *The Enchanter*. In *The Annotated Lolita,* xxxvii, 438, Alfred Appel tells it differently, calling the story "The Magician." According to Appel, the typescript turned up only in 1964 and that, in an interview of 1966, Nabokov said that he would never publish it. He may have reconsidered, recognizing a brilliance approaching that of Thomas Mann's tale of obsessive sexual pursuit in *Death in Venice*. About Nabokov's attitude to women, he tells us that his obsessive theme "had grown in secret the claws and wings of a novel"—suggesting a bird preying on the innocent. This powerful predatory fantasy is no evasion, nor are the onanistic "throb" and "shiver."

It was left for Nabokov's son Dmitri actually to publish the story as *The Enchanter* in 1986. In a testy afterword to the text, Dmitri questions the biographer Andrew Field's opinion (gleaned from an aged emigré critic in Paris, Vladimir Weidle) that the writing had originally been called "The Satyr," a title Dmitri denies his father could have used. Apart from literary reasons, why did Nabokov resurrect this "dead scrap" of a story after it was so far surpassed in thematic development by *Lolita*? He may have wanted his reader to know of the freeing up of moral strictures around pedophilia and incest accomplished by *Lolita*. *The Enchanter*'s self punitive tendency in a predominantly third-person narration is markedly guiltier than Humbert Humbert's first person confession. Humbert deflects guilty self-indictment with mock imputation of beastliness, and other regrets that, as confidences, are intended to win the reader. Humbert is too slyly charming to commit suicide in any way, although that is the effect of his seductions. Whereas Humbert both opens and closes the novel celebrating Lolita's erotic charms, the speaker (never named) in *The Enchanter* begins: "How can I come to terms with myself?" engaging in troubled searching of his divided psyche before the force of obsessive questing for the nymphet spied in the park takes over. The story of sexual involvement with a roller-skating twelve-year-old reaches a terrifying self-negation for the "hero" as he ejaculates over the awakened shrieking girl. Pursued by irate neighbors, "two robed old women" try to block his escape into the street, where all terminates by his willed death under a truck. Idealization of the nymphet and near-apprehension by the crone-like mothers, sum up the fantasy of this story, a fantasy modified in *Lolita*.

Strikingly, a possible etiological glimpse of incest with a sister briefly surfaces in *The Enchanter* but is missing from the novel in just this form. Following a sensuous description of "palpating" the orphan girl, the narration continues:

> Then, in the silence, the whine of a mosquito became inaudible, and for some reason it evoked a fleeting memory of something infinitely remote, late bed times in his childhood, a dissolving lamp, the hair of his sister, his coeval, who had died long, long ago. "My sweetheart," he repeated, and, nuzzling a curl out of the way, cuddling mussily, he tasted . . . her hot silky neck.[14]

This may be an allusion to Nabokov's younger sister Olga (b. 1903), whom he was determined a biographer would never meet, so strangely "infantile" was she, a taboo object. According to Field, Olga was "distanced from the family group," and, while not actually dead, the family tried to pretend it to be so.[15] Perhaps this is the "key" to the repetition compulsion surrounding incest that seems to lie behind Nabokov's storytelling.

In 1949 in Ithaca, New York, Nabokov confides, the "throbbing, which had never quite ceased, began to plague me again"; orgasmic language is quite explicit, making the fantasy seem more compulsively masturbatory than divertingly fictional. The claimed fictional problem of "inventing America" may deflect us from realizing just how urgently compulsive, yet shame-inducing *Lolita*'s theme had always been. When Nabokov considered incinerating what he terms his *Juanita Dark*, "I was stopped by the thought that the ghost of the destroyed book would haunt my files for the rest of my life" (p. 283). This proclaims the strength of the central fantasy, an obsession with psychologically ensnaring and holding captive a young girl; but more than that it is a fantasy of destruction, death, and guilt for causing death. Guilty destruction of pornography collections by addicts is not uncommon, yet the wishes that assembled them persist. So it seems to have been with Nabokov's deliberations whether or not to publish in his own name, the danger being that an allegory of his psyche would be identifiable by the "Freudian voodooism" he so detested. Fear of having an abnormality detected (now classed as a paraphilia) led to a homily on works of fiction as giving "aesthetic bliss, that is a sense of being somehow, somewhere connected with other states of being where art (curiosity, tenderness, kindness, ecstasy) is the norm" (p. 286). This elevates and cleanses the onanistic sexuality by making a fantasy container of the fiction in a realm of pure art. The book becomes "a comforting presence," a "pilot light," with a special "glow," emanating from its "secret points," its "subliminal coordinates" (p. 287). This is an almost religious language of assuagement and consolation, suggesting the afterimaging of autoerotic fantasizing in a psychic cycle that begins again when another provocative nymphet is sighted. For Nabokov, who had no time for organized religion, such desire seems to have a religious ultimacy about it, as though a new cult of the sanctified sexual child were being established. The cynic might reflect that the kiddie porn of literary high culture is given specious seriousness.

Reluctantly, Nabokov concedes that *Lolita* makes "various allusions to the physiological urges of a pervert," going on to warn that "It is childish to study the work of fiction in order to gain information . . . about the author" (pp. 287–88). The warning to post-Freudians (with their unbounded interest in all aspects of childhood) is followed by a most revealing statement of sadistic fantasy: in response to well-wishers who worried about Nabokov's living amongst such depressing characters as those in *Lolita,* he remarks that "the only discomfort I really experienced was to live in my workshop among discarded limbs and unfinished torsos" (p. 288). We must believe that a moral sense did actually bring "discomfort." Revealingly, amidst Humbert's growing remorse over exploiting innocence, Nabokov writes of him: "I have still other smothered memories, now unfolding themselves into limbless monsters of pain," as though a sort of auto-analysis were going on in the creative process (p. 259).[16] A childhood involvement with Olga seems a reasonable hypothesis.

To judge this fairly, Nabokov's reconstruction of his family history in *Ada* (1969) should be considered. Boyd speaks of Nabokov's "almost pathological ability to conjure up the past and bring it to life," an ability perhaps less pathological than therapeutic in that to re-experience conflicted feelings is to begin to master them.[17] This account is literature following an almost psychoanalytic bent, contrary to Nabokov's professed dislike for Freud and all his epigones. Was Nabokov ever in analysis? His personal reconstructions sometimes make it seem so. Adolescent, indeed lifelong, sexual anxiety is palpable in *Ada,* an intricate story of incestuous wishes and their acting out in the extended consanguity of an upper-class Russian family. The fiction must surely touch Nabokov's own relations with his sisters, Olga and possibly Elena, and with girl cousins mentioned in *Speak, Memory.* "The slums of sex were unknown to us," Nabokov wrote, yet tensions around the attractions of little girls appear in the autobiography.[18]

What prompted Nabokov to construct the intricate and obscure

Ada around incestuous relations between the brother and sister Van and Ada, and their erotically frustrated younger sister Lucette? The novel may reflect without being explicit Nabokov's actual childhood relations with his sisters. As Boyd recognizes, the reader of *Ada* always feels that he is missing something in the narrative. This could be because the theme of incest was not so much deliberately chosen by Nabokov as compelling him from a source too deep for him fully to discover. The circling, allusive, time-warped feeling of this novel can be accounted for by its touching on family and developmental truths too sensitive for even Nabokov's subtlety. The reader often feels disoriented and confused, much as Nabokov himself may have felt when contemplating the distressing encounters of his childhood. It is possible that Van was sexually overstimulated by his caretakers, episodes of which he only just manages to pull out of memory and states in a disjointed way; in the following passage Nabokov (speaking for Van) struggles with failure of memory for certain essential elements of experience, while he tries to tease apart those fused elements that are remembered:

> But, personally, Van had not the slightest recollection of that visit or indeed of that particular summer, because his father's life, anyway, was a rose garden all the time, and he had been caressed by ungloved lovely hands more than once himself, which did not interest Ada.[19]

Whose "ungloved lovely hands" "caressed" him: those of nurses and nannies whose hands would not be gloved, as his aristocratic mother's might be? It is speculative to read this passage as a reminiscence of erotic overstimulation in childhood, and the possibility may be dismissed unless it is accepted that Nabokov courageously reconstructed the complications in his own family when writing *Ada*. It is known that Nabokov gave his high-strung sister Olga's birthday to Van and Ada's half sister Lucette, suggesting a discovery he was half revealing.

Lucette is the sexually provocative younger half sister by four years, so her twelve-year-old girlish charms are superimposed on Ada's, aged sixteen. Riding home in the "victoria," the slightly older Van (Ada's full brother) is accompanied by Ada and Lucette, who sits on his knee. As Van gazes on Ada reading a book, he has an erection—"the golden flood of swelling joy"—threatening to "touch off a private crisis under the solemn load of another child." But "no furtive friction could compete with what awaited him in Ada's bower," so there is no ejaculation.[20]

Thus *Ada* seems to switch back in time from the earlier published story of *Lolita*, where a similar incident occurs between Humbert and his child obsession:

> Her young weight, her shameless innocent shanks and round bottom, shifted in my tense, tortured, surreptitiously laboring lap; and all of a sudden a mysterious change came over my senses. I entered a plane of being where nothing mattered, save the infusion of joy brewed within my body. . . . The least pressure would suffice to set all paradise loose. . . . I crushed out against her left buttock the last throb of the longest ecstasy man or monster had ever known. (pp. 57–58)

Lolita is a fantasy version of Lucette/Ada, as they are depicted in "an ardent childhood romance" beginning in late nineteenth-century Russia, and now transposed to the America of emerging sexual liberation. As Nabokov wrote of Van and Ada's sexual attraction, "the relationship is not simply dangerous *cousinage*, but possesses an aspect prohibited by law," a matter pleaded by Humbert Humbert before judge and jury when answering for his crimes in *Lolita*.[21] This pleading may be a reminiscence about Nabokov's sister Olga, or about girl cousins, which Humbert Humbert fills out in a dramatic fantasy of sexually possessing a nymphet. The two novels may thus play with actuality and fantasy in the conflicted area of incestuous wishes. Instinctive overstimulation in childhood never dies in the unconscious, but it can be brought into the light of adult morality. This overstimulation appears in a passage concerning Van's feelings about Lucette's sexual availability: he fears her keeping him "insatiably captive for weeks," and then reverts to childhood association:

> But worst of all, while aware, and ashamed, of lusting after a sick child, he felt, in an obscure twist of ancient emotions, his lust sharpened by the shame.[22]

Shame brings alive the moral sense that actuates these fictional investigations of a common theme needing their quietus in the unconscious. This, of course, is never the novelist's overt concern, but it may be inferred from his use of metaphor.

More than *Ada*'s childhood reconstruction, *Lolita* is filled with the most graphic fantasy, seemingly from the creative unconscious at its most active. Moral torture is palpable, with its analogue in physical contortions. *Lolita* is often grotesque with startling images of persons misshapen or maimed, a man without fingers, a man missing an arm, even a crippled fire hydrant with "red stumps of its arms"—gratuitously overwritten unless seen as an overall pattern of sadistic sacrifice of Lolita herself (p. 99).[23] Just as Humbert's fetishized idealizing fantasies of Lolita's body parts disintegrates when reality breaks in, as will appear, so is Nabokov the novelist left with only the postmortem remains of his creation. The mind's creative workshop is littered with the remains of reparative reconstructions of early experiences of attachment it could not finish yet cannot discard. Obsession leaves its preoccupations futilely active, even though reality testing tells Humbert that his narcissism condemns him to a prison of unfulfillable desires.

II

There is evidence in Nabokov's *Speak, Memory* that his was an obsessional personality, the product of Jocasta Mothering and caretaking, or a least of being a cossetted favorite of his mother's and subject of special attention by English-speaking nurses and nannies. This interpretation is not Nabokov's, yet it is what he says within the confession. As a child of the non-titled Russian aristocracy before it was swept away by revolution, he understands less than might be wished of the forces that shaped him: "Neither in environment nor in heredity can I find the exact instrument that fashioned me," he writes; yet the evidence at least for being a mother's boy is assembled.[24] Not only was his mother his aesthetic mentor, painting watercolors for him, but also she showed him the colors of lilacs and wonders of her jewellery collection—inducement to "mystery and enchantment," the very terms later given to his erotic fascination with Lolita.[25] Numerous childhood illnesses brought him still closer to his mother, he remembers. In contrast to his younger brother, "I was the coddled one; he, the witness of coddling," Nabokov wrote.[26] More than this his synesthesia (seeing colors in words) was sympathetically understood by his mother, implying that from at least age seven, she strongly participated in his hypersensitive imaginative life. Nabokov's first biographer, Andrew Field, reports that his sister told him that Nabokov enjoyed more parental attention than any of the other children: "My mother adored him. Of all the five children. This was really adoration."[27]

Field reports that a close friend of Nabokov's father had written a memoir that before Vladimir's birth "I had the impression that this would be an extremely abnormal upbringing in fatally overabundant circumstances."[28] Born in 1899 to wealth and privilege,

Nabokov was nurtured and raised like an upper-class English child: first a wet nurse, then a nurse, and on to a governess. There seem to be no records showing anything more "abnormal" about this sequence than it was for any European boy of his class. Nabokov himself discouraged enquiry into his early development: "Why should I tolerate a perfect stranger at the bedside of my mind," he asked, implying that, after all, there might be legitimate concern for its well-being.[29] Nabokov admitted to a lifelong fascination with abnormal psychology, observing that "many of my [fictional characters] have sudden obsessions, different kinds of obsessions," speaking of Humbert Humbert as "a man with an obsession" but denying that it had any special origin.[30] Yet his own obsessional nature is amply portrayed in Speak, Memory, for instance, in the scene with his "languid and melancholy governess" Miss Norcott:

> As she strolls on the beach with himself and his brother, Vladimir separates, as he recalled: "I am wearing a toy bracelet. As I crawl over those rocks, I keep repeating, in a kind of zestful, copious, and deeply gratifying incantation, the English word 'childhood', which sounds mysterious and new, and becomes stranger and stranger as it gets mixed up in my small overstocked hectic mind, with Robin Hood and Little Red Riding Hood, and the brown hoods of old hunchbacked fairies."[31]

Here he is innocently in the grip of repetitive obsessional thinking, not only about the word, but also perhaps the very childhood he is experiencing. The "hectic mind" is the embryonic obsessional mind, opening abundant inventive powers.

Field thinks that Nabokov's certainty in his creative powers came of the narcissism produced by "a surfeit of parental love," but this alone is doubtful.[32] Narcissism is not a concept that explains as much about creativity as does obsession, a defense in which the internalized mother is split into accepting and rejecting aspects by which the person gains quasi independence from her by identifying with her. This concept more nearly explains the ambivalence toward women found in Lolita, an ambivalence of love and hate that is surely Nabokov's own whether or not he was excited by nymphets. Early object splitting must be the background of any denigration of mothers coupled with the idealization of pre-adolescent girls, a matter best viewed within the framework of John Bowlby's theory of "anxious attachment."[33] The pedophile's perversion implies forbidden sexual desires toward the mother linked to resistant or avoidant attachment to a narcissistically in-

vested child as object of desire. None of this seems to have occurred to Nabokov.

As Nabokov told Peter Duval Smith, he wrote *Lolita* because it
was "an interesting thing to do" with no social purpose or moral
message, more like a "riddle" he set and solved himself. Dis-
avowing any personal involvement, Nabokov claimed that *Lolita*
"treated of the theme which was so distant, so remote, from my
own emotional life that it gave me a special pleasure to use my
combinational talent to make it real."[34] In response to a question
by Robert Robinson about writers' having one obsessive theme,
Nabokov replied: "If I do have any obsessions I'm careful not to
reveal them in fictional form."[35] Such remarks seem to be definitive rejoinders to anyone wanting to link literary product to psychological process, yet it is on record that Nabokov persisted with
the Lolita theme from at least 1936 to the 1950s before he was
satisfied with its literary incarnation. Alvin Toffler was more direct in an interview of 1964 for *Playboy*, trying to lead Nabokov
first into a discussion of sexuality and then into Freudianism: the
novelist dismissed both. When Toffler opened the question of the
repetitiousness of Nabokov's concern in fiction with middle-aged
men seeking preadolescent girls, Nabokov again evaded answering: "People tend to underestimate the power of my imagination
and my capacity of evolving serial selves in my writings," going
on to deny that his romance at age ten with Colette (referred to
in *Speak, Memory*, p. 149f) was anything other than innocently
normal.[36] The point about Toffler's interview is that Nabokov does
not deny a sexual preoccupation with nymphets: he just slips out
of it. Yet Toffler scores a point about Nabokov's obsession when
leading the author into an admission of a loving preoccupation
with diminutives for Dolores Haze throughout the novel. But
mainly Nabokov (who always prepared interviews, never allowing
for spontaneity) successfully blocked enquiry into motivation. If
his remarks about noninvolvement are not to be taken as simply
disingenuous, the meaning of obsession should be broadened to
include attitudes to all women, not just imaginary nymphets and
their mothers.

The biographer Field does not see Nabokov as a "spoiled"
upper-class child; he is said to have been fathered in a way that
kept him respectful and tutored in a way that sufficiently challenged his intellect. Was Nabokov effeminized by his attentive
mother leading to anxiety about gender and to questions about
sexual orientation? Nabokov's fiction is preoccupied with homosexuality; yet in *Lolita* Gaston Godin's homosexuality, along with

its suggestion in Quilty and in Humbert himself, do not resonate with what so far is known of Nabokov's biography. The more pervasive fantasy in *Lolita* is bisexual: the double (or split) named Humbert Humbert is "a latent repressed homosexual" writes Norman Kiell; he is charmed by Lolita's "beautiful boy-knees" and by her "white wide little-boy shorts, the slender waist."[37] Humbert dislikes mature women with fully formed breasts, and he denigrates menstruating "deodorized career girls" (p. 33). Field agrees that "Humbert's perversity is very close to homosexuality, though Humbert is not homosexual—his double assumes that role for him."[38] A nymphet between the ages of nine and fourteen is boylike, nascently female, perhaps "tomboyish" in a teasing way—a compromise object that becomes obsessive in a repetition compulsion because satisfactory closure is never possible. Thus there is a kind of irrational safety from developmental anxieties incarnate in the boy-girl nymphet; initially she is an androgynous image of a third non-threatening sex, but when adult male sexual desire appears trouble abounds, as Humbert's waywardly violent saga testifies. Thus Nabokov's intended ironic clinical "Foreword" by "John Ray, Jr., Ph.D.," predisposing us to see Humbert as "abnormal," may actually persuade us to do so since child abuse is so much better understood than it was when Nabokov self-indulgently wrote the novel. At the time of writing, Nabokov expected readers to brand the psychologist John Ray as primly narrow-minded for writing: "A desperate honesty that throbs through his confession does not absolve him from sins of diabolical cunning. He is abnormal." We are unlikely to be still "entranced with the book while abhorring its author," Humbert Humbert, not Nabokov who masterminds the pseudoconfession. Rather than a mere reaction of abhorrence, the reader feels the need to understand the obsessive imagination that seems to have been ill at ease with the immorality of its clever invention.

There are further clues. While Nabokov was almost certainly Jocasta-mothered, clear inferences of sexual orientation are yet to be drawn. That his stuttering brother Sergi was interested from age five only in boys argues little about Vladimir.[39] Nabokov appears to have had homosexual uncles on both sides of the family, but was he ever touched, fondled, or seduced by one of them—a possible precursor of bisexuality? There is nothing to show unless a biographer turns up new evidence. Field speaks of *Lolita*'s being "a parodic but very important analogue to incest in the Nabokov family tree," without particularizing or developing the statement.[40] What then is the psychobiographer to do except pick up the behaviors in Nabokov's life that indicate why he would be interested in so perverse a theme as that of an adoptive father's incestuous love for his preadolescent daughter? From the telltale signs of his well-hidden emotional life we can guess at the kind of obsessional imagination Nabokov possessed. Fantasy analysis reveals in *Lolita* an unconsciously coded subtext of death-dealing attractions and aversions that gives the most reliable indication of the imaginative hold this novel had when its perverse prescription for sexual satisfaction was new and provocative. (See chap. 20, p. 82 for its most open plea for nympholepsy.) Ironic and parodic concealment of sexual wishes argue for hidden disreputable themes in the creative consciousness. Shame-enshrouded fantasy material introduced into the public realm as "art" tends to carry disclaimers of personal origins. The Belgian surrealist painter René Magritte, whose sexually charged imagery is unremittingly disturbing, led a highly conventional and correct life to blend in with the world around him. That this lifestyle was a mask is shown in Martha Wolfenstein's psychobiography tracing the effects of the early suicide of Magritte's mother.[41] A more puzzling situation is that of the painter Balthus who, for decades, has painted dreamy girls in early adolescence posed with their legs suggestively spread. Is Balthus a compulsive fantasizer of nymphets? For him, as for Nabokov, art is a sacred preserve where such questions are said to be irrelevant. When asked in 1968 to contribute a biography to a Tate Gallery catalogue, Balthus cabled:

> No biographical details. Begin: Balthus is a painter of whom nothing is known. Now let us look at the pictures. Regards. B.[42]

The ingenuous note of innocence is quite plausible; the artist may not be fully aware of sexist exploitative cruelty in his work. Even so sophisticated a writer as Nabokov, whose fearful fascination for psychoanalysis had lead him to read with some attention from Freud to Melanie Klein, could openly disclaim any sadistic fantasies of his own. When Peter Duval Smith, in a BBC interview, observed that "in your novels there is a strain of perversity amounting to cruelty," Nabokov quibbled about words, noting that as a young man especially he had seen the world as cruel, but finally concluded it had no personal origin. "I don't think that there is a specially perverse cruel streak in my writing. In life I'm a mild old gentleman: I'm very kind. There's nothing cruel or brutal in me whatsoever."[43] The evidence of *Lolita* is far otherwise, yet we should not accuse Nabokov of untruth in speaking for the self of everyday life that is not the creative unconscious with its own urgent requirements. Not to be taken over by an incipient sexual perversion, the gifted artist guardedly confesses it through a fictional persona, an "as if" character who is far more immoral than he could ever be, and whose perverse behaviors may be altered in degree, if not kind, from those worrying his creator. According to Freud (1916, 1917), perversions are the behaviorally active reverse of neurotic urges that are repressed to such an extent that they inhibit life.[44] The writer or artist can displace into a fictional space such enactments, preserving the attitude of an innocent bystander at events that quite fascinate him. Thus neurotic conflict is harmlessly imputed to the imaginary behaviors of persons the artist has created but who are unlike him. If, as Robert Stoller says, perversion is the erotic form of hatred, staged to triumph in the present over traumas in the developmental processes of the past, then the lure and disguise of its hidden elements are more easily understood.[45] With the center of perversions being hostility derived from archaic circumstances of which the artist is largely unaware, it is plausible to think that statements he makes about tangible fantasies of his art will not be denials so much as self-exonerations when there is actual esthetic achievement. Deflection of perverse impulse into "as if" behavioral situations in entertaining fictions seems worthy of culture at any level. Yet when punitive suggestions are directed at innocent persons (e.g., young females) the critic should ask to what extent they are powered by displaced resentments and are unconsciously calculated to settle old scores.

Sooner or later most celebrated writers construct their early lives in the form of an autobiography, in Nabokov's case one recounting his compulsive butterfly collecting. Butterfly collecting, which the writer took to a high level of scientific achievement, was introduced to him by his mother during a childhood illness. "My mother accumulated a library and a museum around my bed, and the longing to describe a new species completely replaced that of discovering a new prime number."[46] After most of a lifetime of lepidopteral collecting and classifying new species, Nabokov blended this collecting obsession with perverse Humbert Humbert's capture of the youthful Lolita about to become a butterfly. Field remarks that Nabokov used "his mother's nickname for Lolita," linking (albeit loosely) mother to butterfly to nymphet with incestuous overtones.[47] *Speak, Memory* emphasizes "the excitement of entomological exploration," serving an "acute desire to be alone" and "amounting to a mania."[48] Speaking of compulsive butterfly collecting, he hopes to "look at my demon objectively," noting that no one except for his parents "really understood my obsession"—a solitary and all-consuming pursuit given its correct name. One of Humbert Humbert's happiest moments of triumph in having captivated Lolita occurs in the "gay town of Lepingville," where he buys her many presents and she capitulates to him, realizing that "she had absolutely nowhere else to go" (p. 130). Lepingville was allegedly the town where Lolita's ill mother was in hospital, but the mother is dead and the town becomes a lepidopterist's paradise where the quarry is finally his own. As Alfred Appel wrote:

> [Nabokov] like a long line of [his] fictional creations, from Luzhin in *The Defence* to Humbert in *Lolita,* had also pursued a secret life, an ardent desire, an obsessive quest. Nabokov went butterfly-hunting every summer, and these adventures as a 'lepist' carried him through two hundred motel rooms in forty-six states, along the same roads traveled by Humbert and Lolita.[49]

A life of restless transience, moving about with his wife, even while lecturing at Cornell, seems to have been necessary to the displaced Russian Nabokov. It stimulated scanning the past induced by recollecting his mother. Appel notes further that "*Speak, Memory* released him to write *Lolita,* and Lolita in her turn released him from the circumscribing spell of *Speak, Memory,* the cul-de-sac of nostalgia."[50] This statement implies that the novel is somehow the product of freeing up a past into which its themes had been bound, having previously entered his fiction in unsatisfactory ways. Pursuit of idealized objects in butterflies resembled the less tangible quest in memory for elusive satisfactions in object relations with parents. In another interview, Nabokov said:

> As for pursuit, it is, of course, ecstasy to follow an undescribed beauty, skimming over the rocks of its habitat, but it is also great fun to locate a new species among the broken insects in an old biscuit tin sent over by a sailor from some remote island.[51]

Butterfly hunting, a pursuit of ideal objects, almost erotic in intensity, prefigures Humbert's compulsive pursuit of Lolita, but it also recalls the less glamorous "broken" objects from remote places in the deep, sometimes unpleasant past. Thus novel and autobiography are connected as products of obsessive collecting—attempts to put structure and meaning to a fragmented past, ambivalently invested with his mother's ministrations.

"A painful birth, a difficult baby, but a kind of daughter," Nabokov at sixty wrote of *Lolita*, reflecting on the literary labor.[52] She was himself reborn, a new condensation probably stimulated by the frenzied adolescent sexuality of America rousing old obsessions less articulated in his European fiction. Mastery of the art of literary masking, even deception, allowed him to be more daring this time. Narcissistic and parodic fantasy avoids being transparently autobiographical, and it also brings changes in the neurotic ego seeking to circumvent the behavioral risks of obsessions. Fantasy displays impulses without necessarily leading to action, if the literary satisfactions are as great as Nabokov's must have been. His portrayal of split, ambivalent feelings about mother and daughter takes us deep into the disturbed male feelings about females that torment Western culture, making it both self-indulgent and violent. Did Nabokov know just how telling his fable of obsessive quest would be, how diagnostic of our alienation from most definitions of healthy sexuality? It is curious that an aristocratic Russian emigré should have stepped into a delegate role to show America its own ambiguity of sexual love and hate. Eroticized American culture has had few moralists of this order, although it is an ambiguous morality entailing a high degree of complicity. Readers who looked to *Lolita* for pornography were partly gratified although ultimately disappointed. The crudity of pornography is refined to a sophistication no living writer could emulate. Nabokov had been at his project for a long time, obsessed by the idea of corrupted innocence, of extreme youth corrupted by age and the consequences thereof.

Field finds the preoccupation with nymphets as early as the sexual story "A Fable" written in Russian in 1926.[53] Appel notes anticipations of *Lolita* in "Laughter in the Dark" (first published as *Camera Obscura* in 1932), quoting Nabokov: "My Lolita had been compared to Emmie in *Invitation,* to Mariette in *Bend Sinister,* and even Colette in *Speak, Memory."* Appel, however, takes on a protective tone, writing, "Nabokov is justly impatient with those who hunt for Ur-Lolitas, for a preoccupation with specific 'sexual morbidities' and obscures the more general context in which these oddities should be seen."[54] Field comments further:

> The basic plot of *Lolita* is sketched out in *The Gift*, which means that it was in Nabokov's mind as early as 1936. There the situation is put very modestly, for in the stepfather's story the man never makes an advance, and the girl grows into a woman who . . . simply looks at him with contempt.[55]

As Erica Jong points out, the fuller "ripening" of Nabokov's obsession is found in "The Enchanter" (1936), in which "all the elements of *Lolita* are present: the Central European lover, the nymphet, the marrying-her-mother theme."[56] The term *enchant* appears repeatedly in *Lolita,* referring mainly to Humbert's place of consummation, the hotel "The Enchanted Hunters." The term evokes Humbert's trancelike conquest of his quarry, an innocent brought down in dream time as though she were no more than Psyche, beloved of Eros, a captive butterfly. Five years in its particular gestation, *Lolita*'s theme of alienated love and incestuous self-indulgence thus reveals a fictional metamorphosis driven by the writer's obsessive imagination.

Yet we still have given no proof that the pedophiliac fantasy was Nabokov's own. Could it be that he was just as fascinated by mothers as by daughters, and that attitudes to women in general are what mattered in the novel? We surmise that obsession for scarcely pubescent girls is a cover for early eroticized feelings about the mother too painful to be acknowledged. The obsession would defend against some nameless trauma that even the most diligent psychoanalysis would have difficulty uncovering. Without a better key than *Speak, Memory,* we are held to speculations about Nabokov's earliest feelings about his mother and caretaking women. What about the succession of English nurses and governesses, Miss Rachel, Miss Clayton and especially the "lovely, black-haired, aquamarine-eyed Miss Norcott" at whose departure Nabokov was inconsolable?[57] And what about the effects on him of the French governess from 1905 known as "Mademoiselle," a lovingly grotesque portrait to which so many pages are devoted? Her authority as Van and Ada's French governess appears to be derided forty years later in *Ada.* And then there are the adorations of young girls such as Zina and Colette, prototypes of Annabel in *Lolita* no doubt: intense sensuality directed to young girls is present in the autobiography. Of a relation he writes:

> On my left, one of my most fidgety girl cousins, a nebulous little blond of eleven or so with long, Alice-in-Wonderland hair and a shell pink complexion, sat so close to me that I felt the slender bone of her hip move against mine every time she shifted her seat, fingering her locket, or passing her hand between her perfumed hair and the nape of her neck, or knocking her knees together under the rustly silk of her yellow slip, which shone through the lace of her frock.[58]

This may be a Lolita creature in the formative stages of the obsession when it was still a buried neuroticism, and compounded by

possible incestuous feelings for his sister Olga. Is this the release
from "cul-de-sac nostalgia" making possible the novel in another
language, and in another land, of which Appel writes? The suggestion is strong but not proven. Nabokov helpfully even tells us
that his father in 1902 had written a paper in criminal law on
"Carnal Crimes" dealing with "little girls . . . from eight to twelve
years being sacrificed to lechers," but this was a later discovery.[59]
Butterfly hunting is linked with the sensual enjoyment of spotting
by chance some naked children bathing, among them Polenka
who emerges from the water chased by other children:

> Before I crept away in a dismal haze of disgust and desire—I saw
> strange Polenka shiver and squat on the boards of the half-broken
> wharf, covering her breasts against the east wind with her crossed
> arms while with the tip of her tongue she taunted her pursuers.[60]

Again, the sensual particularizing, along with the torn moralizing,
of *Lolita* appears; but never in his autobiography does Nabokov
try to explain why esthetic voyeurism is so strong in his makeup.
Perhaps he didn't see it as a symptom of conflict so much as a
fertile resource for creativity, a self-indulgent compromise and,
at the same time, a reparative gesture when enshrined in language. He does not hesitate to tell of his sexual pluralism:

> I see myself as a hundred different young men at once pursuing one
> changeful girl in a series of simultaneous or overlapping love affairs,
> some delightful, some sordid, that ranged from one-night adventures
> to protracted involvements and dissimulations, with very meagre artis-
> tic results.[61]

The link of art to pluralistic eroticism is made, leaving nothing
for the "Viennese Quack" to work with. Is the lover of women
also a fantasy seducer of young girls, and if so what does this tell
us about the origin and meaning of sexual obsession? Origins
must await further evidence, but meaning is readily ascertained
from fantasy analysis of the novel *Lolita*.

Despite hostility to Freud, Nabokov lavishly celebrates the "pleasure principal" weighing up the pleasures and ultimate pains of
Humbert's sensual indulgence with the child Lolita. For him, as
for Freud, sexuality is a fundamental driving force, amoral unless
controlled by social restraints—provided by the court trial of
Humbert, the framework of his confession. He is an erotic animal,
a crude id force whose chosen objects happen to be underaged
girls; and his neurotic conflict, leading to conflict with society and

the law, is an expression of wish-fulfillment in a disordered fantasy life. It is almost as though Nabokov had read Freud's *Three Essays on the Theory of Sexuality* (1905), with its remarks on the unruly life force of libido, and the "polymorphous perversity" of the child, only to reject and try (unsuccessfully) to forget about it. In *Notes Upon a Case of Obsessional Neurosis* (1909), Freud wrote a graphic theory of obsessional neurosis, filling it out with the case history of the "Rat Man." This statement also is too strong and current to simply wish away. In other words, with Freudian assumptions already operating in a fantasy asking us to reject Freud, it makes sense to redouble the effort beyond a psychobiography of either Humbert Humbert or of his cleverly evasive creator. Fantasy analysis can reveal motives little known to Nabokov himself, reveal an intentionality in the fiction perceptible through its artfullness. By close study of repeated words, images, and concepts, fantasy analysis proposes to penetrate the author's defensive system to reach the deep subjectivity of his feelings about primary attachments, especially to women. It assumes that the novel is a multilayered communication, telling a fablelike story to be sure, but also revealing the basic affective tonalities the author brings to the fictionalized attachments. Fantasy analysis thus claims to reveal and to interpret the author's own ego language, uttered in an obsessive trance state in which he freely associates and aggregates meanings of which he is only partially aware. The readers who proclaim the importance of his book as breaking the barriers of taboo subjects are more aware of what the total communication means, but they too may be surprised to realize just how clear the fantasy inversion of love-as-death actually is.

III

In the following fantasy analysis evidence is collected to suggest Nabokov's probably partly unconscious attitudes to the fictive persons portrayed in *Lolita*.[62] So teasingly allusive and self-parodic is the novel, that fantasy analysis is needed to reveal attitudes particularly to women. The principal fantasies in *Lolita* come under two main gender headings, men and women, each of them subdivided about degree of ambivalent desire and rejection. Anomalies of "attachment" are evident throughout, that is types of "anxious attachment," to use John Bowlby's term, with no instance of a healthy attachment developed anywhere in the novel. *Lolita* is a solipsistic, self-absorbed rendering of compulsive pedophilic fantasy, which the novelist can only partially open to inspection through the device of Dr. John Ray, and the judicial proceeding against Humbert Humbert. Nabokov is quoted as writing of himself: "His best works are those in which he condemns his people to the solitary confinement of their souls." As Appel notes, "Nabokov has employed the prison trope in many ways," nowhere more effectively than in the dim reaches of Humbert Humbert's obsessive mind that is likened to a caged primitive ape.[63] Exposing the primitive feeling of the anomalies of attachment in *Lolita* is the task of these pages—to bring light into this particular emotional prison.

Men As Rejecting Objects

Most men in *Lolita* are blocking figures, interfering with Humbert Humbert's quest for the child Lolita as a sexual object; themselves usually prisoners of similar obsessions with nymphets, or at least bizarre sexuality, they pursue or shadow Humbert Humbert, filling him with anxiety, as when the supposed detective Trapp takes pursuit in his Aztec Red convertible. In a more rational moment, Humbert realizes that "Trapp or Trapps" were only "figments of my persecution mania" (p. 218). Not surprisingly Trapp's face becomes "the face of Clare Quilty" (p. 265) who must be punished by Humbert for tricking and sodomizing Lolita (p. 269) as is alleged. The rehearsal of Mr. Richard F. Schiller's "violent death," Humbert's reprisal against Lolita's husband, is a false move. Richard is far too naive to merit such punishment: the real villain is clever "Cue" (Clare Quilty) who had spirited Lolita away (pp. 251, 254). This sets Humbert on a search and destroy mission to Quilty's house, where the murder takes place; the murder can be seen as the self-killing of a double who is more vicious than prurient.

Men As Attracting Objects

Doubling identifies with the persecutor, making a sort of brother, or soul mate, of Quilty who also doubles with Trapp. Both objectify shame and bad conscience, yet as Humbert's double, Quilty, the dandified pervert, is felt to be a mortal danger to be extinguished. To split off Humbert's worst self in Quilty leaves Nabokov as author safely distanced from violent pedophilia, though he created the whole scenario in fascination.

Humbert is powerfully impelled by murderous intent to find Quilty's ancestral home, Pavor Manor on Grimm Road, where the "night panic" will be staged (p. 266f). Quilty's slow-motion execution is a sort of surrealistic farrago of misadventure, of bungled murderous intent in which the antagonists almost become one person (p. 272). Quilty's murder by shooting is a sort of homoerotic consummation as "I was injecting spurts of energy into the poor fellow, as if the bullets had been capsules wherein a heady elixir danced" (p. 276). The attraction-repulsion of male homosexuality is summed up when Humbert plays chess with the ineffectual Gaston Godin who lusts after little boys. The link with Humbert's seeing Lolita as boylike is unmistakable (pp. 44, 47, 111, etc.): both men defend against heterosexual love of somebody their own age. Humbert has associations with Uranists in Paris (p. 17), taught in a school for boys (p. 18), was called "potentially homosexual" by a psychiatric nurse, and is possibly bisexual. Humbert Humbert wishes to annihilate the positive/feminine aspect of self embodied in Quilty, whose feminine characteristics are repeatedly mentioned (pp. 191, 202, 249, 270, 276, etc.). Quilty mirrors Vivian Darkbloom's feminine anagram for Vladimir Nabokov, emphasizing bisexual anxiety.

Women As Rejecting Objects

The bizarre romance between middle-aged Humbert Humbert and the child Lolita is rationalized and mythologized with exceptional power using the traditional and familiar "Beauty and the Beast" legend together with the myth of the Minotaur and the Maiden reworked to support incest. Nabokov drops in such obvious metaphors as "beauty and the beast" (p. 57) and a tiger pursuing a bird of paradise (p. 124), to persuade readers that the turn toward incest is not entirely strange. The metaphors of loved and loathed womanhood, of the madonna and whore, are elaborated in remarkable ways, suggesting powerful unconscious complicity from the author who transmutes the hidden wishes of the society for which he writes.

Humbert's entire self-presentation consists of urgent self-deceptions and rationalizations, but how did Nabokov reach the point where such a performance of forbidden incestuous eroticism was possible? He may have pictured twelve-year-old Lolita as the vulgar sexually precocious carnal initiator to avoid pornographic imputations on his novel. Humbert's "monstrous love" (p. 78) for an innocent Lolita could grotesquely overbalance the power relationship, so Nabokov gave her a forward sexuality to make Humbert seem less guilty of incestuous rape (pp. 104–5).

Revealingly, Nabokov considers three possible attitudes for Humbert to sexual exploitation of a minor. (1) That of the moralist, he bypasses; (2) that of the child therapist he derides, yet grandiosely Humbert Humbert calls himself King Sigmund the second (p. 116) as his is a science of nympholepsy, he claims (p. 199). By derision and satire, Nabokov proposes considerations of mental health, which even in the 1940s and 1950s were emerging into public consciousness. Finally (3) Nabokov-Humbert takes the position of the primitive sensualist driven by obsession to abuse a child, rather as a nineteenth-century chauvinist of a higher class might expect to do with a working-class child (p. 115). The crudeness of this is offset by making a brash American sensualist of Lolita. Humbert's identity as a beast of prey (like Picasso's Minotaur) is reinforced throughout the novel with many animal images: "I lay in wait [for her]" he says (p. 121) and, at last, he condemns himself as "a pentapod monster" (p. 259). With an imagery of aggression so highly developed, it is necessary to furnish Lolita with almost equivalent "polymorphous perverse" desires as is done by giving her precocious sexual experience at camp. With beauty so eagerly libidinous, the beast can take what he wants in the "modern dream world, where everything [is] permissible" (p. 122), including the "rape" of which Lolita accuses Humbert (p. 130). When collusive, the crime against a female minor is made to seem less horrible. Humbert's trance world of desire is loosely linked to the real world of responsible behavior by his "confession" of illicit amours to judge and jury. But the novel's whole atmosphere of contempt for law and convention (the wisdom of the race, against which Humbert pits his perverse wishes) is such that the esthetics of obsession take over the novel. How do we know that Humbert's erotic exploitation is a deep violation of morality? The test is to ask exactly how he sees women (1) as mothers, with age-appropriate men as husbands and (2) how he sees under-aged girls as nymphet sexual objects. When attachment theory criteria are applied to the metaphorical development of attitudes to persons as objects or, perhaps, part objects, the pathology underlying *Lolita* begins to emerge.

To speak of mothers, it will be recalled that Nabokov has Humbert Humbert's mother die when he was only three, leaving him to be brought up by his maternal Aunt Sybil, who died when he was sixteen. His "gentle easy-going" father is said to have "taken advantage" of Sybil, a hint of Humbert's possible incestuous origin—a point Nabokov does not elaborate (p. 12). Aunt Sybil is said to have had a "fatal rigidity," suggesting the two sides

of Nabokov's own mother as indulgent and controlling (p. 12).
Little is known of Elena Nabokov, except that she was "always of
a nervous disposition," a tendency exacerbated by the deaths of
her parents in 1901, and that she delighted in sensuous experience that could be shared, as when she gave the child Vladimir
her glittering jewels to play with.[64] Rigidity is not recorded; it is
more likely to have been characteristic of Nabokov's nurses and
nannies. Humbert's substitute caretaker Aunt Sybil comes to
mind. It is possible only to conjecture from Nabokov's biography
what early female contacts meant to him: "Onya, his pretty coeval;
or the lovely, black-haired, aquamarine-eyed Miss Norcott, with
whom he was a little in love and whose sudden dismissal (she was
found to be a lesbian) left him inconsolable."[65] The governess,
"myopic Miss Hunt" was rebelled against suggesting overcontrol
by her, while the governess Mlle. Miauton (Mademoiselle in the
autobiography) led to derisive fictional portraits.[66] Strong maternal attraction, together with defensive rejection of control by caretakers, seems to have been an issue with Nabokov from an early
age, although the details have not been recovered. There is, however, enough here for us to see how it was that Nabokov could
provide Humbert with a not altogether spurious psychobiography
of perversion, necessary in view of the depressive emotional
breakdowns he is said to have had (p. 33, etc.). Humbert's instabili-
ties may be a magnified and disguised version of Nabokov's own,
with anxiety about incest and pedophilia turned into a monstrous
self-parody.

Nabokov's psychogenesis for Humbert's pedophilia is remarkably in keeping with what is known of the perversion's typical
development. According to Charles Socarides, perversions develop in the pre-Oedipal phase of childhood, before age three.
There is a primary identification with the mother together with
gender confusion and he notes that specifically in pedophilia may
be found: "(1) early loss of the breast (weaning trauma) provoking
strong retaliative tendencies which were alleviated through forc-
ing the love object to gratify oral cravings, and at the same time
dominating and controlling them; and (2) the avoidance of castration anxiety by choosing a love object like oneself."[67] Overly strong
attachment to the mother (whose breast was lost) leads to attempts
to separate being fraught with anxiety, which may be negotiated
by symbolic play to shift feelings to inanimate objects and by fantasy that displaces and dramatizes it in the enclosed imagination.
Both may be tinged with sadomasochism arising from the aggression felt about incomplete separation from the mother. When the

father is not sufficiently in the picture the boy may be traumatized by his mother's emotional demands. Socarides cites a case in which a boy's traumatic experience with his mother's pubic hair resulted in his turning to harmless prepubertal girls.[68] That sadism and exhibitionism can go with this mode of avoidance was long ago pointed out by Krafft-Ebing.[69]

In other words, pedophilia is one of the possible perverse outcomes of initial deprivation followed by instinctual overstimulation in the boy's development. It is a statement by the "false self" of continuing enmeshment in the family to which he belongs as a child, not of sexual liberation but its opposite. That the pedophile is committed to an obsessive pseudosolution to his involvement with his mother who had orally deprived him yet later entranced him, may be deduced from Humbert Humbert's split denigration of older mothering women and idealization of under-aged girls. In a pseudo-reparative exercise, the pedophile identifies with the weak, molested child while exercising power over it, thus also splitting the idealized object. In flight from the traumatizing mother, he sexualizes the child he cannot parent, thus memorializing his inner undeveloped child. With the narcissistic dynamic set going so early, a gifted child is likely to give it the form of fantasy as Nabokov does through Humbert. Norman Kiell cites Humbert as the more worldly sort of pedophile, self-important, even self-righteous, not showing his impotence and immaturity if he can help it. Kiell writes:

[Pedophiles] see sex as an aggressive act that might bring retaliation from a stronger, adult female. In a sense the child molester is picking on someone of his own level of sexual maturity, and is thus regressed or fixated at an immature level of psychosexual development, whereby he obtains primary sexual gratification from a physically immature female.[70]

A writer is unlikely to be interested in such a subject, unless it touches some chord in his own being. Nabokov masterfully disguised any interest he may have had in pedophilia and incest, yet choice of language in image and metaphor reveals the obsessive patterns at work in his imagination. It seems from the hostility to mothers displayed by Humbert that he is reacting against the internalized controlling mother more than he is against the lost mother, who is not a datum of Nabokov's biography, except insofar as nurses and nannies came and went during his childhood. In *Lolita* mothers are typically life denying, blocking rather than enabling agents; ultimately the mother figure joins the novel's most powerful pattern of imagery, that of death. Nabokov used fiction like someone trying to reexperience a childhood perplexed, if not traumatized, by his mother. Humbert's monstrous story magnifies feelings without actually revealing them. Imagery of love and hate, working mainly at the subliminal level, gives a powerful emotional message about the unapproachability of desired older women for whom the nymphet is an idealized safe substitute. Being underdeveloped the nymphet retains boylike features, supplying bisexual excitement, together with a measure of safety as object of desire. Lolita is sometimes a tomboy, sometimes teasingly feminine. By collecting evidence about feelings toward mothers, and toward young girls, underlying patterns of fantasy in *Lolita* will become clear.

Women As Sacrificial Objects: Nympholepsy As Love-Death

Slurs on mothers and older women

p. 14	"fat, powdered Mrs. Leigh (born Vanessa van Ness)"—mother of Annabel, Humbert's first love, "a lovely child a few months my junior."
p. 17	A sexual encounter with Annabel is broken up by "her mother's voice calling her, with a rising frantic note." "That little girl with her seaside limbs and ardent tongue haunted me ever since," Humbert adds.
p. 22	While Humbert tries to engage with an innocent nymphet in a park "groping under me for a lost marble," he is prevented by an "old woman in black," an "insolent hag."
p. 24	Humbert's search in Paris for a girl prostitute leads to a "madam," an older pseudomother, described with a "monstrously plump" fifteen-year-old daughter.
p. 26	Humbert's wife Valeria attracts him because of the imitation she gave of a little girl, a perverse attraction he acknowledges. Humbert likes her "smooth leg," "velvet slipper," and so forth, to start with, but Valeria turns out to resemble "her toad-like dead mama," "a large, puffy, short-legged, big-breasted and practically brainless baba." Valeria takes a lover, filling Humbert with contradictory, murderous feelings; at length he decides only to hurt her "vulnerable" legs. This prefigures special attention to Lolita's legs.

p. 36   On first meeting Lolita's mother, Humbert describes her: "The poor lady was in her middle thirties, she had a shiny forehead, plucked eyebrows and quite simple but not unattractive features of a type that may be defined as a weak solution of Marlene Dietrich."

pp. 41–42   Lolita and her mother are both in two-piece black bathing suits; while Lolita is "my darling, my sweetheart" and Humbert admires "the seaside of her schoolgirl thighs" (a reference to Annabel, p. 17), Charlotte Haze is a "phocine mamma" (a zoological reference to seal-like animals), later called "fat Haze" when she gets in the way of Humbert's amours with her daughter.

p. 47   Mrs. Haze is associated with "a dead something."

p. 48   The Hazes have a neighbor, "old invalid Miss Opposite" who needs a wheelchair.

p. 51   Humbert longs for "some terrific disaster" to eliminate Lolita's mother, now that she hates her daughter for being "sweet on me." By p. 53, Lolita implies the thought that she too would like to kill her mother.

pp. 58–59   With thoughts of sexual joy with Lolita together with loathing of her mother—"busybody Haze"—Humbert sings a fantasy of killing Carmen with a gun.

p. 63   "driver Haze at the violent wheel, rubber-red lips writhing in angry inaudible speech, swung my darling away." while Miss Opposite, the invalid, feebly waved.

p. 67   Murderous thoughts against Charlotte Haze (poisoning) are called up and denied.

p. 68   Humbert tries to think of Lolita's mother Charlotte as her big sister to make her more sexually appealing, only to visualize "too realistically her heavy hips, round knees, ripe bust, the coarse pink of her neck."

p. 72   Humbert fantasizes the nymphet Lolita: "I would manage to evoke the child while caressing the mother" as "she of the noble nipple and massive thigh prepared me for the performance of my nightly duty, it was still a nymphet's scent that in despair I tried to pick up."

p. 75   "A bad accident" to Charlotte is predicted. By p. 79, Humbert is thinking about "the perfect murder" by drowning Charlotte ("my captive corpse," p. 81) but he can't do it. Hatred and violence toward his wife Valeria reappears: "slapping Valeria's breasts out of alignment, or otherwise hurting her . . . shooting her lover" (p. 82). But such fantasies cannot be enacted because "poets never kill."

p. 89 Charlotte discovers Humbert's contemptuous description of her in his journal: "the Haze woman, the big bitch, the old cat, the obnoxious mama," and so forth. Humbert's excuse that these are only "fragments of a novel" is not believed, and when Charlotte runs from the house she is killed by a car (p. 90). Lolita is not told of her mother's violent death until p. 130.

p. 116 Humbert resents the "cow-like mother" of another nymphet.

p. 122 The "frigid gentlewomen of the jury" are asked to believe that Lolita seduced Humbert.

p. 150 A woman who interferes with Humbert's possession of Lolita is called "a full-blown fleshy handsome woman of the repulsive type." (Charlotte's "face in death" haunts him, p. 149).

p. 159 "there are few physiques I loath more than the heavy low-slung pelvis, thick calves and deplorable complexion of the average coed (in whom I see, maybe, the coffin of coarse female flesh within which my nymphets are buried alive)."

p. 161f Headmistress Pratt of Beardsley School for girls is a sort of substitute mother to Lolita. Pratt is "a huge woman, gray-haired, frowsy, with a broad flat nose and small eyes behind black-rimmed glasses" (p. 176). Humbert wonders, "Should I marry Pratt and strangle her," so great is her hold over Lolita (p. 180).

p. 164 Women who enquire too closely into Humbert's relations with Lolita are called "odious spinster" and "loathsome creature."

p. 219 Kindly Mrs. Hays (punning on Haze), "the brisk, brickly rouged, blue-eyed widow who ran the motor court," acts as a surrogate mother when Lolita is ill— the only good mother in the novel.

p. 231 As the novel moves toward seventeen-year-old Lolita becoming a mother herself, her obsessive image merges with those of Valeria and Charlotte "weeping in my bleeding arms and being tenderly kissed by my brotherly lips in a dream of disorder of auctioneered Viennese bric-a-brac, pity, impotence and the brown wigs of tragic old women who had just been gassed." Here brother-sister incest is suggested, along with Freud, impotence, and Nazi death camps.

p. 241   Humbert has an interlude relationship with Rita, whose mother was "a crazy little woman."

p. 245   Searching for Lolita, Humbert sees "two thin-armed, barefoot little girls and their dim grandmothers."

p. 249   As Humbert confronts pregnant Lolita, reflecting that he "had known and adored every pore and follicle of her pubescent body," he sees her "washed-out gray eyes," their sexuality "like a bit of dry mud caking her childhood."

p. 264   Mrs. Chatfield the inquisitive intruder on Humbert's private passion for Lolita "attacked me with a fake smile, all aglow with evil curiosity." She is the last in a series of maligned mothers, appearing just before the murder of Quilty.

The main inference from this stage of fantasy analysis is that Humbert Humbert's marriage to widowed Charlotte Haze, Lolita's mother, is symbolically marriage to any mother, in an Oedipal parody. Nabokov mocks Freud by hating mothers in general, but he also registers negative feelings of his own about sexually needy (overstimulated and overstimulating) older women. Only a means to an end, Humbert's loathing for Charlotte is shown mainly through ridiculing her physical appearance. Charlotte is a blocking agent forbidding Humbert's erotic child fantasy. The pedophilic fantasy with which Nabokov works may arise from the obsessional defense against the anger and pain of some early trauma in being mothered, or cared for by nurses and nannies. Thus the denigration of mothers and idealization of nymphets are the polarized sides of feelings about attachments to females— a self-canceling, "no win" situation for Humbert who can engage with women only on the most limited terms. It seems likely that, for Nabokov, this exercise in the psychopathology of nympholepsy must have brought fully to the surface, if not relieved, anxiety about incestuous wishes.

Idealization of the nymphic daughter

Humbert Humbert is obsessed by young girls as sexual objects, nymphets as he calls them: demon-child lovers "between the age limits of nine and fourteen" (p. 18). These captivating creatures are certainly female while retaining some boylike features that Humbert notes as desirable. Humbert has made an autoerotic study of female development: "The budding of breast development appears early (10.7 years) in the sequence of somatic changes accompanying pubescence. And the next maturational item available is the first appearance of pigmented pubic hair (11.2)" (p. 21). The male lover in pursuit of these girls is "never less than ten I should say, generally thirty or forty" years older (p. 19). Humbert admits to being radically split (as his attitude to mothers clearly indicates) between weak desire for women his own age "having pumpkins or pears for breasts" and raging lust "for every passing nymphet" (p. 19). Of this much Humbert is aware, but he is less aware that he must also split nymphets to lessen the anxiety he feels about them.

Lolita is made into a sort of erotic child-goddess, an obsessive object who merely "individualized the writer's ancient lust" (p. 43); she is turned into a transcendent ideal of sexuality only partially more or less embodied in the actual child who is selfish and vulgar. She is not Eve but Lilith; Eve, the mother, is Life, while Lilith, the winged serpent or winding snake familiar from iconography of the fall in the Garden of Eden, is Death. Nabokov says as much (p. 21) but seems unaware of how much the truth of this is coded into the novel's fantasy.

Repeatedly, Lolita is seen not as a whole person, or even as a potentially complete adult, but as a collection of fetishized body parts; by selective viewing she is eroticized and denied personhood. To pick out a female body part, or an aspect of a body part, or a piece of clothing, is to deflect the full emotional charge of accepting desire for a child. The most obvious example is when Humbert finds in her closet "a heap of crumpled things that had touched her," imaginatively wrapping his "huge engorged heart" in one particularly grubby item of cloth (p. 63). The trance or dream state (Freud's idea of obsessional "deliria" applies here) becomes a nightmare as soon as it starts (p. 129); so how is the unreality of his split off desire to be maintained?

High arousal is maintained by fetishizing Lolita's body parts, especially extremities, arms and legs, with budding breasts and pubic hair less often mentioned. Humbert primes his maleness by thinking of himself as an aggressive beast of prey, albeit a guilty one, whose potency is precariously built on both attack and avoidance. Fetishizing female body parts is, of course, an established pornographic technique that extends well into television and advertising, having originated in art and literature.[71] Humbert's eye contact with the "enchanted prey" (p. 121) is minimized, so that there is no true "meeting" or "being with" Lolita as a person who lives from inside the body features that so excite Humbert.

It is as though he can only deal with her periphery in a tentative noninvolved way. His first autoerotic orgasm with Lolita on his lap is reported as the empty boast of loveless fetishistic discharge, the essence of the pornographic response (p. 58). Only after Lolita has escaped, married, and become "brave Dolly Schiller" (p. 259) does Humbert, the self-styled "pentapod monster," reminisce that there were certainly "times when I knew how you felt" (p. 259). Mainly, however, his part-object obsessions exclude any feeling Lolita may have had, since he is responding to injured narcissism rather than to her as a person. However he may cosset her with favors and lavish gifts, it is not *her* need but *his own* being served, pseudoneed perpetuating the unreality of a triumphant fantasy of possessing that which he cannot truly have. Images of love and death appear as he takes his last farewell: Humbert "knew as clearly as I know I am to die that I loved her more than anything" (p. 253); "come live with me, and die with me" he pleads, adding later "I'll die if you touch me" (p. 254). Humbert knows that he cannot now have married, pregnant Dolly Schiller, no longer Lolita; his strategy to prevent re-experiencing some nameless early trauma that left a residue of fear and avoidance of women is breaking down. Humbert is learning to experience authentic emotions fatal to his fetishized obsessively defensive system. Perhaps Nabokov was not prepared for the way his novel decreed it be ended. He turns death to Humbert's old self in another direction. Deciding on an orgy of violence, madness, death, and Humbert's frantic reflection on his crimes, Nabokov forestalled the fulfillment of authentic feelings about women as persons toward which the novel points.

Depersonalization of Lolita through exhibit of body parts or mere clothing is a technique for controlling aroused, angry, and guilty emotions felt by Humbert in her presence. If he cannot look at her as a whole person, then he will look at eroticized parts of her. Note how Lolita is first pictured following their morning sexual encounter at "The Enchanted Hunters":

> Brown, naked, frail Lo, her narrow white buttocks to me, her sulky face to a door mirror, stood, arms akimbo, feet (in new slippers with pussy-fur tops) wide apart, and through a forehanging lock tritely mugged herself in the glass. (p. 127)

Lolita is turned away from Humbert, self-admiringly gazing into a mirror: there is no eye contact, which is typical throughout the novel. We seldom face this girl to read her inconveniently real emotions; instead, we are invited to ogle her body parts, as does Humbert to self-stimulate, not enter into a relationship that implies responsible reciprocity along with the potential for growth, change, and understanding of one human by another.

Fetishistic ogling is a cinematically perfected fantasy technique in *Lolita*. A prime example is the white sock, or socks (with variations on legs and articles of clothing) surprisingly often singled out. The fashionable post-Second World War "bobby sock" is sharply focused and eroticized, to the exclusion of more personal elements of her being. Evidence that the sock is an emblem of desire associated with nymphets retained from Nabokov's childhood may be found in *Speak, Memory*.

> The little girls in neat socks and pumps whom we and other little boys used to meet at dancing lessons or at Christmas Tree parties had all the enchantments, all the sweets and stars of the tree preserved in their flame-dotted iris, and they teased us, they glanced back, they delightfully participated in our vaguely festive dreams, but they belonged, those nymphets, to another class of creatures than the adolescent belles and large-hatted vamps for whom we actually yearned. (p. 203)

Socks, enchantments, and nymphets may be singled out in this passage, which clearly conveys that young girls belong in a class of their own. The imagery in *Lolita* is surprisingly consistent with this early fascination.

p. 11   In the novel's second paragraph, Nabokov writes: "She was Lo, plain Lo, in the morning, standing four feet ten in one sock. She was Lola in slacks." Dolores is her legal name, but in "my arms she was always Lolita," a kind of erotic wholeness that comes of attending to part objects.

p. 38   When inspecting lodging with Lolita's mother, "I noticed a white sock on the floor. With a deprecatory grunt, Mrs. Haze stooped without stopping and threw it into a closet next to the pantry."

p. 40   A variant: "She wore a plaid shirt, blue jeans and sneakers. Every movement she made in the dappled sun plucked at the most secret and sensitive chord of my abject body." Lolita then picks up pebbles between her feet.

p. 44	"I dared stroke her bare leg." He then "let my hand creep up my nymphet's thin back and feel her skin through her boy's shirt."
p. 47	Humbert notices "the little scar on the lower part of her neat calf (where a roller-skater kicked her in Pisky), a couple of inches above her rough white sock."
p. 56–7	"I managed to attune, by a series of stealthy movements, my masked lust to her guileless limbs. . . . Her legs twitched a little as they lay across my live lap; I stroked them; there she lolled in the right-hand corner, almost asprawl, Lola the bobby-soxer . . . the heel of her slipperless foot in its sloppy anklet."
p. 68	When Humbert announces his marriage to Lolita's mother by phone, Lolita breaks in: "Hold on a sec, the pup—That pup has got hold of my sock."
p. 100	A scarcely disguised sadistic wish is found in Humbert's remark: "I could visualize Lolita with hallucinational lucidity." Buying her clothes, Humbert "examined various pretty articles, sports shoes, sneakers, pumps of crushed kid for crushed kids." "I had next great fun with all kinds of shorts and briefs—phantom little Lolitas dancing, falling daisying all over the counter. We rounded up the deal with some prim cotton pajamas in popular butcher-boy style. Humbert, the popular butcher."
p. 103	"the ribbed cuff of her white socks were turned down at the remembered level."
p. 115	Lolita is described as "Naked, except for one sock and her charm bracelet, spread-eagled on the bed where my philter had felled her."
p. 127	"She wore her professional white socks and saddle oxfords, and that bright print frock with the square throat; a splash of jaded lamplight brought out the golden down of her warm brown limbs."
p. 147	"Dolly wore blue jeans and white high shoes, as most of the other girls did."
p. 151	When the inner Lolita is looked at the result is bizarre and sadistic: "My only grudge against nature was that I could not turn my Lolita inside out and apply voracious lips to her young matrix, her unknown heart, her nacreous liver, the sea grapes of her lungs, her comely kidneys."

p. 154	"Gartered black sock and sloppy white sock" are startlingly juxtaposed as images of Humbert's male age and Lolita's female youth.
p. 166	"Sometimes, from where we sat in my cold study I could hear Lo's bare feet practising dance techniques in the living room downstairs."
p. 171	"Her damp moccasins and white socks were more sloppy than ever."
p. 186	Humbert notices "the heel of an outstretched shoeless foot." "As in terror I lowered my gaze, it mechanically slid along the underside of her tensely stretched bare thigh—how polished and muscular her legs had grown!" He contemplates "the strength of her shapely legs, the dirty sole of her white sock, the thick sweater."
p. 189	"My Lolita peeled off her sweater, shook her gemmed hair, stretched towards me two bare arms, raised one knee."
p. 190	"My Love's striped black-and-white cotton frock, jaunty blue cap, white socks and brown moccasins."
p. 217	"Her obscene young legs."
p. 232	"I cherished and adored, and stained with my kisses and merman tears, a pair of old sneakers, a boy's shirt she had worn, some ancient blue jeans . . . a crumbled school cap, suchlike wanton treasures." (cf. p. 63 where Humbert finds in Lolita's closet "a heap of crumpled things that had touched her.") The clothes fetish is summed up in a bit of verse (p. 234):

Officer, officer there they go—
In the rain, where that lighted store is
And her socks are white, and I loved her so,
And her name is Haze, Dolores.

p. 239	Humbert Humbert obsesses over "Misses' socks, 39c. Saddle Oxfords 3.98."

The white sock fetish is confirmed when, stimulated by one of Lolita's anklets, Humbert masturbates: "Little did the good lady [Charlotte Haze] dream that one morning when an upset stomach . . . had prevented me from accompanying her to church, I deceived her with one of Lolita's anklets" (p. 76).

Thus we have a strongly object dependent attachment pattern

of ambivalently obsessive fantasy. There is much displacement onto objects other than Lolita, the pedophile's ostensible object of desire. While Humbert's confession overcomes denial of his "fatal attraction" he never admits to himself (nor Nabokov to the reader) just how death dealing the composite fantasy really is. Almost all of Humbert's female attachments die in the course of the narrative for what may be thought of as an underlying motive to "get even" with oppressive females: Humbert's own mother dies when he is three, his caretaking Aunt Sybil when he is sixteen. This has something to do with Humbert's wish never to grow up (p. 22) and of the split between "Humbert the Terrible" and "Humbert the Small" (p. 29). Further deaths are of his early love Annabel Leigh, his repulsive wife Valeria, his wife of convenience, Charlotte Haze, the friend Jean Farlow who dies of cancer, and at length Lolita herself who dies in childbirth, along with her baby. This tragedy is well marked throughout the novel: "Mrs. 'Richard F. Schiller' died in childbed, giving birth to a stillborn girl, on Christmas Day 1952." (p. 6); Humbert feels the anxiety of "wrenching open the zipper of her nylon shroud had she been dead." (p. 216); "for she is dead and immortal if you are reading this" (p. 255); "I realized that I could not parade living Lolita . . . publication is to be deferred" (p. 281). Only Humbert's casual girlfriend Rita ("the sweetest, simplest, gentlest, dumbest Rita imaginable," p. 236) lives on, but death fantasy touches even her who, sleeping, is described as being "dead to the world" (p. 243). Humbert himself has died of a heart attack "in legal captivity" the day before his trial for killing Quilty, whose violent and macabre death gives emphasis to the novel's meaning. Even the minor characters Miss Opposite (p. 263) and Charlie Holmes (p. 264) die. Thus there is no ongoingness, no regenerative cycle set up, least of all with the false goddess Lolita. Nabokov could never say outright that pedophilia kills the human spirit, but that is what the novel says for him. This may be what he hinted at in the remark to Edmund Wilson that Lolita "is a highly moral affair and does not portray American kulaks," when there was a flurry of critical disapproval.[72] However, the satirical jibe against moralizing psychologist John Ray, Jr., who prefaces the novel still stands, as does Nabokov's statement that "*Lolita* has no moral in tow," being intended to produce only "aesthetic bliss" (p. 286). No comment on morality can deflect the power of eroticized death imagery, which, at the only partially analyzed level Nabokov works, gives a sort of esthetic bliss.

IV

Nabokov could not decide what his masterpiece really means, nor have his critics fully done so. When *Lolita* is seen as a fantasy production reaching into disturbed relational themes of Nabokov's own childhood, it begins to make sense. Its playing on the edge of necrophilia suggests not only morbidly retributive wishes against women as mothers, but also a disentombing and reanimating of "dead" memories and feelings about them. This doubleness gives the novel its compelled aura, its sense of necessity and inevitability such that Nabokov's own requirement that great art have "beauty plus pity" is approximated. Perverted Humbert does, after all, pay his dues in emotional breakdown, and he begins to learn not to torture but to love "my Lolita, this Lolita, pale and polluted, and big with another's child," albeit to take her away to "die with me." (p. 253–4). This feeling is poignant, not sentimental as it humanizes the monstrosity of Humbert's obsession.

It is as if the clever disguises of parody cover for the Nabokov who was working on the layered obsessions of childhood, obsessions that turn the merely gifted into an artist. The artist is "Humbert the Small" who becomes the "Terrible" creator, the artist-as-pervert. This distinction made by Nabokov gives the book a moral force after all. He knows the difference between narcissistically crude obsessions and the urge to master them in imagined fiction, which converts fantasy into elegantly shaped prose. By extracting and shaping this subconscious material Nabokov reduced its power to hurt him, but he also released it full force into the public realm where it became suggestive. For this the artist disclaims responsibility, execrating as he did all psychologies, especially Freud's. But Nabokov is not beyond criticism as no writer of such influence can claim immunity from being scrutinized. Nabokov knew nothing of the "attachment theory," which reveals how intensive mothering may leave residues of unactably hostile wishes toward women that split into idealizing and destructive fantasies. This unstable condition is one even the most accomplished fiction cannot wish away.

The compromised, half-way-there condition always shows in the very ambiguity of feelings that must invoke the potency of death to nullify illicit sexual wishes. Nabokov's moral straight man, John Ray, Jr., is right to enunciate the seeming intractableness of pedophilia, yet insist on the urgency of probing its sources. Study of male violence toward women would do well to consider the meaning of fantasy in *Lolita*. The full extent of Nabokov's fantasy life will remain unknown until his estate releases the fifty pages of an unpublished manuscript called "Laura." So embarrassing is "Laura" reported to be that it has been suppressed for the next one hundred years.

5

Female Sacrifice in the Novels
of John Fowles

I think a novelist's first duties, oddly enough, are really toward
himself. To be honest to his own imagination, his own total
knowledge of existence. . . . You always write for yourself first,
to discover yourself first.
    —John Fowles, *Maclean's* Interview, 14 November, 1977

JOHN Fowles's novels study the results of a shift from Victorian
restraint to freer sexuality, from a closed to a more open morality.[1]
Quoting at the outset of *Daniel Martin* the *Prison Notebooks* of
Antonio Gramsci, Fowles sees his generation caught between old
and new values and displaying "morbid symptoms." These symptoms reflect the depressing aftermath of Wells's sort of heroic
sexuality and of the moral unsettling that took place during World
War II. The symptoms may be thought of as what Heinz Kohut
calls "Guilty Man," the depressiveness of id-driven males who cannot come to terms with overmastering sexual wishes.[2] Fowles
adopts the Freudian Oedipal concept to interpret the interpersonal material he adduces, leading to a range of insights important for his generation. The historical sweep is impressive in
indicating shifting sexual morality. *The French Lieutenant's Woman*
(1969) traces Victorian Charles Smithson's flight from convention-
ality into an obsessively dangerous pursuit of a mysterious woman,
announcing a sexual quest that Fowles embodies in successive
characters whose lives exemplify the transition to contemporary
sexual mores. An attachment theory of obsessions will help to
appreciate the intentions of Fowles's character portrayals, high-
lighting features that are not immediately evident from his own
formulation of them. It is important to notice the ways in which
Fowles's understanding of male obsessionality is limited even as
he gives perhaps the best phenomenology in recent fiction.

By looking in detail at four novels: *The Collector* (1963), *The Magus* (1965/77), *Daniel Martin* (1977), and *Mantissa* (1982), the changing attitudes of "Guilty Man's" obsession with women as sexual objects and partners can be assessed. Each novel concerns a male protagonist who cannot successfully relate to a female lover (or lovers) and must undergo a purgative experience to atone for mistakes and learn new ways. Destructive obsessions are considered with a view to changing them toward the loving mutuality with women that typically eludes the protagonist. There is a strong reparative urge omnipresent in these novels, an urge reflecting the English Puritan strain in Fowles's makeup. Freudian, Jungian, and existentialist components blend with an even more fundamental Puritan concern with the sinner saved. Fowles belongs to the English nonconformist tradition that individuals are responsible for their actions, and each is held individually accountable. However attenuated Christian-humanist precepts may be in Fowles's novels, the sensitive reader is apt to be reminded of the moral concern with marital fidelity and women's rights inscribed in the English tradition from Milton to John Stuart Mill. When moral concerns combine with piquant erotic fantasies, the literary result is likely to be of compelling interest.

Fowles's novels became the middle-brow classics of a generation trying to redefine its sexuality. Critical acclaim was lavish, with *The Magus* becoming a cult book comparable perhaps only to Hesse's *Steppenwolf.* It can be suggested that Fowles's "page turners" appealed especially to a psychoclass of male readers disturbed by conflict of sexual standards. They were the men raised to think of monogamy as binding yet who recognized other tendencies in themselves, producing acute moral discomfort. Fowles's daring and honesty articulated in fiction the dilemma of fascination with, yet dread of, freer sexuality. He became especially skillful in portraying a precarious balance between a wish to punish women (fearing their control) and guilty male intropunitiveness for having such a wish. A gift for elaborating intrigue and sexual mystification made Fowles unique among writers in the age group born in the mid-1920s and thrust into social change too confusing to define clearly.

A certain blurring of focus in the narratives of male obsessions was perhaps inevitable. Fowles's novels lack the tragic power of his mentor Thomas Hardy's; in keeping with the moral relativism of their times they are more discursive and exploratory. Inspired perhaps by Lawrence's confessional daring in *Sons and Lovers,* Fowles's self-explorations (if that is what they are) remain Oedipally diffuse, never quite delineating the obsessive mother-son relationship so fully realized in Lawrence's masterpiece. Further, Lawrence's burning belief in the redemptive possibilities of sexuality, as in *Lady Chatterley's Lover* (1928), could not go uncriticized after watching it in action as fashionable interpersonal behavior. Fowles could see that apocalyptic sexuality would not be the source of personal freedom that Lawrence and others in his generation supposed. Yet the transition continued toward freedoms on a scale never before known, with Fowles's sensibility attuned to the ambiguities of attraction, fear, and inhibition. He would document new conditions of obsessive arousal, together with the remnants of Puritan guiltiness that made the new age a torture for so many men and a threat to women.

The concept of male sacrifice of females that threads its way through these studies should be addressed with special care in Fowles's novels. It is a cultural theme requiring particular comment in the Christian West where Christ's sacrifice on the cross led to a spirituality in which women were subordinated and sexuality mistrusted. But spiritual exclusiveness need not be the same as mistrust, even hostility, toward women. Why should an intensification of love-hate be a feature of the secularizing phase of our culture? Female sacrifice indeed has ancient pagan origins widely studied by anthropologists. The excesses of the Christian West, such as persecution of witches in the seventeenth century, can no doubt be matched elsewhere. In every society, women of childbearing years have been more at risk for their lives than men, so woman as sufferer and victim is built into our expectations. But beyond this concept is an increasingly obvious male wish to control and hurt the women who are their lovers and the objects of projections from their experiences of having been mothered. Emotional overheating in rearing boys may be an artifact of the nuclear family. Still greater risk arises in one parent families— usually managed by mothers, a risk that we must collectively work to reduce as the numbers of these families increases. Production of gender anxiety in males, in a society already rich in the contagion of violence, is a formula for retaliation against women whoever they are.

Male maladaptations damaging to women are a subject for study in and through the novel, where a moral framework for seeing relationships can be provided. Such a framework is evident in the writings especially of Hesse and Nabokov. It is also present in Fowles's novels as a subtly formed, and forming, conscience in his male heroes; pained and puzzled conscience gives Fowles's fiction its intense interest as we face the worrying fact of increasing violence toward women. It is almost as though the dying goddess, victim of male rage, is the figure typifying our times. The male novelist's quest for self-knowledge through his art, of which Fowles repeatedly speaks, offers a way to improve understanding of this leading cultural problem. It may turn out that Fowles's fantasies of sacrificing women do not fully understand themselves in the fictional context, that his instruments of analysis are not enough to discover the origins of male sexual discontents. Explanations of the interpersonal and developmental origins are lacking, but the novels richly reward speculation about the unconscious meaning of fantasies revealed by Fowles's choice of language. The study of women as sacrificial objects in Fowles's novels is a good way to approach "Guilty Man's" "morbid symptoms" as an index of the self-knowledge so widely lacking among men.

II

To illuminate female sacrifice in Fowles's novels, his view of creativity should be considered, supplemented, and to some extent realigned to account for the obsessional features displayed. Fowles chooses not to investigate the psychology of obsessions itself but to manifest it so consistently to give it the status of a subtext needing explanation. Fowles's explanation of creativity, as a function of early maternal loss, is partial and in some degree unsatisfactory. With the emergence in the 1960s of psychoanalytic studies by John Bowlby and others of the depressive effects of early maternal loss, it is no wonder that writers sensitive to the issue would comment on it. Study of obsessions has not enjoyed the same intensive research, and indeed is so syntonic with social values as to remain nearly invisible.

Fowles cites with approval the psychoanalyst Gilbert Rose's paper "The French Lieutenant's Woman: the Unconscious Significance of a Novel to its Author," which argues that Charles's quest for Sarah arises from an "urge to restore the lost unity with the mother."[3] By Fowles's account, the novel began with an involuntary obsessive image of an "outcast" woman he wished to protect. Fowles's character Charles Smithson's need for mothering is acute, having lost his mother at age one when she gave birth to a stillborn girl. Unable to accept conventional marriage, Charles pursues Sarah as a sort of substitute maternal attachment; he is "reborn," only to lose the surrogate mother-lover he had hoped would complete his life. If we remember the dangers of confusing mother with lover, it is not surprising to see Sarah cast as a sacrifice to rigid Victorian mores. Yet it is Charles's obsessive pursuit of her that leads to his greatest personal danger, as his obsession may (in a Darwinian sense) have unfitted him for survival. Fowles's powerful insight in this novel has more to do with male vulnerability to self-endangering obsession than it does with predisposing loss. Yet his theory frames loss as the main factor in male creative anxiety. In *Islands* Fowles writes:

> There is perhaps no more brilliant antedating of Freud in all ancient literature than that meeting Odysseus has, on the dark shores of the River of Ocean at the end of his furthest voyage, with his own dead mother Anticleia. "As my mother spoke, there came to me out of the confusion in my heart the one desire, to embrace her spirit, dead though she was. Thrice in my eagerness to clasp her to me, I started forward with my arms out-stretched. Thrice, like a shadow or a dream, she slipped through my arms and left me harrowed by an ever sharper pain." In that brief image lies the genesis of all art; the pursuit of the irrecoverable, what the object relations analysts now call symbolic repair.[4]

No autobiographical clues are given about why Fowles might think of artistic creativity as "symbolic repair" for loss of a mother. The theory has much support, for instance in appendix C of Marvin Eisenstadt *et al.*, *Parental Loss and Achievement* (1989), but it is not enough by itself to explain the urgency with which writers ply their craft. A second statement by Fowles is more revealing of the obsessive-compulsive energy so often seen in writers and artists. Fowles writes that added to natural gifts,

> I think you also have to have a sense of loss implanted when you are very young. In other words, I think writers are quite literally born, therefore. I do not believe in creative writing. The Freudian theory of this, that I would apply to all artists, is that some people have had a very peculiar experience after the loss of their mother and the discovery of their own separate identity. Young infants really don't have clear frontiers between themselves and their mother. With some people it's the kind of fluidity of this experience, the changing of shape and the supreme happiness from the sort of union with the mother that probably dominated their adult lives, unconsciously of course. Although I am not a total Freudian, I find this very convincing because I think what is interesting about the novel is the *obsessive repetitive need in true novelists to go on telling stories.* We always have to be telling legends, myths, which very often try in some way to make the world more perfect. Obviously, there is some dim memory some-

where of a more perfect, happier, magical state and we are all trying to get to that. It's very obvious in novelists like Thomas Hardy who was totally fixed on his mother. All the women he fell in love with all through his life even had his mother's physical features (my italics).[5]

This second statement more accurately sets the problem of interpreting Fowles's novels, yet it also lacks completeness in missing the guilt for sacrificing women that often prompts symbolic repair. Reparation is not just resupply of a missing person but making restitution for anger and resentment felt for having been abandoned by the mother, and perhaps having been impinged on either by the mother or by a substitute caretaker. Further, there is no explanation about why novelists persist in telling stories resembling but not exactly reproducing their own. Does creating a new, and in some ways tidier because formalized, story offset the writer's tendency to depression? Creativity can certainly be an affective control system, lifting mood by the exercise of inventive powers over difficult interpersonal situations the artist chooses to portray. By mentioning Thomas Hardy and his mother, Fowles moves toward the guilt feelings and the urge to repair damage implied in "symbolic repair." Hardy did not lose his mother but was himself given up for dead at birth. If anything, Hardy was dominated by his mother, an overly strong presence through his childhood. Thus Fowles's commentary slides away from maternal loss to something quite different that is not fully investigated. It is noteworthy that Hardy's biographer, Michael Millgate, goes so far as to compare Hardy's relationship with his ambitious mother with that of Paul Morel with his mother, Gertrude, in Lawrence's *Sons and Lovers*. Millgate thinks that Hardy identified with his father's passivity while resisting his mother's drive, suffering damage "like Clym Yeobright, by so extreme an emotional dependence upon his mother."[6] Fowles must have realized this without wishing to comment on it or apply it to his own circumstance, clarification of which awaits his autobiography.

Fowles's "Hardy and the Hag" may be reviewed to discover more about the source of erotic obsessions and the moral wish to repair guilt found in his novels. Working obliquely through *The Well-Beloved*, Fowles speaks of "a sense of shared trap, a shared predicament" of the artist's, leading to a sort of "benign psychosis" to which academic critics pay too little attention.[7] Admitting to be a habitual fantasizer "because I have always rejected so much of the outward life I have had to lead," Fowles lays the groundwork of fantasy as producing guilt.[8] He continues, "The simple truth is that novel-writing is an onanistic and taboo-laden pursuit, and therefore socially shameful . . . and morally dubious."[9] No specific content of the fantasies is suggested, although *The Collector*'s erotic and sadistic "Bluebeard Syndrome," in having Clegg incarcerate the innocent Miranda, comes to mind. In later novels, while fascination with capture and control of women is not quite so obvious, obsessively punitive themes persist. Coy about the "morally dubious" and "shameful" aspects of private fantasy, Fowles, like every successful novelist, gauges and exploits latent group fantasy. He gives fictional lineaments to socially repressed urges that may be safely revealed in fiction, or a least so it is supposed, *The Collector* having been too readily emulated in real life. Once revealed, the tensions caused by fantasies may be reduced according to this theory. As Fowles comments, "the more you are aware of a hopeless obsession, the less you are driven by it," a precept presumably as therapeutically good for society as for the individual.[10]

Repeating Rose's idea of creativity as the wish to recover early magical oneness with the mother, Fowles puzzles at "the markedly repetitive nature of their endeavour—the inability not to return again and again on the same impossible journey."[11] He is describing a repetition compulsion, at worst a being stuck in a fantasy for which there is insufficient interpretation, by the artist to himself, of reasons for the complusion. The nostalgic artist working alone tends to reinforce wishes for a lost primal oneness rather than advance into the reexperiencing of narcissistic wounds that show his desires to be tinged with hostility. The persistence of retaliatory hostility leads to sadistic wishes for female sacrifice, for symbolic punishments of the mother for her habits of enmeshment.

Closeness, as well as nostalgia for the unobtainable, is a motif in "Hardy and the Hag." Guilt over anger toward the mother easily translates into guilt over marital punitiveness, as becomes evident in *Daniel Martin,* in which "desire" and "social duty" are at odds. Fowles's concern with Hardy is much more than "anxiety of influence": it is in sharing guilty feelings about lovers and wives who may be thought of as sacrificed on the altar of ambivalence toward mother. Fowles fully appreciates Hardy's overbearing mother, but he does not discuss the ambivalence of his poems of 1912–13, written after his wife Emma's lonely and pathetic death. Hardy's indulgence of guilt feelings, along with powerful nostalgia for their first meeting, makes of these poems a key document of the obsessed imagination. They go far to explain Hardy's concern with female sacrifice, as in *Tess of the D'Urbervilles.* In

Fowles's post-Freudian formulation, flippant though it seems, the elements of guilt and expiation toward the mother and wife are present: "Though the wife is the mortal enemy of the mother as Ashtaroth-Aphrodite, she is also required to assume a rather more practical aspect of maternity—protective Jocasta against the cruel Laius of the review columns." Wife becomes a protective Jocasta but the image is ambiguous, as continuation of the quotation discloses: fictions may "be vindictive as in so much of *The Well-Beloved,* or in any novel where woman is treated as the betrayer of Adam. Both transmogrifications, into the idolized love-object or the unforgiven "whore," may very often be seen side-by-side in the same novel."[12]

Fowles thus speaks of what Freud described as split and internalized love and hate characteristic of the obsessional defense, manifesting in what is popularly known as the "Madonna/Whore Complex." Is it by chance that Fowles invokes Jocasta, who in Besdine's sense, may be thought of as incapacitating her son by her own hungry affect? Fowles was not ready to pursue the psychoanalytic question in the novels to be discussed. Their magical auras seem to be a cloak for investigating split opposed feelings without fully exposing the moral issues. As Fowles says, to generate successful fantasy in a novel "You badly need a thoroughly split personality. I think that is why many, many people can't write novels." He continues in the same interview saying, "I would not like to understand my own novels completely; why I wrote them as they are."[13] Fowles thus repeats the often-heard fear of creative persons that if their emotional disability is fully revealed creativity will disappear.

This is surely a misconception since creativity takes many forms, the novel perhaps being only an intermediary one. Realizing this, many writers, even those such as William Styron who have suffered devastating depressions, write factual autobiography to augment their "confessional" fictions. Without such a document for Fowles, the critic is left to conjecture about the origin of discordant attitudes to women in the novels of a writer claiming to be sympathetic to feminism. Fowles is perhaps best thought of as a writer manifesting unconscious male wishes in a phase of troubled transition in relations between the sexes. Replying to Lorna Sage, Fowles said: "You really have to force yourself to be childlike and in a certain sense impermeable by all your adult critical knowledge when you do that first draft."[14] Fowles communicates child, and especially adolescent, fantasies whose amoral status is inimical to his adult self. His novels speak in the language of forbidden sexual wishes that the "liberation" of our times has made speakable, if only in uneasy tones and with deep moral misgivings. At least it was so for the psychoclass comprising Fowles's generation in England. That his novels were avidly read everywhere speaks for their typifying a male sexual anxiety as yet imperfectly understood.

III

The Magus is appropriately seen by its author as "obsessive" in origin, the product of "compulsive-pattern making," a mythic "trip" into the interior of a male consciousness. It is comparable to Hesse's "All the Girls are Yours" fantasy in *Steppenwolf.* "I teach better if I seduce," Fowles is quoted as saying, a remark with which Hesse might be expected to agree.[15] Stating the obvious, that "Sexual relations have always interested me, and problems of search and quest," Fowles adds that he conjures up "a whole harem of heroines to play out different aspects of the female principle—'I think I'm under a feminine star, quite definitely—mother-dominated, and so on.'"[16] This statement is very different from the one about artistic creativity arising from a sense of loss, but no less true in combination with it. Both observations are necessary, the problem being to find their correct proportions in explaining a text. The act of creation is open-ended, answering to no special formula; as Fowles said, "Books are not planned, they write themselves," but they do so out of a need to clarify conflicted emotions.[17] That is, their themes arise from inner necessity, connecting private with group fantasies at the point where guilt arises over the love-hate surrounding the sacrificing of female lovers. Fowles says nothing further on being "mother-dominated," side-stepping for example in a comment to Raman K. Singh that "I'm totally for the feminine principle, as I hope all my novels prove" because, as he adds, "In a Jungian sense . . . I would say I have a feminine mind."[18] No reader doubts that there is in Fowles's novels a certain sympathy toward suffering women, yet he needs to see them suffer, suggesting fear of an imbalance of power. Speaking to Sarah Benton, he admitted aversion to powerful women. According to Benton, "The woman whom John Fowles would have most feared meeting is Jane Austen. Men are more thoroughly dethroned by women's mockery than by their violent anger, he thinks, and Austen would "see through every pretension—and then record it for posterity." But those he dislikes most are masculine women "like dear Mrs.

Thatcher,'" then the British Prime Minster.[19] As a pre-feminist male writer, trying to assert feminism, Fowles struggles with the bad conscience of "Guilty Man." The most likely source of this would be the ambivalence of a mother-dominated son who strives to create a better reality amidst negative punitive fantasies.

Speaking of *The Collector*, which contains one of the most punitive sexual obsessions in modern fiction, Fowles said, "I've always been interested in the Bluebeard syndrome, and really, that book was simply embodying it in one particular case. It's really a casebook for me."[20] Fowles's first published novel exhibits restlessly obsessive-compulsive energy in its protagonist Ferdinand Clegg. The reader may suspect Clegg's unruly adolescent fantasy to be the author's own, as indeed Fowles in "Hardy and the Hag" confesses it to have been in lesser intensity. In this respect *The Collector* bears comparison to Nabokov's *Lolita* as a long-incubated fantasy awaiting the literary skill fully to empower it. Both authors felt they had a lot of explaining to do. What saves *The Collector* from being sadistic pornography is its brief, but plausible, etiology of Clegg's emotional disorder, together with sympathetic first-person portrayal of his victim Miranda. Clegg is a sadomasochist with necrophiliac tendencies, brought up by a moralistic aunt after his father's death while driving drunk when Ferdinand was two. His mother, the cause of his father's drinking, it is said, abandoned the child, perhaps to go off with a foreigner. Clegg says he feels indifferent toward his mother, resents Aunt Annie, and hates her crippled daughter Mabel. The death of his Uncle Dick when Clegg is fifteen deprives him of his only healthy companionship, the only male in his life. Clegg's main diversion is butterfly collecting, disliked by his aunt but supported by his uncle. Fowles was to distance himself from Clegg by remarking that, while in his youth he had been a butterfly and animal hunter, "I loath guns and people who collect living things."[21] Fowles studies a character who, perhaps like himself, once took out resentments against weak and defenseless creatures. As Fowles remarked, he was the product of dislocated values: "I . . . had to come to terms with my own hatred of [the Victorian Age]. Like every English child of my generation, I grew up with Victorian parents and loathed it."[22] Of course not every child of Victorian parents "loathed it," and we would be grateful for more particulars. Clegg, a "loner," is portrayed as a compulsive butterfly collector, avoiding sexuality as the "crude animal thing I was born without," a parody of the most extreme Victorian denial of sexuality.[23] Sadism is explicit toward his cousin Mabel, the weakest and most vulnerable female in his ambit: Clegg says, "I think people like Mabel should be put out painlessly" (p. 14). It is a study of necrophiliac sadism. Through the "collecting" of beautiful Miranda the novel works out the terrifying effects of Clegg's hostility to the women who brought him up, or failed to do so.

Clegg's new wealth on winning a lottery allows conversion of an adolescent butterfly collecting habit into an obsessive lust for collecting attractive young women. By a sly strategy, he captures and incarcerates the pretty London art student, Miranda Gray. Fowles is a masterful observer of the intricate interplay between sexually obsessed but impotent Clegg and his "guest," Miranda. It is a war of psychological attrition, with rapid adjustments of closeness and distance as the captor enacts a fantasy his captive recognizes with appalled fascination. Clegg's wish to dominate and control Miranda (his inversion of love into hate, allied to a necrophilic fantasy of death and burial) emerges most threateningly when he is unable to perform sexually with Miranda after she decided to use seduction as an escape strategy. "I've discovered his secret. He hates that," Miranda says (p. 223). She angrily states the truth about Clegg: "There's no man in him. I got up, we were lying on the sofa, and knelt by him and told him not to worry. Mothered him. We put our clothes back on. And gradually it all came out. The truth about him. And later, his real self. A psychiatrist has told him he won't ever be able to do it" (p. 221). Miranda is slow to realize the intensity of Clegg's rage against women, especially against mothers. Deprivation of his actual mother and impingement by his aunt have made him both crave and despise mothers, producing impotence and rage. Miranda had also been mismothered, and the concept of mothering altogether breaks down between them: "The kettle boiling and her there. Of course I kept a sharp eye on her [Clegg says]. When it was made, I said, shall I be mother? That's a horrid expression. What's wrong with it? It's suburban, it's stale, it's dead . . . I think you'd better be mother I said" (p. 53). Reacting against her "bitchy, ginny misery" of a mother, Miranda has joined the arty crowd, where she "lame ducks" older male artists such as the womanizing G. P. Thus marginalized, she is a ready prey for Clegg's obsessive misogyny. An admirable feature of the novel is Fowles's ability to show Miranda in the process not only of realizing her peril, but also of seeing her life circumstances for what they are. He gives her insights through recording her thoughts, and allows her clarity in seeing Clegg: "What I fear in you [is] something you don't know is in you," she says (p. 67) remarking later "I could never cure him.

Because I'm his disease" (p. 225). Yet despite her growth in character and feisty attempts to escape, Miranda is sacrificed. There is no ritual killing, only Clegg's bumbling failure to get help as she dies of pneumonia, a disease secondary to the sacrificial incarceration Clegg imposes on her. From the remarks in "Hardy and the Hag," it appears that Fowles had great difficulty in killing his heroine, but the act was nevertheless accomplished with a pathetic finality, leaving Clegg to search for a new "guest" to incarcerate in his Bluebeard's chamber.

As Harry Haller sacrifices Hermine, the person best able to help him, so does Clegg sacrifice Miranda to his intractable emotional disorder. Miranda had a chance of becoming a mature being, but by his perverse photography of her, Clegg turns her into a mere erotic object—a tactic he learned by looking at pornography. She is a trapped Lolita, ogled by a male who cannot understand her personhood. Ritual photography stops her female body dead in suggestive poses belonging to his sadistic imagination. As an artist, Miranda is also a maker of pictures, but neither her drawings nor G. P.'s drawing of the female nude he has her acquire rise to the level of human understanding found in the Rembrandt self-portrait that is the standard of truth in *The Collector*. Clegg lives in a part of society where negation of high culture readily occurs, and Miranda has yet to recognize the full meaning of Rembrandt's self-seeing. The entire tragic performance is enacted well below this level of civilized awareness. Miranda is made into a decadent female sacrifice on the altar of bad parenting and erotomania. Unlike the formally flawless Ucello hunting scene of which G. P. speaks in his attempt to seduce Miranda, Clegg's image of her is mutilated and degrading: "I got the pictures developed and printed that night. The best ones were with her face cut off. She didn't look much anyhow with the gag, of course. The best were taken when she stood in her high heels, from the back. The tied hands and the bed made what they call an interesting motif. I can say I was quite pleased with what I got" (p. 106).[24] Was Fowles also pleased? It is difficult to say, but he powerfully realized a punitive wish dangerously harboring in a society of misparented sons.

Nicholas Urfe, the hero of *The Magus*, is a father-deprived boy but not to such a grotesque extent as Ferdinand Clegg. Urfe in fact predates Clegg, *The Magus* having been written first, and he may better indicate what Fowles wanted to say about male obsessional behavior. When Nicholas was in his second year at Oxford, both parents were "killed off" in a plane crash, freeing him to pursue obsessions closer to the normal than Clegg's. Womanizing in prepermissive times is Fowles's theme as he scrutinizes Nicholas's troubled psyche and chronicles his moral rebirth. The story centers on his relations with Alison, a sexually stimulating Australian girl with notably boyish features.[25] Nicholas is ambivalent about her from the start, finding her sometimes ugly, sometimes not, having sadistic wishes easily prompted by "a characteristic bruised look; a look that subtly made one want to bruise her more" (p. 33–34). After their separation, with Nicholas on a Greek island and Alison with another man in London, he decides not to reply to her letter: "If anything might hurt her, silence would; and I wanted to hurt her" (p. 57). Like Miranda in *The Collector,* Alison is set up as a female sacrifice, made vulnerable by her own dislocated parenting (domineering mother and dead father) and displacement from Australia to England (p. 35). In a sense, Nicholas and Alison exchange ambivalences, being unable to withdraw projections that prevent trust and love. Much of the novel is taken up with deciphering projective double ambivalences. Nicholas says, "I wasn't psychologically close enough to her; something I couldn't define, obscure, monstrous lay between us, and this obscure monstrous thing emanated from her, not me" (p. 39). Nicholas's self-righteous defense is only slowly and imperfectly penetrated in Conchis's "god-game," played with Nicholas on the Circe-enchanted island. Narcissism, together with a self-loathing fear of venereal disease as punishment for indulgence, haunt Nicholas, yet "I began quietly to rape the island" (p. 65). Therapeutic modification of obsessively punitive rage against females is the novel's theme as his urge to rape is discovered. How much "repair" through psychological reorganization of Nicholas's punitive wishes toward women does *The Magus* demonstrate?

The Magus concerns Nicholas's regeneration at the hands of Conchis, lord of the island, who treats Nicholas much as erring Christian is treated in the House of the Interpreter in John Bunyan's *Pilgrim's Progress.* But seventeenth-century regenerative optimism is qualified by the psychological realism that admits to the difficulty of fundamental character change. Conchis is part Priapus, phallic god of lust, and part artist-priest of the creative inner life, a new sort of erotic "elect," or Aristos figure, invented for the novel. A far cry from the resigned wisdom of Shakespeare's Prospero in *The Tempest* and from Bunyan's Puritan allegorizing of the way to salvation, Conchis is a component of the Freudian psyche, the superego or conscience, struggling with Nicholas's powerful id. This Freudian formulation makes the novel phallocentrically relational, centering analysis on Nicholas's obsessional ambivalence toward women. It gives a brilliantly intuitive phenomenology of this characteristic artist's predicament and of the possibility of its symbolic repair.

"Greece is like a mirror. It makes you suffer. Then you learn," Fowles writes (p. 101). It is as if seeing the true self must be not by sensory deprivation but by flooding with excessive imagery of the wanted but feared female object; breasts and mothering are obsessively present, as in the Modigliani portrait, the Bonnard nudes, photographs in The Beauties of Nature, the photograph of the Edwardian girl who died—images of life and death that conjure up Alison, with her affirmation of life counteracted by male punitive fantasies (p. 103f). Female death as an erotic stimulus finds its way into these pages, as do obscene ancient Greek and other erotic images, by which we know that Nicholas's seeing Alison for what she really is will be no easy matter. Is she a "permanent loss," he a "protector of her" or she "a protector of him" (p. 113)? This uncertainty is paralleled by Conchis's experience of Nicholas's alter ego, the superego, or Jungian wise old man within. Conchis's heroic sacrifice in war, his love and rejection of Lily, the bisexual numinosity of the Cycladic head all "mirror" Nicholas's disordered feelings. The showing of Lily as a phantom brought back from the dead prefigures Alison's restoration at the end of the novel and is reminiscent of the reemergence of wronged Hermione at the conclusion of Shakespeare's A Winter's Tale. Fowles too will undo the sacrifice, almost to the point of denial, but he will not let the reader forget sexual threats posed by women as in the de Deukans episode in which the automaton Mirabelle, the naked woman who, grasping her man in coitus, stabs him in the groin with a stiletto (p. 181–82). This shocking and seemingly gratuitous act is at the core of the novel's fantasy of fright at being controlled by women.

The island's magic unfolds under the sign of Apollo's phallus, imaging a new religion of sexuality, with Conchis as high priest and Nicholas as initiate-apostle. But the ritual death and rebirth through Lily is ambiguous, with suggestions of destruction (de Deukans's house fire and death) not far from the idyllic surface. With Nicholas allowed to "love many girls" but "love truly only one," his ambivalence is painfully slow to heal. Desirable women are split into twins, one with a sacrificial scar as though she had been abused. There are two Lilys, one of them scarred by a male, the image being of "an enormous black jackal . . . looming death and the frail maiden" (p. 203). Love and persecution of women in Hesse's *Steppenwolf* is recalled. Images of twinning (June and Julie), Lily's doubleness, male desire, and aggression all bear on Nicholas's indecision about Alison, the suicidal female sacrifice. As Lorna Sage writes, *The Magus* bears the signs of its "obsessive origins"—indeed, Fowles has spoken of guilt about the early death of a woman he knew.[26] "All novels are really metaphors for reality and I personally would not distinguish between the reality and the metaphor and reality and reality," Fowles notes.[27] The reader is invited to consider Nicholas's justification for "all my past relationships with little girls, my selfishness, caddishnesses, even that belittling dismissal of Alison" (p. 215). The story is particular, but its application is general to a male psychoclass entangled in obsessions about mothers and lovers. Rampant phallicism is matricidal, with its only possible corrective in the guilt felt for injuring women. The novel never specifies these matters, only alluding obliquely to them. Self-analysis is a tricky and sometimes devious business, always with latitude for self-deception. Hence *The Magus*'s beguiling complexity, for which a unifying principle can be suggested: an authorial wish to give male ambivalence its most self-aware fictional treatment, a difficult task especially in view of Hesse's achievement in *Steppenwolf.*

The metatheater of transformations in which twinned June and Julie, Lily and Alison combine and recombine is Fowles's fictional way of examining a split and opposed view of women as lovers. Similarly, Conchis is twinned with the militarist Mitford (private school and the Royal Marines), pointing up the split within Nicholas himself. Jungian theory may have taught Fowles something about subpersonalities in a "situational therapy" that tries to make a unity of opposed feelings.[28] Mystical experience is invoked to explain moments of elevated consciousness in the psychodrama of coming to terms with self, but the reality remains overwhelmingly erotic, as might be expected of a novel first celebrated in the late 1960s.[29] The novel's god is Priapus and the disorder was "not something curable like syphilis, but far more banal and more terrible, a congenital promiscuity" (p. 270). "Congenital" is never explained, with puzzlement the dominant note: "'I wish to God I wasn't so complicated—'. 'Complicated!' She snorted. 'Selfish.' 'That's better.' We were silent. Two coupled butterflies flitted heavily, saggingly past" (p. 276).

The crisis of ambivalent eroticism as death dealing comes in chapter 60 of *The Magus,* with its vision of the "living skeleton, a Buchenwald horror." Nicholas becomes furious at the punishment by Conchis and Lily for Alison's death, about which he is sure they know (p. 498–99). He feels violent with Lily, wanting to make a sacrifice of her for his suffering (p. 501). The psychodrama goes forward through a bizarre series of menacingly primitive emblems of fear and aversion to women, ending with Satan as the goat of lust "lampooning the traditional Christ-figure" (p. 511). Nicholas is both subject to the conscience of Christian morality and haunted by Oedipal fears of incest. His psychomachia is reminiscent of Harry Haller's in *Steppenwolf;* like Harry who must answer to his judges after the mock killing of Hermine, his lover and therapist, Nicholas Urfe must submit to judgment by a panel of psychiatrists. Fowles sees Nicholas's hope of change through psychotherapy, not the quasi-religious conversion that Haller undergoes. Fowles's send-up of psychiatry has its serious intention: Urfe's diagnosis is not as silly as it is made to sound. Dr. Mary Marcus's account of his disorder makes sense in terms of what the novel shows of Nicholas's futile relations with women. He does indeed exhibit "an ambivalent attitude towards women, in which they are seen as both desired objects and as objects which have betrayed him, and therefore merit his revenge and counter-betrayal" (p. 517). When the theory is advanced of Nicholas as reacting against an authoritarian paternal regime, and as a bereft only child searching for his lost mother, some credibility develops. But his full story is not spelled out any more than it is in the reworking of this material in *Mantissa*. Fowles's arch dislike of prim and managing women therapists seems to tell another story, but this dislike is not examined in fiction. These are women who are well able to resist being sacrificed, and who threaten the male with fears of his own sacrifice. Such a reaction would be expected of a Jocasta-reared son, less of whose mothering had been cut short. Professor Ciardi's portrait of the new narcissistic character structure that seeks autoerotic pleasures is indeed a plausible variant of this, with some combination of maternal loss and female impingement being necessary to account for it (p. 520f).

The proof of Nicholas's sadistic wishes toward women comes out in a tableau of self-judgment in which he is offered the opportunity, if he wishes, to punish Lily in a "flogging frame." Existential choice making is enjoined by his mentors to reveal true unconscious intentions. His impulse is to whip Lily with a cat-o'-nine-tails: "There was a very real devil in me, an evil marquis, that wanted to strike, to see the wet red weals traverse the delicate skin," Fowles graphically writes (p. 526). Under the influence of Conchis, who reminds Nicholas of his crime against Alison, no violence in the manner of the Marquis de Sade is done. Instead Nicholas himself is fixed to a flogging frame and exposed to lurid sexual fantasies with sadistic and sacrificial overtones: to enter "the elect" he must first be a "crucified Iago," freely accepting the cruelty done him (p. 540). Clegg's crudities are transcended as Nicholas emerges cleansed from the worst self-persecution for murderous feelings toward Lily and Alison.

Nicholas's rage, sadness, and suicidal despair are analyzed before Alison reemerges alive—a sort of restoration of the healthy feminine component of Nicholas's psyche. The learning process inches forward with Nicholas realizing that in using girls sexually "I was the real victim" (p. 619). He further realizes that "I treated Alison very badly. I'm a born cad, a swine" (p. 637). The momentum of inward change in Conchis's "godgame" increases as Nicholas realizes how he has victimized Alison. (The image of the butcher who could not sacrifice Marie Antoinette helps to clarify the moral issue for Nicholas) (p. 641). Exploitation of young girls is no way to live, as illustrated by his sparing seventeen-year-old Jojo, who could so easily have been exploited. Compulsive sexuality abates as feelings for Alison take on maturity. Nicholas must climb off a "cliff of ice" to reach the pinnacle of truth; "Thou shalt not inflict unnecessary pain" begins to take on meaning (p. 652). Yet tortured and resentful feelings toward Alison persist, and there is a pull away from newly gained moral responsibility. Complete "freedom" from the wish to punish her, together with guilt for the wish, seems unobtainable. (The broken Bow plate, with its happy Chinese family, is a poignant emblem of Nicholas's fractured self [pp. 635, 656]).

Reunion with Alison is therefore flawed, and there is an ongoing struggle against the obsessional wish to turn her into a martyr to an only partially named demon: "Whenever I'm with you, it's like going to someone and saying, 'Torture me, abuse me. Give me Hell. Because—.' 'Alison.' 'Oh you're nice now. So bloody nice. For a week. For a month. And then we'd start again'" (pp. 663–64). This scene recalls that of the "bruised face, very near tears" of the woman with the "bruised look," as she appears at the opening of the novel (p. 664). At the novel's end important purgative changes and growth have occurred, but not enough to heal distrust between lovers. Alison accuses him: "You still haven't learnt. You're still playing to their script," meaning that Nicholas remains Conchis's puppet (p. 666). He strikes her on the left cheek, destroying any hope of understanding. The image of "a shattered crystal waiting to be reborn" seems an awkward metaphorical mixing of the inorganic and the organic, of spirit and flesh. The most that can be said is that the separated lovers are both sacrifices to an inability to trust and to grow together. Nicholas's erotic pilgrim's progress into the promised land of self-understanding is far from complete, as the Latin quotation ending the novel seems to say. Having failed a full psychological rebirth, Nicholas will repeat his erotic quest somewhat less cruelly.

IV

Daniel Martin enlarges upon the male protagonist's "terrible Oedipal secret," desire for the lost mother, uncertainty (if not outright fear) of the father, and chronic insecurity in relations with women.[30] In this novel, the span of life studied is longer—from university days into early middle age—and the analysis of guilt over spoiled relationships is examined in a more realistic setting than that of *The Magus*. Gone is the theatricality of Conchis's enchanted Greek island, replaced by real lives in contemporary Oxford and later in Egypt. Self-consciously literary although the narrative is, Dan's first person dominating the narrative as he prepares to write a novel, the effect is that of an intricately reconstructed "confession" of the lives of Dan, English playwright and Hollywood script writer; Nell, his former wife; Caroline, their daughter; Andrew, Nell's new husband; Anthony Mallory, Dan's dying friend who has been an Oxford Professor of Philosophy; Jane, Anthony's wife and former sister-in-law and lover of Dan, with whom the affair is renewed; and Jenny McNeil, an English actress working in Hollywood who is Dan's current mistress. Dan and Jane must work out their destiny against the background of Dan's failed marriage, his affairs with younger women, and Jane's unfulfilling marriage to cerebral Anthony.

The interaction of these characters is worked out from the point of view of Dan's split consciousness-seeking "whole sight; or all the rest is desolation" (p. 1). The novel is again an exercise in moral self-discovery, in purgation of guilt, and making restitution for wrong-doing—a sort of narcissistic paradigm for Kohut's "Guilty Man" by which to bring quietus through self-analysis. By its dramatic particularity in looking at Dan's emotional treachery and infidelity, the novel attains greater sincerity than does the sometimes affectedly mythic *Magus*. Dan represents the exaggerated male ego, which promises abundant life only to cause bitter disappointment. "Whole sight" means considering not only Dan's Oedipal predicament, but also viewing it in the larger historical setting of shift away from restraining Judeo-Christian sexual rules into an era of indulgence in the secular "pleasure principle." Pain, guilt, and lack of fulfillment are the leading terms of this novel's moral discourse; cast as a clergyman's son, Dan exchanges Victorian restraints for the sexual freedoms campaigned for by Edward Carpenter, H. G. Wells, Bertrand Russell, D. H. Lawrence and others who used the written word to reshape values. *Daniel Martin* is a test case in aggressive secularism as it touches the most fundamental of issues, the capacity of man and woman to form solid and lasting partnerships. Fowles clearly sees the fateful historical shift he fictionalizes. At the outset he quotes Antonio Gramsci's *Prison Notebooks:* "the old order is dying and the new cannot be born," a remark repeated in varying forms as the Victorian age gave way to modernism. Fowles's *Daniel Martin* speaks for the post-Second World War generation, which saw massive erosion of the certainties by which sexual relations had been conducted. The novel is a masterful investigation of the tensions between lovers brought by new freedoms.

In the chapter called "Phillida," Fowles presents a rural Devon idyll of young sexuality between the vicar's son and a farmer's daughter, an idyll by which changing values may be judged. Modeled on the relations of Paul and Miriam in Lawrence's *Sons and Lovers,* this sequence shows the traditional rural virtue of a farming family giving way to sexual opportunism that, in time, will change basic assumptions about society. Having resisted homosexual urges at school and having lied about his heterosexual experience, Dan finds rural Nancy a welcome partner in sexual discovery. Fowles develops the theme of sexual closure as reunion with the lost mother, young breasts not just to be fondled but suckled: "Her lips tasted of thyme and caraway seeds, her body was his lost mother's, her giving forgave in a few seconds all he had thought he could never forgive" (p. 382). But gentleness inexplicably turns to roughness and for all the innocent young love, a sexual war results from the mother-lover identification: "She asked if he wanted to see her breasts again; he had his first taste of exploiting the advantage in the sexual war . . . He was allowed to slip down and kiss them, to suckle them" (p. 395). Rural peace has its complications with the lovers set on and separated, consigning Nancy again to the ordinariness of her social position, a sort of sacrifice in the class war. For following the serpent lust, Dan and Nancy are cast out of paradise to go their separate ways. But Fowles makes clear that they are the harbingers of a new religion of sensuality that mocks the Christian church: "He sank facing her and they kissed properly, erect on their knees, clasped, in a blasphemous imitation of that morning's kneeling in church" (p. 387).

The fugitive lovers shelter in nature at Pulpit Rock, and to emphasize the point of their sacramental union Fowles writes, "So endeth the first lesson" (p. 392). Their "beginners luck" in simultaneous orgasm marks the completion of the new sacrament, before religious disapproval and social control separate them. The reader is to remember these scenes when considering Dan's later sexual approach to Jane in all its tentativeness and hesitation. With traditional paternalistic religion and family put aside, the danger of chaos presents. Fowles makes direct reference to the failure of fathering as prefiguring social disintegration, repeating the observation on which the present studies are based (pp. 368–69, p. 403). Fowles seems to say that prevention of disintegration depends on finding a psychology of union and disunion sensitive to human needs, and the search for meaning beyond what Christianity allowed. A "greater humanity" than Dan ever displays was, however, found in the pastoral care given by Dan's father; while recollection of his father keeps him mindful of selfless human concern, it does not arrest the drift into something very different.

Dan's moral sense leads to a microscopic review of his failed loves with Nell and Jenny and of his return to Jane after a brief affair many years before. He is trying to exorcise the dead woman in the reeds, the sacrificed "mother" who presides over this novel with a portentousness not associated with his father. "Dan is a little bit myself," Fowles told James R. Baker without explaining further.[31] *Daniel Martin* gains power by portraying disturbed sexuality as a function of unsatisfactory parenting, an exploration more of effects than causes but highly astute in its tentativeness.

Emotional loading against women is very great in *Daniel Martin*, and its resolution is incomplete. As in *The Collector* and *The Magus*, repeated motifs of female sacrifice bespeak sexual fear and mistrust. "Love is a sickness of my generation," Dan tells Jenny early in the novel, and he is disturbed by the lure of freedom (p. 43). The symptoms are described in varying degrees of starkness: "lay the broad ones," "the old harem fantasy," and "the vile selfishness of romantic love"—but they all come to the same thing (p. 267). Dan needs to admit that adultery is the more selfish, as Fowles seems to want him to do in recounting the sexual exploits of his film career. These passages are put in terms of Circe-like temptations to adultery in the deteriorating marriage with Nell, Dan's proof that romantic love no longer works (p. 144f). He is haunted by the affair with Andrea, an older woman with "something vaguely maternal about her body," and a tendency to depression. She had indeed become a sacrifice: "When she killed herself in 1962, it depressed me for weeks. I hadn't seen her then for several years and it took me some time to understand why it seemed a much greater loss, and guilt, than outward circumstances warranted" (p. 157). Guilt over the brief affair in California with amoral Elaine is much less than that over Andrea, who reminds him of a mother never present except in "my unknown mother's grave" (p. 86). Enough is said of substitute mother Aunt Millie, the dutiful caretaker, to show that her plain, sensible, and kindly exterior, together with her unswerving duty to Dan's clergyman father, is not all it seems. Fowles writes that she misleadingly looked like a Radclyffe Hall era lesbian, and that if his father were running a concentration camp, Aunt Millie would have seen the necessity of genocide. She is fascinated by local tragedies, seeming to live off them rather than in her own right. Fowles seems to be reworking Aunt Annie in *The Collector,* along with the repellent female psychiatrists in *The Magus* and *Mantissa,* as helpers who bring fear and oppression.

Speaking of Aunt Millie, Dan says: "I harried her abominably, like any spoiled son his mother," as if to say that Dan's rejection of her and her "abnormal" world was to be expected (p. 89). This alienation left its mark as resentment of women in general, together with a readily activated guilty conscience held over from Christian teachings. So constituted, Dan cannot easily adopt the guilt-free permissiveness that his emotions compel. The novel strives for an etiological understanding of the wish to sacrifice lovers on the altar of childhood resentments. Its interest is in following the twists and turns of moral pain. Dan tells his dying friend Anthony, "I'm not a Casanova . . . but I have slept around a good deal. I really do have an irredeemable liking for the impermanent" (p. 187).[32] However, Dan's approach to widowed Jane is a bid for permanency, for restoration of more stable marital values. But his history tells against him, and the tortuous relationship with Jane carries less possibility of a fresh start than he had hoped. Fowles worries through Dan about the narcissistic abyss faced by the Don Juan with a conscience, that psychoclass to which the author appears to belong. A sort of spiritual death hovers over Daniel Martin. Its most powerful image is that of the anonymous woman's corpse so shockingly discovered in Dan and Jane's youth during an outing on the Cherwell. "That thing in the reeds," a floating woman's body that bumps against the punt, is a victim of an unsolved murder, or perhaps of suicide (p. 61).[33] There is no clear answer to the possible unconscious source of this obsessive image, which replicates itself in the successive emotional deaths of failed love affairs. This obsessiveness is not *The Collector*'s bizarre necrophilia but a disorder of the emotions becoming endemic in Fowles's world. Radiating through *Daniel Martin,* the motif of female sacrifice is intensified toward the end in the scene with Jenny at Whitestone Pond in Hampstead. By implication Jenny is being sacrificed to Dan's relation with Jane, as he contemplates "the real enemy she had always been pitted against" with a quick suggestive association to "the woman in the reeds" (p. 668). Parting at Kenwood House from his lover Jenny, Dan fantasies being poisoned by bad feelings and dwarfed by the enormity of life in this century. Whereas compassion and consolation are found in the Kenwood Rembrandt self-portrait (much as they are in *The Collector*) desolation assails Dan as he contemplates a permanent return to Jane. Rembrant's "whole sight" seems still to elude Dan who is identified as a "Bluebeard" capable of "junking" Jenny (pp. 668, 670).

In *Mantissa,* a *jeu d'esprit* too easily dismissed, the problem of male fear of female domination is sharply focused. The story of Miles Green's amnesia and his therapy for sexual inadequacy is quirky and involuted. As a satirical comment on modish French postmodernism the fiction appropriately self-destructs, perhaps leaving the reader feeling cheated. However, *Mantissa* clarifies impressions of Fowles's fictions gathered in a comprehensive reading, including the erotic stories about control of women in *The Ebony Tower* (1974), where female sacrifice also operates. As with the therapist Dr. Vanessa Maxwell in *The Magus,* the therapist in *Mantissa,* Dr. Delphie, is a female manipulator of men. She is a kind of professional mother to wayward sons. Not surprisingly she is also the writer of Miles's muse, Erato, both erratic and erotic. As before, promiscuity is the issue, with jibes at monogamy as biological nonsense. The ensuing discussion could only come out of the hypersexualized phase of the "sexual revolution," before a soberer reaction set in. The tones of a newly confident "liberated" professional female are heard in the accusation: "I'm just one more miserable fantasy figure your diseased mind is trying to conjure up out of nothing," a creation on paper of a woman who can be forced "to say and do things no real woman in her right mind ever would."[34] Dr. Delphie/Erato, who is at war with men, calls Miles's "prototypical male bluff." As his Anima, she reminds him of the danger of exploiting women by making sacrifices of them in a necrophiliac fantasy: "You just collect and mummify them. Lock them up in a cellar and gloat over them, like Bluebeard" (p. 95). This brings us full circle to truth telling about the necrophiliac perversion of *The Collector*, but now its adolescent turbulence is controlled in the interplay of Miles and his therapeutic muse. The mother's lost maturational function helpfully surfaces, however wrong it would be to say that the novel gives this event its full effect.

Nevertheless, *Mantissa* makes plain that, for Fowles, novel writing is self-therapy for disordered feelings he considers to be characteristic of his generation of males. When asked by Raman Singh whether writing was therapy, Fowles answered, "It is therapy, isn't it? All writers must have a tremendous fix; they're obsessive. This is what's so marvelous about this psychiatrist's analysis of why people write. Why it is that you're never satisfied? Why do you go on trying, trying, trying again? Obviously what you're trying to do is—this is my theory—trying to achieve some primal state of perfection and total happiness, which you're doomed never to experience because you'll never be one-year-old again."[35]

Fowles has said that he does not wish to be cured of the "benign psychosis" that fuels writing: "I am in love with my own disease (or need to repair loss) and could not bear to be free of it."[36] Yet he seeks a new source of morality beyond the frivolous near-pornographic intent of which *Mantissa* might be accused. There are fundamental doubts about literature as pathological: Erato/Dr. Delphie "simply happens to have specialized in the mental illness that you, in your ignorance, call literature" (p. 143). As in *The Magus*'s diagnosis of Nicholas's "only partly resolved Oedipus complex," so repressed feelings of Oedipal rejection" are transmuted into a "need for revenge" against the mother, that is, the need to humiliate symbolically a woman doctor (p. 517). The sexual embrace of Miles and his therapist (p. 154f) is a hard-won achievement, a capitulation for each in the verbal battle for domination staged by the author for the general edification of obsessive men. Transformed into a satyr (with enormous phallic size, mocking maleness, p. 191f), and then transformed back, Miles almost enjoys his worst fear of manipulation when the narrative turns from not very satisfying myth making into broad comedy. Dr. Delphie's Greek guise tells us that this is another island of transformations, but now the riddle of maleness is only a spoof. Or is it? Adolescent phallocentrism is made to self-destruct in a comic farrago possible only for the middle-aged author reflecting on repeated attempts to see clearly the failure of compulsive sexuality.

V

Fowles's heroes are transitional figures who suffer their way from Victorian guilt toward a new morality they cannot quite define. The quest for insight is never completed because parenting of the hero is not seen complexly enough, left unstudied in the detail necessary to establish how the obsessional character is formed. Fowles's vehicle for understanding the male psyche is Freudian Oedipal theory, uninformed by object relations or self-psychology revisions. The psychoanalyst Heinz Kohut, speaking of the Oedipal origins of "Guilty Man," could have clarified Fowles's endeavor.[37] Kohut turns Oedipal theory in an object relational direction, showing the force of early defective parental relations with the child in producing depression. Fowles's depressed, angry yet struggling heroes clearly need more said of their mothering. The interactive precursors of sexual ambivalence need spelling out, but Fowles is a novelist with moral intent, not a psychologist. He is first of all an imaginative storyteller, whose fictional insight into male punitiveness toward women is gain in itself. It is for others to bring his imaginative insights into the cold light of psychological truth—discovering why it is that there are few satisfactions and no winners in the obsessive war of the sexes. Fowles puts confessional fiction to a new use by interrogating the conflicts of the driven, promiscuous male, not just celebrating his exploits as Fitzgerald or Hemingway were wont to do. Clegg, Nicholas, Charles, Daniel, and Miles are uneasily probed for what is wrong with them as the perception of their hero status dwindles into recognition of confused and dangerously obsessive emotional lives. With the male-centered brutalities of World War II as moral watershed for Fowles, there is no complacency about what violence man does to man and to woman. In this sense, he is an original investigator of the deepest troubles of our times.

Romantic love is over, Fowles seems to say, with male-female relationships heavily sexualized but often unrewardingly impermanent. With traditional marital rites and obligations thrown in question, what is the source of social cohesion? What does marriage mean in an era of "sleeping around," of casual noncommitted sex? Fowles is among the first postwar writers seriously to address this question, doing so as a participant-observer whose moral perspective was formed in an era of heterosexual monogamy. As a critic of the restrictiveness of this, but tasting the woes of its alternative, Fowles comes forward as a prime diagnostician of our confusing age. But does he write about the typical male as

Bruce Woodcock and other critics imply?[38] Or is he writing especially about a subset of an obsessive psychoclass, "Guilty Man,"
who is better described as suffering from sexual obsessions than
enjoying them? It is not difficult to see that Fowles speaks for
guilt-ridden Don Juans who would wish to do other than turn
the women in their lives into suffering sacrifices. When Don Juan
fully immunizes himself to guilt, then civilization really is in trouble, Fowles seems to say.

There is marked progress through the novels in understanding
the motives and interior states of obsessively driven erotomania.
The quest for the right woman, who will finally end the search
for perfection, is shown to be futile. His fictions' airless, closed-
in, and "islanded" feeling is perhaps inevitable as this truth is
produced. Styling himself as an English "existential" proponent,
Fowles shows that there is no easy exit from the moral ambiguities
of sexual pluralism. His novelist's imagination works relentlessly
over the dialogue of persons in relation, with little relief for their
exertions. Not only are his novels devoid of the transcendent, they
are little informed by the healing powers of nature, as is surprising for the author of *Islands* and *The Tree* with their Words-
worthian overtones.[39] That Fowles himself takes consolation from
wild nature, both land and sea, does not seem to help him form
new norms by which driven conflicted humans might right themselves. Magic and mystification cannot do it, while the numinous
in world mythology is strangely missing from his psychological
scheme of things. Nevertheless, the novels show a progressive
emergence of awareness of the destructive side of maleness, of
driven sexuality as death dealing. This insight is perhaps gain
enough in an era clouded by the erotic fantasy falsehoods of mass
communications, with manipulation of desire at the level of narcissistic gratification. Fowles sees much beyond the common group
fantasy of sex as salvation, but falls short of a solution to the
moral dilemma.

Part of the reason lies in the struggle to make sense of his
own experience of closeness to and distance from his parents. In
"Glacier Men" (1992) Fowles expands on his portrait of his father
published in *The Tree* (1979). The edgy, somewhat constricted
memoir of how the younger Fowles learned from the elder to
appreciate orchards becomes a confession that "I never really
knew my father, or rather, our relationship: or more precisely
still, sensed the distances between us." Fowles realizes that not
only was his father psychologically damaged by being in the
trenches during World War I, but also he belonged to a genera-

tion of middle-class Englishmen who could not communicate with their sons in a direct and open way—in fact, Fowles's father (never named) seems to have been chillier than most. Correct, conformist, and deeply private, his father belonged to "the stiff, almost Prussian, middle-class culture and code, the caste system, in which we were both brought up." He adds disarmingly, "I can see now that it very seriously warped his life, and I'm far from sure whether it has distorted mine in many ways I don't like to have to admit."[40]

But what of his mother, who is only alluded to and never named or described in relation to his father? It is puzzling why the father should be so much the focus of these autobiographical remarks. The reader might suppose that the father was being asked to alleviate a stressful maternal attachment or make up for an absence of mothering. But there is nothing to go on, leaving speculation unproductive. The piece is nonetheless deeply felt, and it ends with the question whether or not Fowles disliked or even "detested" his father. Having written a poem to him twenty years before, Fowles admits that he could not show his father the poem, nor state his actual love. This evidence is enough to put Fowles in that psychoclass under study, and the fictionalized modelings of the idealized father are Fowles's attempts at symbolic repair.

Appeal to the father as deliverer in *The Magus* and *The Ebony Tower* diminishes in *Daniel Martin* to vanish in *Mantissa*. More than an exercise in erotic frivolity, *Mantissa* accepts woman as a guide, as the goddess she always was, who, when trusted, leads man to fulfillment. Purged by the banter and irony of play therapy, Miles must learn simply to "be"—awkward jokes being inevitably part of an uneasy new sexual order. High seriousness has hurt people too long, Fowles implies. It may after all be that the mother/analyst muse-lover, if allowed the dominant role in a play relationship, can solve the Oedipal puzzle. If woman is no longer idealized, as she had been in *The French Lieutenant's Woman*, if "she has fallen from true divinity," then Don Juan's urge to control and punish her may be eased if not banished.[41] In *Mantissa*, the female sacrificial object, the mother who, in other novels, stands behind Miranda, Sarah, Alison, the dead woman in the reeds, Jenny, Jane, and others, turns slyly benevolent and therapeutic. This is not to exonerate *Mantissa* as fully successful; it is only to identify a positive nurturance displacing the unreality of thinking that a magical male guide (artist, magus) will save the obsessed psyche from guilty self-immolation.

An implicit homoeroticism (Conchis with his too studied

womanizing, Dan's obligatory reunion with dying Anthony, leading to revival of a relationship with Jane, his wife) plays off the Oedipal theme of killing the father to marry the mother. The loved and arousing father is finally "killed," while the distant and impossibly wonderful woman becomes shrewish in a wit contest, giving as good as she gets. If this is disappointingly throw away humor, we should remember that the Dr. Delphie/Erato part of Fowles knows that the split high romantic and punitive intentions toward woman, if unchecked, are enough to wreck the world. Overtly playful eroticism is better than secretive and sinister sadism as it operates in perverted Clegg. Collecting women can take different forms, some of them harmlessly fictive seductions. Derepressed sexuality need not be a killer, and depressive guilt need not overshadow the delights of being human as long as those with power to hurt refrain from doing so. As Dan says, it is important to realize the difference between Eros and Agape.[42] Following Freud's dictum that the unconscious be made conscious, Fowles examines in each novel the compulsive theme of damaging and undoing damage to women. This is Fowles's most important contribution to the growth of male awareness. In *A Maggot* (1985), Fowles goes over some of the same ground as in *The French Lieutenant's Woman* but with a difference. Again there is pursuit and exploitation of a woman of doubtful morals, whose fortunes are followed in the eighteenth-century English class system. Again Fowles is fascinated by the damaged woman, but this time the seductively "bad mother" does not have so obvious a male victim. The increments of understanding are slow and hesitant, sometimes doubling back on themselves. There is nevertheless an evolution of human consciousness in which the obsessional mode is just one phase, a staging point for something more forgivingly humane for men and women. Dan thinks of "the freedom to know oneself" as "the driving-force of human evolution."[43] Such awareness may help us out of the impasse so brilliantly portrayed in Fowles's fiction of obsessed "Guilty Man" and his sacrificial women.

6

Eros and Death in John Updike's Fiction

> For it was my sin, that not in Him, but in His creatures—
> myself and others—I sought for pleasure, sublimities, truths,
> and so fell headlong into sorrows, confusions, errors.
> —Saint Augustine, *Confessions*

THERE is no better guide to the effects of the "sexual revolution" in middle America than John Updike's fiction. Updike's is a voice of the people speaking from its confusions in the midst of the largest revamping of sexual morality ever to occur. Both agent of that change and assessor of its effects, for more than thirty years Updike has chronicled the declining fortunes of marriage. To do so is appropriate as Updike is more deeply American than almost any other writer of his generation. A descendant on his father's side of the seventeenth-century Dutch settlers of New Netherland and on his mother's of Germanic "Pennsylvania Dutch," he partakes of two established moral traditions. Church records in both traditions show the sanctity and inviolability of marriage, a theme that in Updike's life and art is more honored in the breach than in the observance. As he says in *Self-Consciousness* (1989):

> My notions of heterosexual love had been derived from Hollywood movies and pornographic comic books and then such modernist benchmarks of sexual realism as *Lady Chatterley's Lover,* the last chapter of *Ulysses,* Henry Miller's *Tropic* books, *The Story of O,* and the memoirs of Frank Harris.[1]

The ground-shaking effect of such a powerful combination of moral revisionists is felt throughout his fiction; thus he is perfectly positioned to take the measure of shifts in moral and relational standards as they affect monogamy and its maintenance in Christian marriage. In dozens of stories and novels, Updike chronicles marriage and family breakdown, failed recombinations, and fail-

ure of the sexes to understand each other's emotions and expectations. With uncanny subtlety of insight, Updike explores and
reexplores the sources of mistrust that make our sexually overstimulated times different from the more ordered past. No moralistic pointer of lessons, Updike nonetheless remains a Christian,
holding to the source of traditional morality while looking steadily
at its disintegration. He is the chronicler of religions in collision,
Protestant Christianity and the new heresy of salvation through
sexuality as taught by D. H. Lawrence, Henry Miller, and many
others. Quite apart from his exceptional powers of observation
and character depiction, Updike's stories make his books documents in social change unparalleled in our time. Future historians
studying the perilous moral conditions of midcentury America
should put these writings alongside the statistically based trend
spotting that so often passes for truth.

If H. G. Wells and Hermann Hesse are the early twentieth-
century writers who most accurately identify the theme of obsessive sexual ambivalence toward women, then Updike speaks for
the consequences of monogamy's breakdown. Closer to the bone
than Fowles's erotic fantasies, Updike's fictions look at the ordinary lives of men and women caught up in unimaginable sexual
freedom. He writes in a hypersexualized America that is also
deeply mistrustful of women, often to the point of misogyny. Neither a misogynist nor particularly sympathetic to the cause of
women, he remained with that early 1930s generation that welcomed the loosening of sexual restraints but could not naturally
take the woman's point of view. That Updike strives to understand
the minds of women is much to his credit; but mainly it is of the
sexually uneasy predatory male, released from bondage by the
"new morality," that he writes. Updike both partakes of the group
fantasy of limitless sexual pleasure and criticizes it by showing
consequences in marriages and family life. He is the historian-
theologian of sex-as-salvation in secular society where everything
is permitted, at least until lethal consequences appear. That Updike demonstrates dangers from permissiveness is arguable from
the imagery of death that pervades his fictions. While it should
be allowed that death fantasies have contributing sources other
than Updike's personal history (the dangerous cold war, for example, and the Korean and Vietnam political atmospheres), I believe
that Updike tells us that the promised new life of sexual freedom
is ultimately death dealing.

For Updike freedom for the individual and connectedness to
family and past are hard, if not impossible, to reconcile. The epi-

graphs to his autobiography, *Self-Consciousness,* smack of individualism, even complacency (Woolf, Bellow, Bishop West of Ely), yet the quotation from Emerson, about a thread running through all things, is also part of Updike's consciousness and leads to some of the book's most moving passages, where sexual self-serving is put in abeyance. He writes:

> Evidence of God's being lies with that of our own; it is on our side of the total disparity that God lives. In the light, we disown Him, embarrassedly; in the dark, He is our only guarantor, our only shield against death.[2]

This statement is not a cliché of a "born-again" Christian but the authentic voice of someone who in an earlier age might have found consolation inside the church for the guilt of sinning. In the seventeenth century "Jack" Donne of the risqué *Songs and Sonnets* (1633) became Dr. John Donne, Dean of St. Paul's, a "second St. Augustine" as a biographer called him. Updike's words sound like one of Donne's death-obsessed meditations, but in Donne's instance excessive selfhood was overthrown by God's grace, not a likelihood in Updike's secular frame of reference. The urgent confessionalism of his fiction, never far from autobiographical truth, hints at an Augustinian or Donne-like repentance that would not find favor with readers today. Updike is no Thomas Merton who saw the beauty of austerity and withdrawal to serve a higher truth.

The chronicle of "man for himself" in post-Christian America goes on extending through such remarkable studies of interpersonal tensions in marriage as are found in *Couples* (1968), *Too Far to Go: The Maples Stories* (1979), and the *Rabbit* series (1960–90), to name only leading examples. So prolific is Updike that it is hard to select even the most telling examples of his insights into marital difficulties; one must read virtually his entire production to catch the nuances of what he is saying within a thematic preoccupation. Contrary to the critics who charge that Updike is a marvelous stylist, especially gifted with visual imagination, but that he has nothing to say, we will assert that he has unsurpassed understanding of the sexual discontents that are tearing apart the social fabric on which civilized life depends. That Updike has no corrective, Christian or otherwise, should not detract from the brilliance with which the problem is defined. He fully realizes the obsessional hypertrophe of eroticized love in our time, and he offers much evidence about reasons for it. As long ago as 1963, in a review essay on Denis de Rougemont, author of *Love in the Western World* (1940/1956), Updike commented on the sex-driven dynamic of the West compared to "the technological torpor of the sexually sane East." He continues:

> It would seem that . . . de Rougemont is dreadfully right in asserting that love in the Western world has by some means acquired a force far out of proportion to its presumed procreative aim.[3]

Updike helps us greatly to comprehend what that "force" actually is and how its ambiguous power came about.

Couples, a novel of rampant sexual individualism in upper middle-class America, may be taken as Updike's most original statement. Both provocative and diagnostic, *Couples* caused a shock wave in a society being shaken by the sexual revolution; its sexual explicitness has been extensively commented on. The novel's impact is made more understandable by *Self-Consciousness,* Updike's lucid reflection on his art and life. His role as spokesperson, or delegate, of a generation in transition from traditional Christian morality to permissiveness becomes even clearer from the autobiography. Updike the novelist is nothing less than the agent of an emergent psychoclass of persons caught between two moral systems, one time-honored but shaky, the other enticingly new but of doubtful durability. Paul Strietz writes that the most significant art signals "the development of a new psychoclass by crystallizing the emotions of a generation, thus causing a heightened insight into that generation's emotional dilemmas."[4] While the earlier psychoclass, whose problems of adaptation were different, protests outrageous new departures, the innovative artist proposes a way of reconciling the moral dilemmas of his own age group. "The artist is only a cultural hero because he publicly confronts what is previously an unexpressed mass problem for the group," Strietz writes, adding that the problem must be the artist's own personal problem if its formulation is to have validity.[5] Working with taboo material, the artist gives the emergent psychoclass a language in which to voice its predicament and consider the moral options. This, I believe, is what Updike did, especially in *Couples,* a novel that let prosperous suburbanites in their early thirties see just where permissiveness was leading. If the womanizing hero Piet Hanema is an Updike projection, then his breakaway from traditional restraints is understandable in terms of *Self-Consciousness.*[6]

In the autobiography we learn that Updike spent his first thirteen years living with his parents and maternal grandparents in Shillington, Pennsylvania, where his father was a mathematics teacher in the local high school. A wry melancholic with a delight-fully poignant self-deprecating sense of humor, Updike's father only just managed to survive the depression with his self-respect intact. A remarkable and moving fictional appreciation of him appears in John Updike's *The Centaur* (1965), while John's son David writes appreciatively of his grandfather in a short story, "The Cushion of Time":

> My parents were still very young and beautiful, and in an odd way they seemed more like my peers to me than my parents. My grandpar-ents were older, clearly of another time and place and there was some-thing about being with my grandfather that made the world seem safer, more stable, as if in his presence I was protected.[7]

And so were John Updike's grandparents of a different, more traditional generation than his parents who had entered the "knowledge industry" in however marginal a way. College educa-tions and exposure to the arts made a decisive difference, marking off his parents' generation from all preceding it. As an only child, Updike received the full force of this difference together with an awareness of his mother's family having once enjoyed a more advantageous status before societal changes compromised them. Poverty and fierce pride combined to make Updike want to avenge his father's humiliation at being made to feel an ineffectual teacher. As he explains in "A Letter to My Grandsons":

> the world I grew up in was raw and rough enough to threaten the survival of decent people, who paid their dues, revered their flag, honored God and their parents, tried to do the right thing. How often, in the household of my childhood, did I hear of people trying to do the right thing! That there *was* a right thing seems an old-fashioned notion now; the family I grew up in was so old-fashioned we quoted proverbs aloud.[8]

The lurch into moral relativism, and drastic revision of sexual mores, is surely an example of what Strietz is talking about as change of psychoclass. Updike's fiction investigates the special conditions and pressures in childrearing in the 1930s that brought his talent forward to become spokesman for the sexual confusions of his generation. He speaks for the psychoclass whose fathers' absence, or diminished or compromised presence, left their sons doubting manhood. One family scenario for the pro-duction of Don Juan flight from and to women, and for the rise of agonized moral self-consciousness, stems from Updike's semi-autobiographical and autobiographical writings.

Updike's feelings about being mothered are not as easy to ascertain from *Self-Consciousness* as are those about being fathered. The autobiography does not favor this angle on its material, being concerned instead with Updike's self-perception as "defective," battling to overcome multiple disabilities: the skin disorder psoriasis; asthma; a stammer; and a tendency to choking. The reader's sympathy is easily won for the boy and man who had to endure the suffering these brought and to look for ways to cure, or compensate for them. The theme of loss of sense of a whole self, a constant awareness of the need for repair, is central to the autobiography. While creating an Updike with whom the suffering side of ourselves finds it impossible not to identify, he also effectively masks the Updike who would be talking about what God sees, were he a new St. Augustine or John Donne. Perhaps the psychological sophistication of our times is what makes this difficult, if not impossible, for the would-be confessional writer. Updike does not want to make explicit autobiographical ties between actual life events and those parts of his novels drawing on them. A canny mixture of hinting and avoiding prevents anything like the self-indictments of Rousseau or the solemn candor of Frank Harris. It is more self-consciously constructed than a spontaneous outpouring; Updike is selective in what he reveals, leaving intriguing gaps between the vignettes and the fantasy surrounding them. A probable further consideration of Updike's childhood appears in "A Sandstone Farmhouse," a story written after his mother's death in 1989. Here Joey views his mother and father as ill-suited to each other from the start of marriage; and he sees the futility of his mother trying to please her own mother. His feelings about his mother's sexuality as a young woman, and about her rugged individualism as an older one, are sensitively developed. But I wish to stay with Updike's earlier poetic attempt to portray his developmental experience as this better reveals the relational confusions, characteristic of his generation, which power his best fiction.

II

> The child's ego-sense does not come at birth but slowly emerges from a confusion of its self with the mother's.
> —*Self Consciousness*

In the game of creating a credible semblance of life that might produce an artist, Updike never quite comes to the point of saying what he really feels about mother, and hence about women as lovers and wives. Not that this is forbidden; it is more that concepts and vocabulary are not developed. He rightly says that "Most of the best fiction is written out of early impressions, taken in before the writer became conscious of himself as a writer."[9] Early impressions are the writer's most important resource precisely because they are so deeply felt and mainly preverbal. Replenishing this stock in later life is almost impossible, and to use what one has is to gain the mainly poetic associative skills that manifest in images of the feelings available from childhood intensified by the changes of adolescence. Although not successful in its entirety, Updike's autobiographical poem and photographic resumé *Midpoint* (1969) has moments of seeing into the past, before adult sexuality became all encompassing. Of his grandparents he wrote:

> My mother's father squeezed his Bible
> sighing, and smoked five-cent cigars
> behind the chicken house, exiling the smell.
>
> His wife, bespectacled Granma,
> beheaded the chickens
> in their gritty wire yard
>
> and had a style of choking during dinner;
> she'd run to the porch, where one of us
> would pound her on the back until her inner
>
> conflict had resolved. Like me, she was nervous;
> I had sympathetic stomach cramps.
> We were, perhaps, too close,
>
> the five of us.[10]

The sense of menace in grandmother cutting off chicken heads yet being herself afflicted with choking is perhaps significant, as is the sense that grandfather is subordinate, as father was to mother, the lot of them "too close." But interpretation is not so certain in the intensely sexual later parts of this poem, with its intermittent focus on and withdrawal from mother. A steady look at her seems impossible for the poet, a mother's boy obsessed by femaleness but inclined to avoid emotionally charged relations with females.

Feelings about women that need clarification emerge in section 4 of *Midpoint*, "The Play of Memory," a composite of ambivalently sexualized associations from childhood and later erotic encounters. Following some overheated passages, the Don Juan figure appears at his most sensitive and reflective. Juxtaposition and merging of images from memory make of several women—lovers, mother, daughter—a set of dissimiliars who flow together in the mind space. Evocations of mother become primary, however, and seem closely associated with the sexual provocations of "pubescent daughter" as well as with love trysts, as in the lines immediately preceding those to be quoted at length below:

> you who demurely clinched
> your thighs and came and might have snapped my neck

We are back with grandmother's chicken and woman's threat of castration in a family "too close." A sense of continuity, if not causality, develops in this part of the poem; mother is seen as a figure of caring and conflict:

> you who nursed me
> and fed me dreams of Manhattan in the cloudy living-room
> and rubbed my sore chest with VapoRub
> > and betrayed me with my father
> > and laughed it off
> and betrayed me with your husband
> > and laughed it off
> and betrayed me beneath the pines
> > and never knew I thought I knew
> your underpants were ghostly grey and now
> > you wear them beneath your nightie
> > > and shy from my hug.[11]

What is "betrayed" with husband and father if not Jocasta's allegiance to son, the son having been led like Oedipus to expect more than his due? In the first paragraph of "At War with My Skin," *Self-Consciousness* discloses the sense of intimacy with mother. Treatment for the skin disorder psoriasis was sunbathing:

> I was lying on the upstairs side porch of the Shillington house, amid the sickly, oleaginous smell of Siroil, on fuzzy sun-warmed towels, with my mother, sunbathing. We were both, in my mental picture, not quite naked. She would have been still a youngish woman at the time, and I remember being embarrassed by something, but whether by our being together this way or simply by my skin is not clear in this mottled recollection. She, too, had psoriasis; I had inherited it from her.[12]

While most sensitive boys sooner or later experience their mothers as "too close," his age at this episode was not given, so we are unsure whether to see it as seductive or merely unsettling. To return to *Midpoint,* the sense is of importunate mothering by an overly concerned but articulate woman who conferred the gift of language, even as she disapproved of its tentative literary uses.

> you fed me tomatoes until I vomited
>   because you said you wanted me to grow and you
> said my writing was "a waste" about "terrible people"
>   and tried to call me down from the tree
>   for fear I'd fall
> and sat outside nodding while I did toidy
>   because I was afraid of ghosts
> and said to me "the great thing about us is
>   you're sure of things I'm unsure about and
>   I'm sure of the things you're unsure about"
>
>   and you blamed yourself for my colds
> and my skin and my gnawing panic to excel, you
>   walked with me on Penn Street
>   the day I tried to sell cartoons to Pomeroy's
> and they took our picture LOANS
>   Oh mother above
>   our heads it said
>
>   LOANS[13]

The mother in *Midpoint* is both overbearing and enabling, over-feeding and overstimulating to a son rightly recognized to be a prodigy. The sense of "LOANS" may be that a son is only on loan to his mother, not her possession for life. The passage following, on mirroring, is about the emergence of increasingly complete images of self, from emergence in birth though a "crack," to growth in stature as evidence of approaching manhood. But there is a moment of doubt, hesitation, and arrest that must stand for the charged intimacies of mother and son: Updike writes of a little round mirror

> with which you
> conducted arcane examinations by the bedside
> I lying on the bed and not daring
> look over the edge

Soon we are told in bold capitals that "MIRRORS ARE VA-GINAS," women as lovers now mirroring his initial feelings of

attraction and fright. We learn from the next bold type that "PE-
NISES ARE EYES," a metaphor of male need to be fully mirrored
to overcome sexual insecurity. The poem is carried forward by
powerful evocations of marriage, adultery, and perhaps even fantasized incest.[14]

Updike's theorizing about his creativity touched only tentatively
on the role of mother; moving from the farfetched theory that
creativity is a parody of the skin's overproduction in psoriasis,
he remarks that a psychiatrist would say "by Freudian lights my
mother's failings (if any) matter far more than my skin's."[15] Whatever maternal failings, there were inducements to follow the arts,
as though his mother had provided an attractive exit from the
threatening enclosure of her influence. A well-educated admirer
of the arts and an unpublished novelist, she saw to it that Updike
was given painting lessons and that he had art supplies "to feed
my 'creativity.'"[16] Although she was overbearing and critical of his
speech to the point of producing a stammer, through her impera-
tive an esthetic line of psychological self-help was established in
the visual arts, which Updike seriously pursued. It was perhaps
an essential detour before returning to the relentless visual realism of his prose.

As he relates in "What MoMA Done Tole Me," "My first museum I would visit with my mother." What excited him the most in
that provincial Pennsylvania museum was the sculpture showing
female nudity; but I felt myself a furtive animal stirring in the
shadow of my mother."[17] The ominous shadow of woman as caretaker and erotic object extends through the account of his many
quasi-religious pilgrimages to the Museum of Modern Art, to
which his aunt later introduced him. Similarly, he felt under her
"shadow" while delighting in the exhibits as a kind of toy shop.
Most noticeable about Updike's selection of female images from
repeated visits to the museum is their bulk and quality of shadow,
their ambivalent menace along with attraction, as in Picasso's "Girl
Before a Mirror" (1932). This picture may indeed be taken as
showing the sinister side of pregnancy, the split mother-to-be as
witch. Updike remembers Braque's "Woman with a Mandolin"
(1937) as towering over him with "frozen sadness." He looked
also at Giacometti's "Woman with Her Throat Cut" (1932) as "a
dreadful subject." There are bulky women in Maillol's "The
River" (1938/39) and in Lachaise's "Standing Woman" (1932), all
of them products from the years of his birth and early childhood.
In fairness, a work of Brancusi, "Maiastra," is said to be "mounted
at a height suitable for manifesting a goddess," a more benign

icon.[18] But woman as threat is more often manifest in these objects of art, products of the defensive maleness to which Updike himself would contribute richly.

Updike articulates the sexual anxieties of that age group of American boys, the emergent psychoclass that took shape in the early to mid-1930s, depression years leading to the upheaval of World War II. Economic uncertainty and the immanent dislocations of war further undermined the security of family in which father as head pursued a traditional livelihood by farming or small trade. The shift to maternal influence (even dominance) in childrearing, requires a psychosocial study beyond our scope; here it is enough to suggest that the balance of power tilting toward mother in Updike's family induced him to help shape a sexual mythology for an America in which mothering had acquired a new power. From this point of view, the most important biographical feature of *Self-Consciousness* is the imbalance between passive, fatalistic father and active, ambitious mother. Updike remarks on there being "enough suffering in the Shillington house—my mother's fits of anger and my father's fear of poverty."[19] His mother's frustration and rage at blocked talents, at having been educated only to fall back into economic hardship and isolation, are of more than personal relevance. Updike's mother was overly dedicated to him because her energies and talents were allowed no other outlet. That her frustrations became intolerable appears from this remark:

> As I remember the Shillington house, I was usually down on the floor, drawing or reading, or even under the dining room table, trying to stay out of harm's way—to dissociate myself from the patterns of conflict, emanating from my mother, that filled the air above my head. Darts of anger rayed from her head like that crown of spikes on the Statute of Liberty; a red "V," during those war years, would appear, with eerie appositeness, in the middle of her forehead. Her anger was aimed rarely at me.[20]

He remembers a harried family life of highly verbal adults, his mother's perfectionism the main driving force, his speech overcorrected and his hair cuts scrutinized for flaws.

The sort of mother-son relationship documented in *Self-Consciousness* is fictionalized in *Of The Farm* (1965), with its struggle of wills between a mother and a son who was about to marry for the second time. This source of conflict is worth remembering when thinking of later fictional studies of marital discord in *Couples* and *The Maples Stories*. In *Of the Farm* the new woman in the farmhouse is seen by the possessive mother, Mrs. Robinson, as a rival for her son's affection. The story thus centers on difficulties with the widowed mother, whose portrait is not so lovingly drawn as that of the father, George Cadwell, in *The Centaur* (1963). Here the mother is seen as a "witch," is said to have destroyed her husband, and is pictured as being chronically interfering.[21] The son is given such pointed lines as:

> You poisoned one marriage for me and I want you to leave this one alone. You be polite to my wife. She didn't have to come here. She was frightened of coming. You asked us to come. Well, we're here.[22]

There is struggle for separation and autonomy reminiscent of Paul's with Mrs. Morel in D. H. Lawrence's prototypical *Sons and Lovers.* In this syndrome the would-be lover is a mother-bound little boy who can hardly feel otherwise since he is always striving against interference, most of which is internalized. Contact with the mother renews a tyranny:

> I avoided my mother's glance, lest with facial nakedness I overcommit myself to her again.[23]

The dynamic reappears in *Rabbit Run, Couples,* and elsewhere, but nowhere is it studied quite so sensitively as in *Of the Farm;* yet Updike seems more interested in exploring the further consequences of mother domination than in looking at its fraught beginnings.

Connections with the general and typical sexual anxieties of American males of his generation are clear enough in *Self-Consciousness,* the more telling perhaps for not being consciously made. Anxiety about girls and dating is palpable, with something sinister attributed to female teenage sexuality. The passage on high school formal dances is a sardonic masterpiece of recollection; "darkened gym" with "drooping twisted streamers of crepe paper," "wilted" corsages, and tuxedos "rumpled in the heat"; partners separated stickily, the boy remembering moving his hand up to "the hard ridge of the bra strap," with breasts unnaturally "plumped up," "waists cinched and their hips widened by crinoline petticoats." The fingers have "scarlet fingernails" matching lips, lips that in the high school yearbook are dark and black though smiling. The death trap images are concentrated into one astonishing sentence: "But what heats, what shadowy, intense glandular incubations came packaged with that five-dollar purchase of a baby orchid in a transparent plastic box!"[24]

Adolescent loves led to separations, a more insistent artistic mission outside of Shillington beckoning; interestly, it is "my mother's vision" of small-town inadequacies that propelled him away from the perfectly nice girls: "I was not allowed to be a normal boyfriend but had always to be sneaking and breaking up and saying goodbye."[25] This gives Updike a particular angle of vision on women as interchangeable, replaceable, the hallmark of this psychoclass. In 1968 he told the *Paris Review:* "I have attempted a number of portraits of women, and we may have reached that point of civilization, or decadence, where we *can* look at women."[26] Does he really see women in his fiction? There is something of the disengagement, the sardonic detachment of the high school dance retained throughout, as though protective distance were necessary for safety. And what does "decadence" mean, if not that looking at women really means managing them, manipulating their pleasures? We do not hear precisely why his first marriage ended in 1974, with much in the personal realm remaining undisclosed to protect the living. His first girlfriend is named, not his wife, and there are only glimpses of the liberated sexual style that suffuses *Couples:* for instance, the return journey from a ski trip, with his wife in the front seat, Updike

> patiently masturbating my back-seat neighbour through her ski pants, beneath our blanketing parkas, and taking a brotherly pride in her shudder of orgasm just as we hit the Ipswich turn-off.[27]

This is the Tarbox set of *Couples,* the dalliance of Piet and Foxy, the breakup of trust and fidelity in a welter of illusory sensual pleasures. Nobody in that novel gets to fundamentals, all seekers of new delights being creatures of a new sexualized *zeitgeist* whose origins are not understood. Updike asks, "Will the future understand . . . how much sex, with Freud's stern blessing, meant to us . . . . ?"[28] But this is not quite the question, and Freud as originator of the Oedipal theory, as well as of brilliant insight into obsessional behavior, cuts both ways. Without Freud we would not be so quick to see the transitory excitements of *Couples* for the relational dead ends they are. A remark of critic John Romano accurately sums up the failure to see women as fully relational beings, with their own sexuality.

> What gives poignance to so many scenes of intimacy in Updike's fiction is that they are "done" in the voice of someone who has some stubborn difficulties in truly *being* intimate. For isn't it, after all, the

failure of intimacy that preoccupies him? It is the refusal to give, to yield, to share, to forego, and above all the refusal to stay, the decision to leave, that relentlessly creates the dilemmas in the lives of his characters. They hurt each other by persisting in their privacy when they shouldn't; what they lack is the means of doing otherwise.[29]

Updike's fiction is constrained along a pathway that allows limited means of "doing otherwise." Early in *Self-Consciousness* there is an outbreak of fantasy around "normalcy." Concealment and the narcissism of endless self-examination are the psychological concomitants of psoriasis; the sufferer is left alone with his "self-contempt," which is reinforced by living on a farm in comparative isolation after the family moves from Shillington. Somehow his mother's presence accentuated the misery:

Perhaps the unease of my first memory has to do with my mother's presence; I wished to be alone with the sun, the air, the distant noises, the possibility of my hideousness eventually going away.[30]

Seasonal in nature, it did go away, but the sense of being singled out did not and it, in a sense, was the precondition of art. In the masterful story "Should Wizard Hit Mommy?" the little skunk's mother actually disapproves when the Wizard finds a cure for its bad smell. The question is, should the Wizard as good doctor punish the mother who did not want a cure—an allegorical irony of the author's situation.[31] This is a reworking of Edmund Wilson's famous theory of creativity in "The Wound and the Bow," but Wilson omitted mother as a reinforcer of the difference that mother and son share and that holds her son to her. Updike's language of difference is indeed strong:

An overevaluation of the normal went with my ailment, a certain idealization of everyone who was not, as I felt myself to be, a monster.[32]

The artist, whether or not he has a skin disease, is a sort of sacred monster, like Kafka's Hunger Artist. He becomes addicted to his performance regardless of who is watching. But in Updike's autobiographical presentation the "monster" is joined to the sexually rapacious, Picasso-inspired Minotaur. The Minotaur is a sexually active shaggy beast, who rules women by brute energy. Not subject to social codes, the Minotaur works on his own terms in a lonely, predatory way; he will not be restricted. Updike dislikes writing an autobiography this close to his real life and work, but the full delineation of the psychoclass for which he speaks would seem to need it.

The American "Ladies' Man" does not like being fenced in; seeking fresh sexual contacts to prove his manhood, he shies from full commitment that would be felt as entrapment. Cruelty is often implicit and may be indirectly expressed rather than dwelt on. Updike undoubtedly felt entrapped by his skin, but fantasies of entrapment go far beyond this in the autobiography. There is the incident (at thirteen) in which the dog, Copper, is caught in a pipe and freed, then coaxed by the young Updike back into the pipe's mouth to reexperience its terror. Death by suffocation is the self-punitive fantasy. Updike wisely comments, "What is our tremendous human cruelty, after all, but the attempt to discharge our pent-up private nightmares onto the open ground of actuality?"[33] He continues: "Our lives depend upon an interior maze of pumping, oozing tubular flow whose contemplation itself can induce claustrophobia," and he refers in a note to a submarine fantasy made less terrifying by having Raquel Welch along—glamorous, sexualized woman as antidote to existential fear.[34] It is true that much fear of suffocation is on the physical level: a terrifying asthma attack recounted (p. 92f), followed by discussion of emphysema (p. 96), yet he sees the asthma as occasioned by too much pressure on him as "son, husband, and father, and the demands from each side slic[ing] my inner freedom thinner and thinner."[35] The chicken beheading fantasy reappears as threat from wife as well as mother and grandmother.

The real test of restriction and suffocation comes in the passage on ending his first marriage. Here the language is that of earlier fantasies of suffocation: the walls of the house "seemed to be shrinking around me," "the squeezing, the panic crept in and were suddenly there," and he felt an "inner clenching" as he was overcome by feelings of captivity to wife and family.[36] The physical, the psychological, and the marital are tied together in one claustrophobic nightmare from which divorce is a desperate escape. As Richard Maple says, he feels "glued fast" and prone to feeling guilt.[37] In the Maples Stories that lead to a "no fault" divorce, imagery of hostility, guilt, and death is rampant, yet many readers will not be quite sure why. The problem in these stories is that the male feels so restricted by marriage that he projects resentment on his quite well-meaning wife. "All those years, he had blamed her for everything . . . No longer: he had set her adrift from omnipotence."[38] But how did wife and mother become "omnipotent"? That is the cultural problem Updike can't directly address, although he sees that America had become a "nation of temporary arrangements" in consequence of this very sort of breakdown of trust.[39] A close reading of Updike's fiction helps to determine how the conjunction of mother and wife in the obsessional psychoclass can be understood. His impulse to understand and correct a bad situation is positive; as he told John Halpern, "I enjoy writing as a form of self-administered therapy," an echo of D. H. Lawrence's famous statement that "one sheds one's sickness in books, repeats and presents again one's emotions to be master of them."[40] Judging from such a story as "The Fairy Godfather," Updike does not think much of psychiatry, nor does he seem especially enlightened or even curious about depth psychology. But this is not to say that Updike is unwilling to use his unconscious as a means of mediating in fiction the most urgent interpersonal anxieties of our time. If his "self-administered therapy" through writing fiction has left him "depressed," we should not wonder, given the gravity of the questions he continues to address.[41]

III

"It's a real mess."
—*Couples*

The imagery of mess, messiness, and entanglement, along with guilt and death, is frequent in *Couples*. It implies a standard of order and regularity from which the sexual adventuring in Tarbox, Massachusetts, is a deviation. The novel shows that experimental adultery, sex as a pleasurable exploit against Puritan mores, leads to destructive emotional entanglements. Nothing really works out for the antihero, Piet, and his women; today's glowing erotic promise is tomorrow's dust and ashes. But why couldn't the women see this and avoid the miserable aftermath of misdeeds that it does not take much astuteness to realize will depress and taint all involved? The unconscious fantasy message of *Couples* is not life abundant but all-consuming death: the death of the hamster, to which repeated references are made, the Kennedy baby's death, Kennedy's assassination, and the death of John Ong are the most obvious manifestations of this novel's dwelling on death amidst a vital set of young characters. Emotional mess leads to personal and societal disorganization and thence to death, the novel seems to say. But why at this moment in history should such an outbreak of permissive sexuality, of flouting the wisdom of the race, occur? Updike caught and formed danger signals emanating from anxieties that I am attributing to the imbalance of mothering over fathering in increasingly mobile industrial society. His central metaphor, "Tarbox" as the City of Destruction, a new Inferno, captures the consequences of moral decay: a sticky mess from which it is almost impossible to extricate oneself. The distressed mother's son plays out the game his creative unconscious knows to be lethal. Enacted sexual wishes and metaphoric reflection combine throughout the novel, making it a moral statement rather than pornography. *Couples'* tension between the glamorous new arena of sexual liberation and its lethal underside is unique in contemporary literature, but not entirely unprecedented. Updike sensed something endemic in American culture.

Flight from women and denunciation of mothers are recurring themes in American fiction—Huck Finn's escape from Miss Watson's reproofs by sliding into the river, Rip Van Winkle's flight into the woods to escape his termagant wife, Hemingway's damaging portrait of the mother in "The Doctor and the Doctor's Wife," Philip Wylie's *A Generation of Vipers* alleging women as the cause of modern man's "gutlessness"—examples could be multiplied. Flight into love affairs with many women may be the equivalent of flight from woman as enchantress and as engulfing maternal goddess. "You can't live with them, and you can't live without them," goes the saying. Hypersexuality is a means of flight, of evading female control by distorting the sex act into a "conquest" rather than a sign of commitment to new life. Woman is de-idealized and made into carnal object, an easier container for feelings of attraction-repulsion. Without our realizing just how drastic a change was taking place, the monogamous ideal upheld by Christianity was assailed from within the popular and artistic culture in the name of sex-as-salvation. As Peter Gardella points out in *Innocent Ecstasy: How Christianity Gave America an Ethic of Sexual Pleasure* (1985), through the eighteenth and nineteenth centuries there was a steady erosion of the doctrine of original sin.[42] Gardella shows how the churches themselves became active in removing the taint of the Fall, especially from women, and how the Christian mystical tradition mutated into a quest for ecstatic orgasms. From St. Augustine to Luther, lust of the flesh had been condemned, with sexuality for Christians officially restricted to procreation. Through the teachings of such anti–Victorian, psychoanalytically informed Americans as G. Stanley Hall and Margaret Sanger, sexuality rightly used was made to seem godly, a way back to a "lost paradise." Sanger sponsored birth control and sexual pleasure for women, while Hall aligned sexuality with true religion. Other psychological writers such as Erich Fromm, Norman O. Brown, and Herbert Marcuse (with various provisos) joined the crusade for self-realization through sexuality. Does sexual pluralism have to do with increasing fear of women, with increasing male anxiety at mothers having become too close to their sons? The evidence of Updike's novels points to the use of sex as ecstatic escape from the realities of actual feelings brought about by a committed relationship. The pseudoreligion of sex, in other words, is an escape from authentic feeling into fantasies of control, mastery, and depersonalized transcendence.

Sex as a redemptive ritual, a sort of secular communion, became a popular crusade through such publicists as Hugh Hefner of *Playboy*. Hefner's cry for almost forty years has been for "freedom" in sexual relationships; believing that "nothing lasts forever," Hefner himself has been serially monogamous with many beautiful women. Beginning in December 1953, *Playboy* became successful beyond all expectations by tapping the collective unconscious of a sexually insecure generation of mother's boys. They were offered a way out of the intolerable anxiety of being permanently close to one woman. Aimed at the college crowd, *Playboy* defined a voyeuristic style—ogle the centerfold as a masturbation fantasy, and, actually dating girls, think opportunistically and pluralistically. Leonard Glass's "Ladies' Man" became a celebrated hero, the latter-day Don Juan. Girls were defined as "bunnies," cute and cuddly, while Playboy himself was pictured as a black rabbit with erect ears and a bow tie, retaining something of the old *Esquire* motif's dapperness. Is Updike's skittishly running hero, Rabbit Angstrom, the anxiety-ridden incarnation? The prolifically breeding rabbit runs after females, while the anxious one runs first toward, then away in fearful fright. That having it both ways was a serious adaptational attempt is clear from the difficulties with intimacy evident throughout Updike's fiction. In publishing his fiction in *Playboy*, Updike spoke directly to the emergent element in the psychoclass he represents, the obsessionally driven boy learning to become a man in a setting of radical ambivalence to women and sex. With the Women's Movement gaining strength, many men took this "false solution" as their own, almost to the point of making it a new religion.

Updike's view of religion as Eros, especially in *Couples*, also resonates with Hefner's views. As Updike said of *Couples*, "I was asking the question, After Christianity, what? Sex, in its many permutations, is surely the glue, ambience, and motive force of the new humanism. Freddy Thorne is a prophet who brings, with his Grove Press books, the new gospel into the backwoods of Tarbox."[43] He adds that, as God withdraws from the new Sodom and Gomorrah that is Tarbox, the only churchgoing Christians, protagonists in adultery Piet and Foxy, feel "relief." This seems to back Gardella's point about the church being complicitous in the dissolution of its own morality. However this may be, a religious coloration is thrown over sex in the novel, while at its terrifying culmination the Congregational Church in Tarbox burns, ignited by "God's own lightening."[44] The suggestion could be that the flames of lust are their own judgement—a sort of test of *Playboy*'s assertion that sexual liberation was the only needful condition of a new humanism. In a preface to some extracts from "The Playboy Philosophy" (a twenty-five installment series begun in 1962), Hugh Hefner quotes the Reverend Roy Larson's comment:

> *Playboy* is more than just a handbook for the young man-about-town: It's a sort of Bible which defines his values, shapes his personality, sets his goals, dictates his choices and governs his decisions. The *Playboy* philosophy has become . . . a sort of substitute religion.[45]

Reinforcing this, Hefner writes:

> The existence of two sexes, and their attraction for each other, must be considered the major civilizing influence in our world. As much as religion has done for the development and growth of society, sex has done more.[46]

It is as if *Couples* were testing the truth of such a fulsome assertion as this, wishing it to be so, hoping for a new sexual humanism, but far too honest and intelligent in its formulation of experience to give uncritical support. Those who took *Couples* as pornography were mistaken; its sheer excess of sexuality tests the reader's sensibility, which may become one of sated apathy and disassociation rather than of stimulation. As John Ditsky pointed out, novels such as *Couples* and Philip Roth's *Portnoy's Complaint* (1969), to which it is compared, may be "the early signs of a new post-Judeo-Christian moral orthodoxy, a stiffening of the grounds of situational ethics."[47] To judge the moral significance of *Couples,* we must look at Updike's treatment of women as lovers and mothers and of men who are the sons of mothers.

Couples is a kind of collective confession, subtle in its observation of the early 1960s generation of privileged, upper middle-class Americans anxiously living their most vital years anticipating middle age. In pursuit of the abundant pleasures of affluence, metaphysically they are lost. Echoing Hesse's idea of two ages overlapping, Updike writes of his generation being:

> suspended in . . . one of those dark ages that visits mankind between millennia, between the death and rebirth of gods, when there is nothing to steer by but sex and stoicism and the stars. (p. 389)[48]

The lyricism is not misplaced in this richly imagined novel, but it is to the psychosocial dimension that we must attend. Updike pictures less a swingers' haven, a "post pill paradise" where no guilt need attach to free sexuality, than he does a set of decent characters deluded by the false hopes of sexual deliverance. Tarbox (dubbed "Sex-pot") is based on Ipswich, Massachusetts, the early seventeenth-century Puritan settlement where Updike spent his early married years. Tarbox is a sort of laboratory of the "new humanism," brought by sacralizing sex in the era of "man for himself." Here progressive thought is put to the test. Angela (Piet Hanema's wife and sacrificial victim) reads Freud and believes in the power of psychiatry to put right her failing marriage. But Angela finds no application for her insights as she is victimized by relentlessly womanizing Piet. Marital decay and death thwart reconstructive efforts attempted in the endless discussions amongst the group of ten men and women, each dedicated separately in some degree to the god Sex. The more private conversations take this form:

> "I was never mocking God."
> "No. Your God is right there, between your legs,
> all shapeless and shy and waiting to be touched." (p. 360)

This is Piet in conversation with Foxy Whitman, his partner in adultery who is carrying his child. But he is determined that she will not bring the baby to term.

> In Foxy's silken salty loins he had planted seed that bore his face and now he wished to be small and crawl through her slippery corridors and, a murderer, strike. God forgive. No: God do. God who kills so often, with so lordly a lightness, from diatoms to whales, kill once more. (p. 363)

This death to life is more than the issue of abortion and "right to life"; it is Piet's own ambivalence working itself out on a sexually insecure woman. The novel is astute about Foxy's own psychological disability attributed to a missed relationship with an absent father (pp. 47, 78, 276).[49] As Foxy has already given birth to her husband Ken's child, there is an opportunity to test Piet's reaction to motherhood. When they come together after a separation, Foxy remarks: "You can't fuck a young mother," yet that is precisely what Piet feels compelled to do against a gripping fear: "Ever since you've had the baby I've been frightened to death of you. I assumed it was the end of us" (pp. 344, 327). This statement belongs to the strongest fantasy evoked in the novel, that of motherhood as death bringing, with abortion as confirmation of the death message mothering seems to be. So emotionally over loaded for Piet is mothering that Updike must test it by having Piet break the most basic of all taboos, "mother-fucking." Foxy is not his own mother, but by projection she is a Jocasta.

Love-hate of mothers is found throughout *Couples*. It comes with various inflections, as in a passage recalling John F. Kennedy's similar background to those of Piet's Tarbox circle of "swinging" friends. (Kennedy is earlier cited for his promiscuity, pp. 104–5.) Invoking Kennedy gives the early 1960s ambience of Camelot permissiveness in which the pansexuality of Tarbox took hold. There is discussion of

> the similarity of JFK's background to their own, the differences, their pasts, their fathers, their resentment and eventual appreciation and final love of their fathers, their dislike and dread of their mothers, sex. (p. 148, see also p. 105)

The most sexually cynical of Tarbox's adventurers, the dentist Freddy Thorne, is reported by Foxy to have admitted fear of his mother: "He said I reminded him too much of his mother, and he was afraid of her" (p. 377).[50] Piet is perhaps Freddy's more complex and sympathetic alter ego—more frightened by the certainty of death and more in need of comfort. In a conversation with his old mistress Bea Guerin, she suggests that Piet, now down on his luck, is rumored to be "keeping a nest of girls." But Piet has more archaic longings and isn't jesting when he comments:

> Everybody's wrong. I only liked married women. They remind me of my mother. (p. 441)

This may be the novel's most revealing insight into Piet's character, its neediness surpassing wishes to control and punish women. Fascination with pregnant Foxy but inability to accept paternity plays up her "love [of] being used/abused" by the unreliable father-lover (p. 276).[51] Making love with Georgene Thorne, a past mistress, feels "incestuous" to Piet, a "betrayal" (p. 54). This is said just after a loving recollection of his mother's warm ironing board, on which he had laid his head to sooth earaches in childhood—just as he lays his head on Georgene's belly in a reentry fantasy. The sudden leap to power saws' "rasp and spurt" on the Indian Hill building site suggests a male's hostile rebound into the destruction of virgin territory. This defensively "cuts him off" from feelings too powerful to entertain. Sex with Foxy in her fifth month of pregnancy is surely regressive and punitive: regressive in the wish to be a baby again and punitive in the violation of her marriage and preparation for motherhood. It is a kind of interference, even abuse, she invites, with Piet and Foxy locked in a destructive codependency. Significantly, he comments: "I'm afraid of abusing you." To which she replies, "Don't be. Do" (p. 213).[52] Sex does not work; perversion is discussed, blame canvassed, fright declared in Updike's brilliant observation of these lonely and confused persons. More orally dependent (obsessed by oral stimulation) than hostile, Piet nonetheless wishes to dominate while Foxy "would give herself to him in slavish postures" (p. 455). In the final love scenes, just before the church burns, animality obtrudes, as if Piet's fear of Foxy is finding its true words: "she clawed his back and came. Could break his neck. Forgotten him entirely. All raw self" (p. 456). The chicken's neck fantasy is recalled. "Raw self" in Piet, as in Foxy, begs to be understood. We are told little about Piet's parents, except that they were growers of flowers in Michigan, traditional Dutch Calvinist immigrants, snuffed out in an automobile accident. Thus a contrasting background of religious strictness is established, but there is no analysis, the novel's whole emphasis thrown on the sexual obsessions. A dynamic of ambivalence to mothering is, however, offered, *Couples* being among the most intuitive of American novels depicting the destructiveness of male sexuality.

Callous and promiscuous, Piet tries "to lull himself to sleep with bodies of women he knew" (six are named), a bizarre remothering for some nameless pain, but the only result is to kill God, not salve the wound. As Robert Detweiler points out, there is a mythic consistency in *Couples*, which combines the Tristran and Don Juan legends in a framework of courtly love. Passion is expected to reconcile spirit and flesh, substituting for the Incarnation, a sort of erotic Gnosticism or antinomianism:

The same kind of pattern appears with the Gnostic Mater Sophia, the Mother of Christ who becomes the Eternal Feminine and then, in the courtly love tradition, the subject of erotic worship. All of Piet's women are mothers.[53]

But however dignified by myth, critics recognize a predominance of religious nihilism and death in the novel. Piet's unconscious is activated by a dream of a plane crashing, the "fall" of the artificial, mechanical world that supports his promiscuity. A fall from grace is studied throughout, a matter to which Updike returns in the same context of obsessive-compulsive eroticism in *A Month of Sundays* (1974) and *Roger's Version* (1986). The false hope of salvation through adultery is a matter he must view from every angle, so critical is it to assessing the moral meaning of "our new morality." In *Couples* loss of faith is harsh and final, evoked in condemnatory imagery:

> Piet tried to pray. His up-pouring of thoughts touched nothing. . . . Whosoever lusteth in his heart. . . . Dead Sea. One more dismal sect. . . . He had patronized his faith and lost it. God will not be used. Death stretched endlessly under him. Life a scum, consciousness its scum. (p. 271)

Nothing so final is proposed in *Roger's Version*, a searching, teasing reexamination of a Christian's sexual guilt, while in *A Month of Sundays* it seems that morally compromised Reverend Thomas Marshfield's penitential retreat and confession bring a tortured kind of forgiveness for his promiscuity.

Couples' Nietzsche-like, aphoristic cynicism is not, therefore, the more true: "Nothing sacred. Triune like cock and balls. . . . The voracious despair of a woman had swallowed God" (p. 271). Here the linkage is made with poetic deftness, at a level of imagination Updike's later novels do not reach. Piet is vulnerable in a dangerous world; he clings to women, yet victimizes them. His wife Angela is his most conspicuous lover-victim, his captor who might crush him, he fears. She is the dutiful mother of his children, inoffensive, even intuitive and wise (an active dreamer, she thinks of entering therapy); yet "to him she was exhausted, a stale labyrinth whose turnings must be negotiated to reach fresh air and Foxy" (p. 223).[54] First and last Angela is heavy: "going heavy in her haunches and waist"; when "she stood in the tub, Angela was colossal"—like the overpowering female sculptures pictured with Updike's essay on The Museum of Modern Art (pp. 7, 424). Their estrangement is marked by Angela's words: "You've abused me horribly. I've asked for it, sure, but that's my weakness and I've been indulging it" (p. 425). Piet, feeling violence, almost flares; even in his days of admiring Angela's physical person, he could fantasize her decapitated—struggling into a dress she is seen "Without her head . . . all full form, sweet, solid"—the cutting fantasy again (p. 11). It is Updike's genius to give sacrificial Angela the novel's most devastating truth about Piet's promiscuity: "You sleep with women when you're really trying to murder your mother" (p. 218). It is a gratuitous piece of psychologizing, but Angela's words are Updike's way of obliquely conveying his fullest insight, his ambivalent compassion.

IV

Only truth can be built upon. From a higher, inhuman point of view, only truth, however harsh, is holy.
                    —*Self-Consciousness*

The self-perpetuating swings of ambivalent feelings about heterosexual relationships may be Updike's final depressing message. The persistent oscillation of male-female relationships, their unceasing pain, limits the transcendent hinted in moments of sexual ecstasy. Perhaps, like the sexual antinomian Wilhelm Reich, Updike is too focused on the orgasm, mistaking it for the mystical unitive state reported by Christian ascetics; too intent on bliss, he is perhaps not Buddhist enough in mindful acceptance of what arises and passes from awareness in the great cycles of existence. Updike's reading of the crisis of belief in our time can be criticized in several ways, but in describing the phenomenology of erotic obsessions and their consequences he is unassailable. No other writer has so effectively pursued the truth that has gradually become visible in the criticism of Freud's Oedipal theory: that Jocasta's maternal reach goes right into the most intimate areas of male loving, oscillating it fatefully between the poles of life and death.

In *Rabbit, Run* (1960), Harry Angstrom or Rabbit (who is twenty-six as was Updike at the time of writing) hates the way his mother speaks about his wife Janice:

He hated it when his mother went on like that; maybe she did it just to kid him, but he couldn't take her lightly, she was somehow too powerful, at least for him.[55]

Rabbit Angstrom is in league with death, suffering under a net more complicated than that entangling Peter Rabbit in the children's story. The net is associated to "the high perfect hole with its pretty skirt of net," a basketball net with other connotations of entrapment.[56] Rabbit is an escapist, a runaway from marriage and family who cannot find the freedom he craves. It is not found with Ruth Leonard, his lover who becomes pregnant but refuses to have his baby. The child he and Janice have is accidentally drowned when the despairing Janice is in a drunken stupor—one of the most terrifying death scenes in recent fiction. Rabbit's religious crisis, much remarked on by critics, is certainly that, but more it is a crisis of bad faith in relationships—of obsessive fending off of women while desperately needing them. Rabbit is Piet in a different light, the conscience-haunted Don Juan whose psychogenesis in maternal conflict is hinted but never spelled out.

Updike is the master observer of marital tension and breakdown in America, the epic writer of a people whose soaring divorce rates have been the cause for much comment but little understanding. As a modern phenomenon, the breakdown of the family has coincided with increasing awareness of the "needs" of men, women, and their children, and of helping, enabling modes of childrearing rather than the repressive styles of former times. Updike's fiction monitors the age of rampant marital and family instability, calling special attention to the plight of the male. It is the male who cannot be content, settle, or feel an essential part of domestic arrangements that are made and run by women. When lovers become wives and wives become mothers, male discontents set in as if the fact of motherhood itself were the trigger. Typically, the male wavers between maintaining commitment and escaping it, fitting Freud's perceptive description of the obsessional defense. Sometimes the marriage fluctuates, as is seen in *The Maples Stories* in the preface to which Updike comments that "the seesaw of their erotic interest rarely balances."[57] Ambivalence, separation, yet inability to part company is the dynamic of these brilliantly observed vignettes. In *Marry Me* (1977) the story is largely about Jerry's attempt to leave his family to marry Sally and run away to a ranch in Wyoming. But self-centered Jerry cannot decide; a sense of suffocation and desire for freedom paralyzing him to the extent that he lives in fantasy. "In intermittences of rage and despair Ruth felt sorry for [Jerry], he looked so 'torn,'" Updike writes in a narrative suffused with imagery of violence, hurting and death—the most powerful emotions being generated by domestic strife.[58] This is indeed a novel about the "twilight of the old morality," as the epigraph has it.

Male dominance of ex-wives and mothers appears in *The Witches of Eastwick* (1984), too far-fetched for most readers but making a point not made before with such force. It is about the exploitability of middle-aged divorcees whose sexual needs govern their lives. Darryl Van Horne (a double-entendre name, suggesting both colonial Dutch virtue and the male member) is a rich and libidinous sponsor of female creativity. Darryl is in fact a Hefner-like playboy figure, a Satanic Don Juan who would devour women if he could; perhaps his inspiration is J. P. Donleavy's *A Singular Man*. However Updike shaped this portrait, he makes of it the epitome of male rage and female self-destruction. The sexual romp turns nasty when witchcraft is used by three of the women to destroy a fourth rival who dies of cancer. Fear of death by cancer is a metaphor for decadent society attacking itself—an extension of the death fantasy so noticeable throughout Updike's fictions about marriage. Furthermore, all the women in the novel are witches of one coven or another, and no marriage is healthy. It looks as if the breakdown of this society should be attributed to women empowered by the Women's Movement, but aren't the likes of Darryl Van Horne still the real villains; or is it something about the way he was mothered? Updike gives Darryl only one comment that leads to this surmise: "If my mother had neglected me a little more I might be a better all-round guy."[59] Sex for Darryl is a substitute for relationship, the defining characteristic of a "Ladies' Man" who cannot stand intimacy but "loves" women promiscuously.

There is no Updike fictional hero who, having sampled love's delights, fails to succumb to the sexual revolution's ravages. A sort of relentless judgment for carnal interests seems to tear its way through the lives of his men: the more Christian they begin, the more their misdemeanors make them look culpable or ridiculous. The Reverend Thomas Marshfield's mid-life crisis leads him to write a sermon on the sacrament of adultery, secondary only to that of marriage: "Adultery is not a choice to be avoided; it is a circumstance to be embraced," he argues.[60] Sacred and profane become hopelessly confused, as they are in the mind of Roger Lambert, a divinity school professor in *Roger's Version*. His attempt to rescue fallen Verna lands him in a sexual trap, cheapening his relation to a God for whose presence evidence was, in any case, wanting. The problem of mothering agitates this novel too, although incestuous wishes are displaced from mother to sister and niece. Updike's general comment is:

> Foolishly or not, we do associate females with safety, all history's murderous mothers, frenzied Bacchanites, and self-mutilated Amazons to the contrary.[61]

For Roger Lambert women are not safe but an enticement in the absence of God, making him feel cheapened and wretched for his carnal indulgence in the age of AIDS and the other sexually transmitted diseases of casual relations. He flees from woman to woman with no seeming escape from his ironic entrapment:

> Those musty, doughy women of home: they had been too much for me, I had successfully fled them, why was I courting this disaster?[62]

No reasons for male entrapment in such absurdity are given, other than those hinted but left undeveloped by Updike in his fictions. He is, after all, a writer and poet, not a psychologist bent on tracing the origins of emotions, nor a psychohistorian looking for fundamental processes in society as evidenced by its dominant fantasies.

John Updike did not invent the sexual revolution in America but inherited it in the formative stages. A neo-Puritan might argue that his fiction greatly stimulated sexual excesses, but a fairer view is that, while Updike's fiction was certainly propelled by and helped to propel a torrent of change, it also reached for the securer shores of traditional values. Updike could not know that Christian teachings of monogamy and family solidarity would be unable to hold against the psychological disturbance of overmothered sons. He could only give evidence of the demise of centuries of understood values no longer enforceable once a sex-obsessed male psychoclass had asserted itself. It might be argued that among such American writer-prophets of sexual revolution as Henry Miller, Norman Mailer, and Philip Roth, Updike is the most sensitive to what was being lost. Further, his powerfully intuitive fiction reaches into the unconscious for new bearings, only to give evidence that "love" promiscuously pursued leads to satiety, emptiness, despair, and finally to death, which itself becomes an obsession.

Updike's story "Aperto E Cuiuso," in the January 1991 *Playboy*, is about a nearly sixty-year-old man in a third marriage to an attractive forty-year old woman. On holiday in Italy he is captivated by the hypermasculinity of the writer Gabriele D'Annunzio who died in 1938, while she is repelled by it. D'Annunzio lies entombed with comrades in pompous marble, a memorial the death-obsessed husband admires. Husband and wife never understand each other on this point, D'Annunzio the writer, warrior, and womanizer dividing them, and they don't know why. While the ingredients of fuller understanding are present, Updike does not press for it.

Commenting on the last novel in the Rabbit series, *Rabbit at Rest,* Updike sees it as "a depressed book about a depressed man, written by a depressed man," but this is to greatly underestimate its achievement.[63] While the mood is beyond questioning, it should not deflect attention from the novel's deepened humanity. The best measure of Updike's increased compassion for human ambiguity and self-caused suffering is taken by reading consecutively the four Rabbit novels, as they chronicle the life of Rabbit Angstrom from young manhood by the passing decades. Most remarkable is the viewing of tension, its complications and remissions, between Rabbit and his son Nelson, minutely observed particulars becoming symbolic of the difficult generational transitions in recent American society. Through marital infidelities and disruption of family ties runs the question of how male sexual energy is to be responsibly used—how to be a man whose life has meaning and not merely an overenergized rabbit bounding about in search of illusive fulfillments. Little is resolved or resolvable within materialist America where the inner life is not easily nourished. But one thing is clear: driven sexual pursuit, as enacted by Piet Hanema in *Couples* or the early Harry "Rabbit" Angstrom, only further breaks down an already fragile social fabric. This breakdown is followed with deepening compassion and understanding in *Rabbit at Rest.* If depression is its inescapable outcome, then the reasons are revealed along with compassion for the personal weaknesses and spiritual poverty of post-Christian man.

Rabbit at Rest's obsession with death is the inevitable outcome not only of Updike's personal experience, but also of relational and sexual preoccupations in his fiction over many years. As he explains in *Odd Jobs,* two weeks after completing the first draft of *Rabbit at Rest,* his mother died, contributing "to the hospital scenes of this book and to its overall mortal mood."[64] Death imagery of many sorts permeate this novel (played off against recurring imagery of eating that both feeds the hungry psyche and kills the overfed body): death is the cumulative effect of Rabbit's unfulfillment and spiritual destitution in the society he inhabits. Glutted and sated, American society is still unfed, Updike perceives in this deeply depressing assessment of America's spiritual decay. In purely moral terms, "the wages of sin is death," as the Rabbit series testifies; in human terms Rabbit's life runs out into mere oblivion because he has no consuming purpose for his life beyond serving the appetites society teaches him. Updike's fictional triumph is to follow Harry's aging with a relentless eye, reporting what he sees with unswerving stoicism. As the novel ends Rabbit indeed slips into nothingness but, as readers, we know that he has increasingly known himself. This is humanity of an order only the finest fiction can produce.

Piet Hanema's brassy surface resistance to true feeling, his narcissistic and often callous sexual adventuring, is replaced by acceptance of the ambiguities and limitations of any individual life. When death imagery invades *Couples,* as it does with Piet's failures to turn eroticism into meaningful relationships, it comments on the futility of his pursuits. In *Rabbit at Rest,* death imagery spreads to the entire society that has missed the rich promise of a fresh start for European civilization on a new continent. By their long span of time the Rabbit novels allow such an assessment. Piet's defensively manic assertion is outgrown, and depression is seen as an achievement beyond his reach. If Updike has not fully uncovered the destructively obsessional dynamic of mother-dominated males, he has made a brilliant start at doing so. No other American novelist has done so much "to publicize the otherwise obscure, and to throw complex light, from many angles, upon issues that tend to be badly lit."[65]

7

Obsession: The Driving Force of Culture

In psychoanalytical and allied work it is found that all individuals (men and women) have in reserve a certain fear of *woman.* Some individuals have this fear to a greater extent than others, but it can be said to be universal. . . . This fear of *woman* is a powerful agent in society's structure . . . [and is] responsible for the immense amount of cruelty to women.

—D. W. Winnicott (1965)

In these closing remarks I should like to enlarge upon the meaning of obsession as customarily used in psychoanalysis and psychiatry to describe an intrapsychic defensive system. In the technical sense (as described by Freud, Fairbairn, and others) the obsessional defense is an internalization of bipolar impulses to both accept and reject the same attachment object, usually the mother to begin. This defense is characterized by a high degree of ambivalence and by a ritualized wish to control that becomes the leading feature of the adult male's relations, especially with women. Beyond this is the popular meaning of the term *obsession,* including the new verb "to obsess," which means to be persistently preoccupied about something, usually an unsatisfactory relationship. The popular press frequently has stories about men who are "obsessed" with celebrity women, for instance, who do not reciprocate the fascination and feel menaced by it. The two meanings are yet to be convincingly connected, yet there is a certain continuity between them. The obsessing man may well have an obsessionally organized ego defense as understood in psychodynamic theory. It is simply that what was once privately held in the imaginative realm of fantasy production (whether literary or not) has broken the limits of social control to be produced as an aggressively disconcerting act. It is plausible, therefore, to see manifest obsessions with antisocial consequences as the escaped forms of controlling ritualization designed to hold compulsive behavior in check.

The overall argument of this study is that a psychoclass was formed around imaginative externalizations of obsessive impulses that threatened to escape the controls of male writers. Sexually active though these writers sometimes were, they were not at peace with their inclinations and sought moral expiation and symbolic repair by fictional rituals. By picking up the signals of widely shared male distress, these writers were able to shape a new fictional language of obsessional distress and its ritual neutralization. High artistry is most evident in literature, but the same motifs and sexual preoccupations are to be found in film, the visual arts, and popular music as well as being widely discussed by pundits and journalists at all levels. It is remarkable how the once little-used term *obsession* has come to permeate our language. Thus an entire cultural period may be described as dominantly obsessional, producing and feeding off ritualized controls on fearful attraction to women. Each new phase of culture acquires a set of imaginatively mediated instructions to guide emerging male consciousness. Beginning as subliminal and suggestive, they move through fictional articulation before becoming banal scenarios described in decadent metaphors at the point where the psychoclass becomes too obvious to be exciting. With the disintegrative effects of obsessionalism taking its toll in family relationships, mutant forms of the psychoclass claim their expressive rights. Thus the early to mid-twentieth-century literary manifestations discussed here transformed by degrees of crudity in the misogynistic themes of pop and rock subcultures. To understand this broadened popular sense of obsession, however, entails recognition of the individual psychogenesis of its most imaginative forms, as has been attempted here. I recognize that fully to substantiate this thesis a much broader survey than that attempted in the five studies would be necessary.

How great a factor in twentieth-century fiction is male obsession in which fear of women manifests itself as control? A preliminary sampling shows the likelihood that almost all fiction by men about women contains some elements of fear, avoidance, and accommodation by glamourization and idealization. A proportion would be found to contain the controlling and punitive elements noticed in the work of the five writers here studied. The distribution of these elements across the decades and the actual amount of fiction replaying defensive male obsessional tactics remains to be tallied. How much of it actively promotes a pseudoreligion of love as unlimited sexuality is also unknown and this, too, needs to be assessed. From evidence already in, it would not be surprising to find that sexually ambivalent and destructively driven male discontent is the single most prevalent theme in twentieth-century fiction. In the novels of such American writers as F. Scott Fitzgerald and Ernest Hemingway, the glamour and tragedy of male sexual drivenness infused itself into the core of culture. From Fitzgerald's glamourisation of wealth and sexuality in *The Great Gatsby* (1925) to Hemingway's bizarrely fetishistic *The Garden of Eden* (begun 1946), male obsessions came to dominate writing. Artistic emulation in fiction and film produced an "amplification of deviance" such that obsessive and addictive sexuality were virtually normalized. It is a difficulty of studies such as the present one that pathologies of gender anxiety have become almost invisible in the great mass of art in which they are the governing factor. There is, however, beginning to be recognition among psychotherapists of the destructiveness of sexual addictions transmitted in the very culture. For instance, Patrick Carnes cites an example of an abusive father trying to normalize his sexual behavior with his daughter by giving her a copy of Nabokov's *Lolita:* "She and her father intellectualized their own sexual experience as an affair and an outgrowth of the Lolita role."[1]

The literature we have been considering took shape in the midst of the largest shift in morality during modern times, the so-called sexual revolution, made possible by birth control techniques and high mobility and the decline of Judeo-Christian religion. The history of this psychosocial mutation of culture away from Judeo-Christian restraint to a new secular religion of permissive eroticism remains to be written. First evident in the European Renaissance and seventeenth century, its fullest expression came in the America of our time and deserves to be fully chronicled. Obsessively driven sexuality appears to be the single most powerful force at work in our lives. With parental restrictions under attack and youth subject to media "hype" of sexual availability, successive shifts of mores produced an urban jungle where the driving force is sexuality. We need to reflect on why our entire culture so rapidly became sexualized.

In the glare of this social change, mere fiction pales, but its influence does not disappear, nor does its importance as a channel to unconscious wishes and fantasies. The mid-twentieth-century sexual revolution has resulted from several forces, including electronic communication and mass distribution of sexually suggestive or explicit visual and verbal materials. Sex has been cynically commodified by filmmakers and by the magazine publishing industry. But why have men especially been such easy targets for commericalized stimuli promoting promiscuity? To discover reasons we have had to discuss changes in family structure, with fathering subordinated to mothering, leading to sons' unconscious angry fantasies against dominating women. Perhaps, the fantasies and wishes fiction reveals should be termed preconscious, having almost reached the level of articulation when the prescient writer puts them into words. Writers are the first detectors and purveyors of group fantasies, the provisional mythmakers who reinterpret (and sometimes distort) the archetypal urgings of the timeless unconscious. The writers studied here speak for what might be called the sexually ambivalent unconscious of an overmothered psychoclass. To speak through their narcissistic and self-willed characters in the timeless language of religious awareness is not part of their program. It is enough that writers probe into, and resonate with, the actual erotic and punitive wishes that inhibit harmonious relations between the sexes.

Gender distress is widely evident in modern fiction—distress over what it is to be essentially male and female and how the sexes happily combine to produce healthy successive generations. Gender formation and identity are endlessly played over in recognizable scenes from life, yet literary criticism is reluctant to confront this aspect of its subject, studiously avoiding the language of psychodynamics. For too long, academic teachers of literature have accepted at face value writers' special pleading for various obsessional fantasies, refusing to see much correlation between art and the childhood experience of the artist. As biographical and psychological evidence mounts, they have abandoned this increasingly untenable position for the equally stultifying study of texts as linguistic structures and as parodies of each other. There is no dishonor in being frightened by the power of destructive fantasy, especially if one is, in some measure, involved in it. It is difficult to work past our own self-serving interest in the deviant forms of relationship and sexuality, but in a world increasingly aware of violence against women, there is no other way forward but to look critically at writers' fantasy messages in the light of healthy developmental principals. If literature is to retain its value to society as the deepest communicator of psychological distress crying out for disclosure and repair, then this function should be recognized in criticism and teaching.

The novels studied here seem to belong entirely to the disintegrative phase of the twentieth-century sexual revolution discernable as far back as the writings of H. G. Wells. By pleading for new erotic freedoms, they break decisively with the inherited wisdom of their culture that lifelong monogamous heterosexuality is desirable for both men and women. But their rebellion against a restrictive past is not all they convey; there are also healthy confessional, ritualizing, and reparative urges at work. Obsessional rituals, of course, mainly ward off dangers rather than fully facing them, but by repetition, they do call attention to the source of danger, in this case, fear of being dominated by a woman reminiscent of one's mother. Repetition of ritual leads to a certain desensitizing to gender distress, and it is arguable that repeated obsessional fictions have implanted a new but unhealthy set of relational expectations. Young readers may no longer think of marriage breakups as unusual and pathogenic for children. Writers' confessional and reparative urges, on the other hand, may be valued as productive of new moral insights lacking in society and as a source of awareness that transcends male urges toward treating women as sacrificial objects.

The writer's examination of guilt and remorse, of confused, loveless, and emptied-out states, brings much needed moral enlightenment. When the writer examines how it happens that Don Juan promiscuity, to say nothing of outright punitiveness toward women, offers no rewards for anyone, a service is performed. In this sense, writers do test runs of most, if not all, variations of conventional forms of relationship. First person narratives—as found from Wells through Hesse and Nabokov to Fowles—give the illusion of a speaking presence who knows whereof it speaks. In this sense, the novel is adaptive behavior, a way society invented to see its most fateful players modeling and reflecting on beguiling but often destructive fantasies. Arguably without fiction to display aggressive male fantasies, protesting feminism would have been slower to gather momentum. By calling attention to male oppression, feminists have deepened male fright; but the good result is that unconscious fears in both genders are beginning to be appreciated for their real power. Literary creativity is thus an essential part of the feedback loop by which we catch sight of ourselves as the actors we are. Self-consciousness, in the sense that Updike uses the term, is the inevitable consequence of lost innocence and of chewing the bitter fruits of broken relationships. "You saw it here first" may be but a small literary comfort in the midst of an actual marital crisis, but the attentive reader will also find the causal analogy to his own case and possibly be forewarned of rocks ahead—especially if criticism further clarifies the creative writer's insights.

If psychodynamic criticism can find a plausible language to interpret what writers leave unsaid, the full "story" of our obsessively driven culture may be pieced together. The "story" of self-blinded male marauding and punitive exploitation, not only in intimate relations but right through nature and society, would become a cautionary tale. A turning point has been reached when it is at least acceptable to hypothesize that our destructive onslaught on nature is connected with chronic inability to find contentment in personal relationships. Aggression displaced into working relationships, and into exploitations in the realm of nature, poses questions about maladaptations in child development. It is now possible for the social sciences and humanities to address questions of obsessional destructiveness by looking at the successes and failures of basic human attachments. Insight in literary creativity is the start of this fuller process of human self-recognition and might change our course for the better.

Literature emits society's distress signals, even as it purveys seductive fantasies. By giving significant form to distressing relationships, it makes them into objects of esthetic contemplation, but also opens them to critical awareness. That we are frequently posed with choices between love and death is seen in the novels studied here. Without sustained and sustaining love, death (accompanied by fear and despair) inevitably begins its inroads. The marital casualties of technologically accelerated life, predicted so blithely by Alvin Toffler in *Future Shock* (1970), can now be more realistically appraised.[2] By working in the subjective realm the disconnected drivenness of the late twentieth-century male, exemplified in Updike's masterful *Rabbit at Rest*, is seen pushed to its unsatisfactory conclusion. If death imagery prevails in this novel, it is not only because its author chronicles the depressing life cycle of a typical American male, but also because he seizes on the unconscious fantasy of death as the outcome of an unlived life, of repeated relational and erotic frustrations. In this sense, obsession may be said to be the driving force of culture, a perverse force that needs to be seen for what it actually produces when death as Nemesis triumphs in the midst of life rather than providing a peaceful ending to the natural course of events.

Hermann Hesse thought that "Human life is reduced to real suffering, to hell, only when two ages, two cultures and religions overlap."[3] Early in this century, Freud's psychoanalysis propelled the avant-garde away from traditional morality founded in Judaism and Christianity. Freud argued, in "'Civilized' Sexual Morality and Modern Nervousness" (1908), that the neuroses "originate in the sexual needs of unsatisfied people ... we must regard all factors which operate injuriously upon sexual life and suppress its activity or distort its aims as likewise pathological factors in the psychoneuroses."[4] By suppressing and redirecting powerful sexual instinct a freeing of culture had been achieved, but a terrible price in neurotic suffering had also been exacted. Certain of Freud's followers, such as Otto Gross and Wilhelm Reich, singled out sexual emancipation as their special cause. While Gross advocated sexual license, Reich advocated orgastic sexual satisfaction as the aim of therapy. Both suffered the opprobrium of their excesses, but their teachings had undoubted influence over those ready to relinquish the sexual restraints enjoined by traditional religion. Clearly obsessional in their insistence on the primacy of sexual fulfillment, they began gathering the psychoclass for which creative writers would become powerful spokesmen. Gross's doctrine of free love greatly influenced the life and work of D. H. Lawrence, which in turn may be seen as a bridge to the fictional material under discussion. Lawrence, in his erotic fiction, began playing out the implications of Freud's theory of sexuality as an instinctive drive, and other writers followed suit. As long as drive theory held sway, fiction celebrating Eros flourished, but, as drive theory was questioned, so attitudes to sexuality in fiction changed.

In *The Origins of Love and Hate* (1935) Ian Suttie, an early Tavistock Clinic psychiatrist, questioned Freud's insistence on sex as a biological drive that excludes love defined as a state of responsiveness.[5] With the subsequent development of attachment theory by John Bowlby and his associates, the reciprocity of love, beginning with mothers and their infants, came into sharp focus. For attachment theorists, procreation is a natural function of father and mother, whose children exhibit instinctive attachment behavior that is more or less successfully reciprocated. The language of psychoanalysis became dyadic and interactional, eventually including family dynamics. Sexuality took its place in the sequence of growth and development without the excessive emphasis it had been given by many Freudians.

Freud's insights into obsessional behavior have been amended and enlarged on, but the task is incomplete. Reorientation from classical drive theory, through object relations and self-psychology, to attachment theory, points to further study of how defenses are built in actual infant, child, and parental interaction. If the obsessional, driven, aggrandizing and sexually destructive tendencies in modern culture are to be understood, then a convincing account of their psychogenesis is needed. Faulty male gender development should be made a priority in the study of attachment behavior. Literature and art can signal the danger points as they arise within a culture; they may even supply partial and coded explanations of their causes but they cannot tell us enough. Novels in particular are adaptive in showing assumptive models of relational reality in action, and in suggesting which of them work better than others. It is clear from the examples cited that obsessive Don Juan sexuality is a perversion with a built-in death-trend because it prevents full reciprocity between man and woman. To establish this much is an advance in the evolution of culture and society, an advance that can be consolidated best by understanding the malign psychodynamics that produce male punitive fantasies, wishes, and actions.

It is easy to be pessimistic about the picture of distraught human relations everywhere present in the arts. The cardinal signs of infant and child defeat as described by Bowlby-Protest, Despair, Detachment—are easily seen, while full engagement with life and celebration of its multitudinous possibilities is all but missing. The chronic suffering that men and women cause each other is virtually taken for granted, as though the alternatives had been used up. We try to draw back from the self-destructive promotion of technology and from our onslaught on nature, thinking that change of heart will repair past mistakes. But surely only a more realistic view of ourselves, as angry, resentful, and driven destroyers of whatever will take our projections, can make much difference. We seem to be on the verge of a new accession of self-awareness arising from the interaction of literature, the arts, and psychodynamic theory. Self-enclosed, "imaginative" literature is changing into a way of seeing how faulty assumptive models of reality acquire their power to subvert healthy life.

The sexual revolution has been a mixed blessing, with promises of "liberation" loading new shackles on many. Women have gained less and lost more by sexual freedom than have men. Seeing that their plight as victims of male aggression has not been alleviated by liberation, women have begun enquiring into the cause of male menace. Studies such as Jessica Benjamin's *The Bonds of Love* (1988), David Holbrook's *Images of Women in Literature* (1990), together with his many other studies in applied psychoanalysis, and Liam Hudson's and Bernadine Jacot's *The Way Men Think* (1991) are defining with new clarity the problems of male gender formation. Benjamin writes that "the deep source of discontent in our culture is not repression or, in the new fashion, narcissism, but gender polarity," an over statement containing some truth.[6] Hudson and Jacot spell out the developmental reasons why male gender formation is more difficult than female, leading to greater male angst and perversion yet also to more art, scientific discovery, and innovation.[7]

Thus when psychodynamic criteria are admitted into evaluations of cultural materials belonging to the humanities, a different pattern emerges from that of liberal humanism. Creative products should not be assumed to confer themselves moral broadening of the reader, as conventional liberal education assumed. Imaginative literature is better seen as attempting to understand relational maladaptations, beginning with those in the writer's own formative years, and including those he chooses to portray in fictions as symptomatic especially of the sexual tensions of his time. The writer's "solution," however, may not be fully representative of human possibility, only a testimony of the limits he has reached. If the humanities are to deal with literature in recognition of its intrapsychic and interpersonal problem-solving function, they need to consider more psychodynamic theory and less of the intricacies of textuality and inter-textuality. This, however, can be demanding personally as obsessional phenomena, for example, are all-pervasive, and we may little like finding them in ourselves, or if found we may shrug them off as unworthy of further attention because they have so nearly become social norms.

Nonetheless, it is in the methodologically exacting and rigorous researches of attachment theorists that the fullest promise of improved practices of child rearing are to be found. As Mary Ainsworth's "strange situation" technique of assessing mother-infant reunion styles becomes more widely known, as Mary Main's "Adult Attachment Interview" develops, and as the work of Patricia Crittenden gains recognition, our understanding of the variables in human nature will greatly improve. With the varieties of "anxious attachment" aligned with early interactions with mother, father, and other caretakers, it will be easier to see that deformations of gender are less fated than programmed as faulty internalization, programmed in ways that might have been different. When this information comes into social awareness, some parents at least will be more sensitive to how children, and boys in particular, are raised. By avoiding confusions, double messages, and impingements on the integrity of the forming personality (instinctual overloading) the pathways to secure gender formation can be cleared. With narcissistic pressures reduced, there will also be less male inclination to control women. As Bowlby writes, "because a child's self model is profoundly influenced by how his mother sees and treats him, whatever she fails to recognize in him he is likely to fail to recognize in himself. In this way . . . major parts of a child's developing personality can become split off from, that is out of communication with, those parts of his personality that his mother recognizes and responds to, which in some cases include features of personality that she is attributing to him wrongly."[8]

Through psychological interpretation of split and repressed male fantasy, the distortions of gender caused by early emotional overloading can be seen for what they are. It is the cumbersome but necessary work of culture to transmit back to us through novels, and the other forms of art, the sources of social distress. Our collective failures of self-recognition, the troubled group fantasies of psychoclasses sharing certain styles of upbringing, are brought into the light of understanding, their power to harm defused. After the manic assertion of anxious maleness we have witnessed in the novel, a reaction of reflective sadness, and relational re-alignment, may occur.

Notes

Chapter 1. Introduction: The Obsessive Imagination in Writers

1. Paul Streitz, "Art and Psychohistory," *Journal of Psychohistory* 10, no. 2 (Fall 1982), p. 254.

2. Quoted in Peter Gay, *Freud: A Life for Our Times* (New York: Doubleday, 1989), p. 92.

3. Quoted in Humberto Nagera, *Obsessional Neuroses: Developmental Psychopathology* (New York: Jason Aronson, 1976), p. 87.

4. Peter Gay writes: "Freud's professions of ignorance [about women] appear almost wilful as though there were some things about women that he did not wish to know." *Freud: A Life*, p. 505.

5. Quoted in Humberto Nagera, *Obsessional Neuroses*, p. 44.

6. *The Portable Jung*, ed. Joseph Campbell (New York: Penguin, 1971) pp. 165–66. In "Aion: Phenomenology of the Self" (1951) the mother-son bond is put in a mythological framework, pp. 148f.

7. Ibid., p. 150. As Marie-Louise von Franz writes in *Puer Aeternus* (Sigo Press, 1981): "The Great Mother makes a religious cult out of her son and then he becomes the dead Tammuz, Adonis, Attis: he replaces the image of God. He is really also the crucified Christ and she is the Virgin Mary crying beside the Cross" p. 17.

8. D. H. Lawrence, *Fantasia of the Unconscious* and *Psychoanalysis and the Unconscious* (London: Penguin, 1971) p. 124f. In *Where D. H. Lawrence Was Wrong about Woman* (Lewisburg, Pa.: Bucknell University Press/ London, Toronto: Associated University Presses, 1992), David Holbrook shows how throughout his writings Lawrence "tends to enlist us in the fear of woman and the impulse to control her" (p. 20). See especially the discussion of *Sons and Lovers*, p. 60f.

For a cross-cultural analysis of maternal ambivalence and narcissism, see Philip E. Slater, *The Glory of Hera: Greek Mythology and the Greek Family* (Boston: Beacon Press, 1968). Slater sees both Greek and American (and presumably recent British) family systems encouraging "a vicarious involvement of the mother in the life of the son" (p. 461). He adds, "I have . . . suggested that maternal overinvestment in the mother-son relationship, a resulting commitment to oedipal fantasies, and a narcissistic orientation to the world, all tend to produce societies which historians would call 'energetic'—restless, fitful, and competitive—and that under optimal conditions this output of energy can lead to what are usually felt to be positive cultural achievements, even if in the majority of cases it leads only to some extremely unpleasant dead ends" (p. 462).

9. Harold I. Kaplan and Benjamin J. Sadock, *Synopsis of Psychiatry* (Baltimore: Williams and Williams, 1988), p. 326.

It is important for those who incline to psychodynamic explanations of obsessional ideation and behavior to realize the severity of challenge from biological psychiatry, with its arguments for genetic and neurochemical origins of disorder. For instance Judith L. Rappoport, M.D., argues for nature over nurture in *The Boy Who Couldn't Stop Washing: The Experience and Treatment of Obsessive-Compulsive Disorder* (New York: E. P. Dutton, 1989). Rappoport claims that severe OCD, such as that displayed by Freud's Rat Man (1909), "must come from an inborn program in the brain," that it is "more like a tic, more like a medical illness than we in the medical professional have believed" (pp. 17, 78). She adds:

> It remains one of the greatest ironies of psychiatry that Obsessive-Compulsive Disorder, the illness most cited to illustrate the fundamental principles of psychoanalysis, should be the disorder that benefits the least from this treatment. (p. 101)

Her treatment of choice is the psychotropic drug Clomipramine (tradename Anafranil), an antidepressant belonging to the tricyclic group. Rappoport is little interested in family studies conducted according to styles of maternal attachment by John Bowlby, Mary Ainsworth, and Mary Main, which take us far beyond Freud's theory of fixation at the anal level. Intrusive and ambivalent modes of maternal attachment raise levels of instinctual stimulation of infants, themselves biochemically programmed for optimal stimulation; in the two-way exchange biochemical susceptibilities in the infant may well be overtaxed with permanent maladaptive results. This possibility is insufficiently studied, nor are the cultural forms of obsession found in artists' concern with confession, relaxation of intellectual control, and expiation for moral excesses.

10. Daniel M. Wegner, *White Bears and Other Unwanted Thoughts: Suppression, Obsession, and the Psychology of Mental Control* (New York: Penguin, 1989), p. 162.

11. Ibid., p. 170.

12. H. R. Beech and S. Perigault, "Towards a Theory of Obsessional Disorders," in *Obsessional States*, ed. H. R. Beech (London: Methuen, 1974), p. 115.

13. Daniel M. Wegner, *White Bears*, p. 165.

14. First endorsed by William McKinley Runyan in *Life Histories and Psychobiography: Explorations in Theory and Method* (New York: Oxford University Press, 1984), the application of attachment theory seems more promising as research advances. See John Bowlby, *A Secure Base: Clinical Applications of Attachment Theory* (London: Routledge, 1988).

15. Patricia M. Crittenden, Mary F. Partridge, and Angelika H. Claussen, "Family Patterns of Relationship in Normative and Dysfunctional Families," *Development and Psychopathology* 4 (1992), p. 504.

16. Kay Redfield Jamison, *Touched With Fire: Manic-Depressive Illness and the Artistic Temperament* (New York: Free Press, 1993), p. 137. See pp. 252–3 for her indecision about the true proportion of genetic, biochemical, and environmental influences on manic-depressive creative personalities.

For a survey of work on bipolar disorder and creativity see Constance Holden, "Creativity and the Troubled Mind," *Psychology Today* (April 1987) pp. 9–10 and chapter 14, Manic-Depressive Illness, Creativity and Leadership," in Frederick K. Goodwin and Kay Redfield Jamison, *Manic-Depressive Illness* (New York: Oxford University Press, 1990).

17. Erwin W. Straus, *On Obsession: A Clinical and Methodological Study* (New York: Nervous and Mental Disease Monographs, 1948) pp. 17, 41f. For an illuminating discussion of Swift and other creative obsessional personalities see Anthony Storr, *The Dynamics of Creation* (London: Secker and Warburg, 1972), p. 72f.

18. Martha Wolfenstein, "The Image of the Lost Parent," *The Psychoanalytic Study of the Child* 28 (1973), p. 444f.

19. Lenore C. Terr, "Childhood Trauma and the Creative Product: A Look at the Early Lives and Later Works of Poe, Wharton, Magritte, Hitchcock, and Bergman," *Psychoanalytic Study of the Child* 42 (1987), p. 545f.

20. Lloyd de Mause, *Foundations of Pyschohistory* (New York: Creative Roots, 1982), pp. 136, 142–43.

21. J. Laplanche and J.-B. Pontalis, *The Language of Psychoanalysis* (New York: W. W. Norton, 1974), p. 281.

22. Robert Burton, *The Anatomy of Melancholy*, vol. 3, ed. Holbrook Jackson (London: J. M. Dent, 1961), p. 149. In "The Dread of Woman" Karen Horney suggests that "Man strives to rid himself of his dread of women by objectifying it," by attribution of the sinister to her. "May not this be one of the principal roots of the whole masculine impulse to creative work—the never-ending conflict between the man's longing for the woman and his dread of her?" (*Feminine Psychology*, New York: W. W. Norton, 1973), p. 135.

23. Otto Rank, *The Don Juan Legend*, ed. David G. Winter (Princeton: Princeton University Press, 1975), p. 109. For further psychological discussion of the more than five hundred known versions of the Don Juan legend see Alice Miller, *Thou Shalt Not Be Aware: Society's Betrayal of the Child* (New York: Meridian, 1984), p. 79f.

24. David G. Winter, *The Power Motive*, (New York: Free Press, 1973), pp. 172–73. Dallis Pratt, M.D., points out in "The Don Juan Myth," *American Imago* 17 (1960) that "machismo" is primarily a reaction against female dominance or identification" (p. 330). In this sense, Don Juan is "the pursued rather than the pursuer" (p. 330), which was Shaw's point. Karl Stern calls Don Juans "hit and run lovers," tied to mother and virtually homosexual, "they are mysteriously compelled to go through this act of conquest and flight in an eternally repetitive experience," *The Flight from Women* (New York: Noonday, 1965), p. 221.

25. Quoted in Nagera, *Obsessional Neurosis*, p. 96.

26. Ibid., p. 88. Anna Freud's rival, Melanie Klein, saw obsessional neurosis arising from reaction to the earliest "danger situation" in which paranoid disturbances are defended against (pp. 99–100).

27. Quoted in Paul L. Adams, *Obsessive Children* (New York: Penguin, 1975), p. 201.

28. Ibid., p. 202.

29. M. Masud R. Khan, *The Privacy of Self* (London: Hogarth Press, 1974), p. 53f.

30. Ibid., p. 55.

31. Ibid., p. 56.

32. In Paul Adams, *Obsessive Children*, pp. 203–4.

33. Heinz Kohut, *The Restoration of the Self* (New York: International Universities Press, 1977), p. 193–94. Apart from the theoretical differences between Kohut and Otto Kernberg, it is worth mentioning the latter's "Barriers to Falling and Remaining in Love," *Journal of the American Psychoanalytic Association* 22 (1974), as a contribution to understanding envy and rage against mothers in boys who develop sadistic wishes. Kernberg examines how the narcissistic personality achieves the "capacity for concern and guilt" that allows "falling in love" to develop into stable "being in love" (p. 510). For a discussion of our "matricidal, depressive, guilt culture" in which mothers are dominant, see John Carroll, *Guilt:*

The Grey Eminence Behind Character, History, and Culture. (London: Routledge and Kegan Paul, 1985).

34. G. Legman, *Love and Death: A Study on Censorship* (New York: Breaking Point, 1949), p. 78.

35. Matthew Besdine, "The Jocasta Complex: Mothering and Genius," part 2, *Psychoanalytic Review* 55 (1968) p. 595. A scale of mothering styles is given by Besdine, "Cradles of Violence," in *The Neurosis of Our Time: Acting Out* (Springfield: Charles C. Thomas, 1973) p. 5. See also his "The Jocasta Complex, Mothering and Woman Geniuses," *Psychoanalytic Review* 58 (1971/2), pp. 574–600.

36. Richard C. Friedman, *Male Homosexuality: A Contemporary Psychoanalytic Perspective* (New Haven: Yale University Press, 1988), p. 67.

37. Matthew Besdine, "The Jocasta Complex, Mothering and Genius," part 1, *Psychoanalytic Review* 55 (1968), p. 271. Further useful studies of this complicated myth are Harold Stewart, "Jocasta's Crimes," *International Journal of Psycho-Analysis* 42 (1961) and John Munder Ross, "Oedipus Revisited: Laius and the 'Laius Complex,'" *Psychoanalytic Study of the Child* 37 (1982), 169.

38. Matthew Besdine, 1, p. 274. See Alice Miller, *Drama of the Gifted Child* (New York: Basic Books, 1981), who speaks of obsessional neurosis as a tormented survival into adulthood of the child's thwarted "true self," p. 87f.

39. Ibid., p. 273. For indications of feminine identification and interest patterns in poets who grew up lacking fathers see Colin Martindale, "Father's Absence, Psychopathology, and Poetic Eminence," *Psychological Reports* 31 (1972), pp. 843–47.

40. Besdine, "Cradles of Violence," in *Neurosis for Our Time*, p. 10.

41. Besdine, 2, p. 577.

42. Henri Ellenberger, *The Discovery of the Unconscious*, (London: Allen Lane, Penguin Press, 1970). See especially p. 447f.

43. Estela V. Welldon, *Mother, Madonna, Whore* (London: Free Association, 1988), p. 65.

44. Ibid., p. 81.

45. Ibid., p. 83. Dr. M. F. Stewart who has read this Introduction comments on this point, drawing on her work with distressed young adults: "I think that the narcissistic issue of the avoidance of humiliation (and often the punishment of *someone* if a humiliation occurs) is central in the functioning of obsessionals and I think that this arises out of repeated humiliations in early childhood, most of which would not be recognized by the surrounding adults. I think that this is frequently the recurring trauma which gives rise to obsessional pathology and it arises out of the mother's profound lack of self-esteem, her tendency to long for/demand rescue from this state from an external source, usually male, and her unconsciously taking the boy child as the repairer of her inadequacy." She adds that although currently politically incorrect, this situation is common clinically (Personal communication).

46. Ibid., p. 83.

47. Christiane Olivier, *Jocasta's Children* (London: Routledge, 1989), p. 40.

48. Ibid., pp. 40–41.

49. Ibid., p. 43.

50. Ibid., p. 64. Fantasies of domination are characteristically male, she argues (p. 88).

51. Ibid., pp. 131, 142. See Valerie Monroe, "The Erotic Image that Unnerves Women Most," *Self* (September 1988). "From birth a boy has his mother's heart on a string—and the pulls can be disturbingly strong" p. 108.

52. Dorothy Dinnerstein, *The Mermaid and The Minotaur: Sexual Arrangements and Human Malaise* (New York: Harper and Row, 1977), p. xii.

53. Ibid., pp. 5–6. Pleas for reform of parenting as shared by mother and father are found in such popular books as Jane Swigart's *The Myth of the Bad Mother: The Emotional Realities of Mothering* (New York: Doubleday, 1991) See especially pp. 250–1.

54. Ibid., p. 69. See also pp. 100–1. See David Holbrook, "The Symbolism of Woman," in *Images of Women in Literature* (New York: New York University Press, 1989) for evidence of the pervasiveness of images as split good and evil attributed to women in literature.

55. Ibid., p. 72.

56. Ibid., p. 205.

57. Robert J. Stoller, *Perversion, the Erotic Form of Hatred* (New York: Pantheon, 1975), p. 150.

58. John Leopold Weil, *Instinctual Stimulation of Children: From Common Practice to Child Abuse* vol. 1, (Madison, Ct.: International Universities Press, 1989), p. 9.

59. Ibid., vol. 1, p. 31. (See tables p. 14f, and pp. 91–93.)

60. Ibid., p. 74.

61. Ibid., See vol. 1, p. 41f.

62. Ibid., See vol. 1, p. 239f.

63. Leonard L. Glass, "Man's Man/ Ladies' Man," *Psychiatry* 47 (August 1984), p. 274. For focus on narcissism see Otto F. Kernberg's "Barriers to Falling and Remaining in Love," *Journal of the American Psychoanalytic Association* 22 (1974), 486.

64. Ibid., pp. 262–63. In *The Don Juan Dilemma* (New York: William Morrow, 1989), Jane F. Carpineto distinguishes four types of parent-son relationship that may lead to womanizing: (1) son abandoned by mother (2) son overattached to mother (3) son disapproved of by both parents (4) son unattached to either parent (p. 123f). It can be suggested that these configurations are not always mutually exclusive, intergrading in some cases, with (2) the commonest element in the subjects under study.

65. Ibid., p. 265.

66. Ibid., p. 274.

67. Peter Trachtenberg, *The Casanova Complex: Compulsive Lovers and their Women* (New York: Poseidon Press, 1988), p. 19.

68. Ibid., p. 216.

69. Ibid., pp. 188, 188–89, 191, 192, 193.

70. Ibid., p. 201.

Chapter 2. H. G. Wells: The Confessions of a Sexual Rebel

1. H. G. Wells, *H. G. Wells in Love: Postscript to an Experiment in Autobiography* (London: Faber, 1984), p. 222.

2. St Augustine, *The Confessions,* trans. E. B. Pusey (London: Dent, 1957) p. 51.

3. Theodor Reik, *The Compulsion to Confess: On the Psychoanalysis of Crime and Punishment* (New York: Farrar, Straus and Cudahy, 1959), p. 205.

4. Peter Kemp, *H. G. Wells and the Culminating Ape: Biological Themes and Imaginative Obsessions* (London: Macmillan, 1982), p. 77.

5. J. R. Hammond, *An H. G. Wells Companion* (New York: Barnes and Noble, 1979), p. 169. See *H. G. Wells in Love*, ed. G. P. Wells (London: Faber, 1984), p. 201f, for Wells's thoughts on temptation to suicide.

6. H. G. Wells, *Experiment in Autobiography: Discoveries and Conclusions of a Very Ordinary Brain* (London: Victor Gollancz, 1966), p. 79. Wells was thinking of Freud's idea of the Oedipus complex of which he first wrote in *The Interpretation of Dreams* (1900); Wells seems to have read *Three Essays on the Theory of Sexuality* (1905), especially chapter 2 on infantile sexuality.

Wells's own attempt to theorize about sexual development does not get very far: "For the normally constituted human being there must be two contrasted types of phase, fixation upon an individual as one end of the series and complete promiscuity of attention and interest as the other. Anyone, at any time, may be in one or other phase, or moving from one to the other. We are not monogamic by nature, or promiscuous by nature, but some of us happen to get *fixed* for longer or shorter periods" (*Experiment in Autobiography*, p. 425).

There had been little suggestion in theory at this time that the affect-starved mother might have something to do with later promiscuity. That emerges most persuasively in Mathew Besdine, "The Jocasta Complex, Mothering and Genius," *Psychoanalytic Review* 55 (1968), parts 1 and 2, and in the article by Leonard L. Glass (see n. 24).

7. Wells, *Experiment in Autobiography*, p. 22.

8. Ibid., p. 25.

9. Ibid., p. 47.

10. Ibid., p. 67.

11. Ibid., p. 69.

12. Ibid., p. 58.

13. Norman and Jeanne MacKenzie, *The Time Traveller: The Life of H. G. Wells* (London: Weidenfeld and Nicolson, 1973), p. 15.

14. Jeanne MacKenzie, "Introduction to H. G. Wells," *Ann Veronica* (London: Virago, 1984), p. i.

15. MacKenzie, *The Time Traveller*, p. 16.

16. Wells, *Experiment in Autobiography*, p. 64.

17. MacKenzie, *The Time Traveller*, pp. 20–21.

18. Wells, *Experiment in Autobiography*, p. 64.

19. Ibid., p. 66.

20. MacKenzie, *The Time Traveller*, p. 21.

21. Anthony West, *H. G. Wells: Aspects of a Life* (London: Hutchinson, 1984), pp. 180–81.

22. Lovat Dickson, *H. G. Wells: His Turbulent Life and Times* (Toronto: Macmillan, 1969), p. 315.

23. Wells, *H. G. Wells in Love*, p. 197.

24. Leonard L. Glass, "Man's Man/Ladies' Man: Motifs of Hypermasculinity," *Psychiatry* 47 (1984), p. 263.

25. Ibid., p. 265.

26. Wells, *H. G. Wells in Love*, p. 16.

27. Ibid., p. 17.

28. Ibid., p. 60.

29. Ibid., pp. 53–54.

30. Ibid., p. 56.

31. Ibid., p. 55.

32. Ibid., p. 56.

33. Ibid., p. 60.

34. Ibid., p. 113.

35. John Fowles, *Mantissa* (Toronto: Collins, 1982), pp. 85, 148.

36. MacKenzie, *The Time Traveller*, pp. 250–51.

37. Ibid., p. 83.

38. H. G. Wells, *In the Days of the Comet* (New York: Airmont, 1966), p. 30. Further page references to the novel are given in the text.

39. Wells, *H. G. Wells in Love*, p. 83.

40. MacKenzie, *The Time Traveller*, p. 248.

41. H. G. Wells, *Ann Veronica* (London: Virago, 1980), p. 250. Further page references to the novel are given in the text.

42. Wells, *H. G. Wells in Love*, p. 53; H. G. Wells, *The New Machiavelli* (Penguin Books, 1985) p. 359. Further references to the novel are given in the text.

43. Juliette Huxley, *Leaves of the Tulip Tree* (London: John Murray, 1986), p. 114. Anthony Storr writes that "C. P. Snow records his talking with Wells about suicide; and my own guess would have been that Wells used new sexual conquests as a defence against depression which was liable to descend upon him when he was unoccupied. He seems always to have exhibited a frantic need for activity—whether writing, playing games or seducing women." (Letter to me of 1 February 1993).

44. David C. Smith, *H. G. Wells: Desperately Mortal* (Yale University Press, 1986), p. 375.

45. Vincent Brome, *H. G. Wells: A Biography* (London: Longmans, Green, 1951), p. 112.

Chapter 3. Hermann Hesse and Bisexuality

1. Hermann Hesse, "Life Story Briefly Told," in *Autobiographical Writings* (New York: Farrar, Straus and Giroux, 1972), pp. 43–44. Pietism began as a late seventeenth-century movement in the Lutheran church away from dogma and hierarchy toward Biblical precepts and religion of the heart; rigid by Hesse's time, it nonetheless helped legitimize religious experience.

2. Hermann Hesse, "A Child's Heart" (1919/20) in *Klingsor's Last Summer* (New York: Harper and Row, 1971), pp. 7–8.

3. Hesse, "Childhood of the Magician," in *Autobiographical Writings*, p. 3.

4. Ibid., p. 7.

5. Ibid., p. 9. See p. 16 for a more balanced view of parent and grandfather.

6. Hermann Hesse, "Casanova," in *My Belief* (London: Triad/Panther, 1978), pp. 305, 308.

7. Hesse, "Life Story Briefly Told," pp. 59–60.

8. Ralph Freedman, *Hermann Hesse: Pilgrim of Crisis* (New York: Pantheon, 1978), p. 16. Hesse calls her "the epitome of liveliness" in "Childhood of the Magician," p. 16. Alice Miller's discussion of Hesse's intense relations with his mother supports the obsessive and narcissistic interpretation of his personality; however, Miller neglects the father's role. *Drama of the Gifted Child* (New York: Basic Books, 1981), pp. 84f.

9. Ibid., p. 22.

10. Ibid., p. 19.

11. Ibid., p. 19.

12. Ibid., p. 21.

13. Hesse, "Childhood of the Magician," p. 16.

14. See Sandor Rado, "A Critical Examination of the Concept of Bisexuality," *Psychosomatic Medicine*, II no. 4 (October 1940), 459.

15. Quoted in Volker Michels, *Hermann Hesse: A Pictorial Biography* (New York: Farrar, Straus and Giroux, 1971) p. 119.

16. Miriam Reik, "Translator's Introduction" to Hesse's "Artist and Psychoanalyst," *Psychoanalytic Review,* 50 no. 3 (1963), p. 5. Ralph Freedman, *Hesse: Pilgrim of Crisis,* p. 184.

17. Ibid., p. 184. Hermann's mother recorded in her diary for 1889 that Hermann's doctor had given him electrical shock treatments for pain in his limbs.

18. Joseph Milech, *Hermann Hesse: Life and Art* (Berkeley: University of California: 1978), p. 107f.

19. Hesse, "Artist and Psychoanalyst," pp. 9–10.

20. Hermann Hesse, *Demian,* (London: Panther, 1969), p. 7. Further page references are given in the text. Of *Demian,* Martin Green writes "This novel was published in 1918 and had great international success. By 1925 it had sold 140,000 copies, and was translated into every literary language. It formed part of that literary propaganda for eroticism which was so prevalent at that moment; in English literature one can point to Maugham's story "Rain" and Lawrence's stories like "Sun" as parts of the same project. In an earlier version, Hauptmann's novel [Der Ketzer von Soana] was entitled *Die Syrische Gottin* [The Syrian Goddess], one of the titles of Magna Mater, the Great Mother, then current. Lawrence spoke of Syria Dea in *Women in Love,* his 1920 novel, which echoes the ideas of Ascona. Otto Gross, the Asconian psychiatrist, was trying to restore the cult of Astarte in his last years, 1918 to 1920." Martin Green, *Mountain of Truth: The Counter Culture Begins, Ascona, 1900–1920,* Hanover and London: University Press of New England for Tufts University, 1986), pp. 4–5. As Green explains, the Asconans (especially Otto Gross) impeached modern man for his violence against women, enthroning Magna Mater on the sacred mountain of Truth. Hermann Hesse was associated with this movement using its mythology worked out in *Demian,* as a way of solving his own intrapsychic problems.

It is interesting that from J. J. Bachofen's study of matriarchy, *The Law of the Mothers* (1861) onward, German culture should be so preoccupied with idealizing and compensating the wronged mother when it was Germany that produced Europe's most aggressively masculinized army, culminating in that which fought the Second World War under the Nazi banner. Hesse's fiction reflects this group fantasy yet is remarkable for its ability to see war making as a false solution.

21. Alexander Mitscherlich, *Society without the Father* (New York: Schocken, 1970), p. 141.

22. Ralph Freedman, *Hermann Hesse: Pilgrim of Crisis,* p. 53.

23. Previously in his troubles "my mother's amiability brought me no comfort; it was heavy and distressing" (*Demian,* p. 22). Significantly, Sinclair confesses stealing from his mother's money box to pay tribute money to Kromer (p. 43)— leading to a temporary family reconciliation.

24. Hesse's apotheosis of Eva as a goddess may owe something to the trend in German culture toward replacing Christianity with paganism as indeed *Demian*'s teaching of the Abraxas cult seemed to do. As Martin Green writes, Gerhard Hauptmann's popular novel *Der Ketzer von Soana* [The Heretic of Soana] finds a Catholic priest leaving Christ for Eros and enjoying the sexual favors of a female child of nature (*Mountain of Truth,* p. 4f).

25. C. G. Jung, "A Letter on Hesse's Inspiration" (March 24, 1950), *Psychoana-*

lytic Review 50 no. 3 (1963), p. 15. Hesse's own comment was that after reading a number of Jung's books between 1916 and 1922, his interest waned, and in any case he had been more impressed by Freud's writings. In 1950 he recalled that while he had a "fine impression" of Jung, "I began to see that for analysts a genuine relationship to art is unattainable: they all lack the sense for it"; in his essay on "Artist and Psychoanalyst" he had certainly not praised analysts for special insights into art, acknowledging only what analysis could teach artists. Nevertheless, Hesse continued to appreciate Jung's unique insights as an interpreter of symbols.

26. Hermann Hesse, "Back to the Womb," in *Crisis, Pages from a Diary*, trans. Ralph Manheim (New York: Farrar, Straus and Giroux, 1975), p. 21. The poem may owe something to Jung's *Symbols of Transformation* (1912).

27. Hermann Hesse, *Steppenwolf* (New York: Bantam, 1970), p. 22. Further page references to the novel are given in the text.

28. In "For Marulla" (1953) in *Autobiographical Writings*, a memorial to his just buried sister (and a tribute to his father's sainthood) he speaks of the "painful warmth around the heart that I felt in conjuring up the irrecoverable" (p. 262). Adele is called "the creature of fantasy with her love of festivity and great hunger for beauty" while Marulla was "soberer, cooler, more critical, but always ready for fun" (p. 264).

29. See Klaus Theweleit, *Male Fantasies*, 2 vol. (Minneapolis: University of Minneapolis Press, 1987), vol. 1, pp. 22–3.

30. Bisexuality is used descriptively rather than to write Hesse's psychobiography. Not only is a sufficiently detailed account of Hesse's parenting lacking, psychological studies of bisexuality are too few to support speculations. For the complications surrounding the study of male bisexuality see Ron Langevin, *Sexual Strands: Understanding and Treating Sexual Anomalies in Men* (Hillside, N.J.: Lawrence Erlbaum Associates, 1983).

31. The comment on p. 102 "You must be difficult if nobody sticks to you" is relevant.

32. Possibly this image is derived from Thomas Hood's comic poem "Miss Kilmansegg and her Precious Leg" in which the lady in question makes "a model, in small, of her Precious Leg." *The Poetical Works of Thomas Hood* (London: Henry Frowde), p. 578.

33. Of course he is also killing "my distant, angry love, my poor [Erika]," p. 160.

34. The violent attack on Hermine must be taken seriously: it is not just imaginary. As Eugene Stelzig remarks: "the violence or the impulse is real enough (in *Klein and Wagner*). Klein's temptation to murder the sleeping Teresina and the *Crisis* persona's confession of having stabbed to death his beloved Erika Maria Ruth (the last two names match those of Hesse's first and second wives) are vividly realized in this bloodly nightmare." Eugene L. Stelzig, *Hermann Hesse's Fiction of the Self: Autobiography and the Confessional Imagination* (Princeton: Princeton University Press, 1988) p. 221. Stelzig also reminds us of the "recurring nightmare" of a "murderous assault" on the father displaced from Hesse to Sinclair to Kromer in *Demain*, p. 150. These are not just attacks on anima and animus but indirectly on Hesse's actual parents, p. 216.

35. See Michael Lach Fleischer, "Twin Fantasies, Bisexuality and Creativity in the Works of Ernest Hemingway," *International Review of Psychoanalysis* 17 (1990), p. 287f.

36. Quoted in Eugene L. Stelzig, *Hermann Hesse's Fiction of the Self: Autobiography and the Confessional Imagination*, p. 233.

37. Edmund Remys, *Hermann Hesse's Das Glasperlenspiel: A Concealed Defense of the Mother World*. (New York: Peter Lang, 1983), pp. 170–73. See Erich Neumann, *The Great Mother: An Analysis of the Archetype* (Princeton: Princeton University Press, 1955), p. 148f; Bram Dijkstra, *Idols of Perversity: Fantasies of Feminine Evil in Fin-de-Siecle Culture* (New York: Oxford University Press, 1986), pp. 359f.

38. See Erich Neumann, *The Great Mother: An Analysis of the Archetype*, p. 150f. See also Bram Dijkstra, *Idols of Perversity*, p. 359f.

Michel Leiris's *Manhood: A Journey From Childhood into the Fierce Order of Viriliy*, completed in 1935, is another literary rendering of the split female archetype who both attracts and repels. Together Lucrece and Judith are death dealing, the one a suicide, the other a murderer of men. Leiris's goal in the confession of personal experience was to liquidate "certain obsessions whose weight oppressed me" (p. 14), a literary continuation of psychoanalytic treatment by which he had hoped to overcome his obsession with guilt and punishment.

A post-World War I example, belonging to the same despairing frame of mind as Hesse's *Steppenwolf*, *Manhood* probes the male obsession with women as sorceress: "I both desired and feared her, the enchantress containing all sweetness, but also concealing all danger" (pp. 90–1). Impotence, bisexual desire, and suicidal ideation disturb him.

Chapter 4. Love and Death in Vladimir Nabokov's *Lolita*

1. Vladimir Nabokov, *Lectures on Literature*, ed. Fredson Bowers (New York: Harcourt Brace Jovanovich/ Bruccoli Clark, 1981), p. 251.

2. Elizabeth Ward, *Father Daughter Rape* (London: The Women's Press, 1984); Judith Herman, M.D., Diana Russell, Ph.D., and Karen Trocki, Ph.D. "Long-term Effects of Incestuous Abuse in Children," *American Journal of Psychiatry* 143 no. 10 (October), 1986. Successive books by the ex-psychoanalyst Alice Miller trace the emergence of childhood trauma as the central issue in both later psychopathology and creativity. See especially *The Untouched Key: Tracing Childhood Trauma in Creativity and Destructiveness* (New York: Doubleday, 1990), *Banished Knowledge: Facing Childhood Injuries* (New York: Doubleday, 1990) and *Breaking down the Wall of Silence: The Liberating Experience of Facing Painful Truth* (New York: Dutton, 1991).

3. Brian Boyd, *Vladimir Nabokov: The Russian Years* (Princeton: Princeton University Press, 1990), p. 10.

4. Ibid., p. 5; see also p. 336 for "his own idyllic childhood." In *Vladimir Nabokov: The American Years* (Princeton: Princeton University Press, 1991), Boyd asserts that in writing *Speak, Memory: An Autobiography Revisited*, Nabokov was in "total command of the past"—very doubtful from a psychodynamic view, and probably an impossibility even for the most thoroughly analyzed of persons, p. 153. Boyd riskily takes Nabokov's part in dismissing psychoanalysis arguing that Nabokov had such "an extraordinarily precise memory of his early childhood that he had good reason to trust better than Freud's, and an abnormally sharp eye for the unique patterns of his own life." Boyd adds that Nabokov "detested the way Freud befouled something he held as precious as family love," pp. 160–1.

5. Quoted by J. P. Shute, "Nabokov and Freud: The Play of Power," *Modern Fiction Studies* 30 no. 4 (1984), p. 637.

6. Ibid., p. 644. Digs at psychoanalysis are found, for example, on pages 75, 105, 115, 116, 143, 152–53, 162, 234, 250, 261, and 275 of *Lolita* (New York: Berkeley Medallion Books, 1966). As Jeffery Berman writes: "Nabokov's virulence [against Freud] is astonishing and unsoftened by time. The invective is bitter, mirthless, and unprecedented. It is as if Freud is the central figure in Nabokov's life, always shadowing the novelist." (*The Talking Cure: Literary Representations of Psychoanalysis* [New York: New York University Press, 1987], p. 213). Berman rightly observes that this virulence is "obsessive," that is defensive (p. 219). In *Freud and Nabokov* (Lincoln: University of Nebraska Press, 1988), Geoffery Green likens Nabokov's case study of obsessive Humbert Humbert to Freud's study of the "Rat Man," suggesting that Nabokov thought of art as "a special kind of obsessional neurosis," a sexualized narrative that he both cherished and wished to be rid (p. 104).

7. Vladimir Nabokov, *Lolita*, (New York: Berkeley Medallion, 1966), p. 7. Further page references to the novel are given in the text.

8. Nabokov's cunning psychology of narcissism is filled out by having Lolita's brother die at age two when she was four—making her the sole object of her mother's care (p. 65).

9. In Greek mythology nymphs, who often guarded springs, had supernatural powers. As divinities of birth, they brought up heroes who shared in supernatural powers. But they also stole children and so were feared as well as venerated. Whoever saw a nymph emerging from water at midday went mad with a nympholeptic mania. Mircea Eliade, *Patterns in Comparative Religion* (Cleveland and New York: Meridian, 1963), pp. 204–5. See *Lolita*, p. 18.

10. Alfred Appel, Jr., "Lolita: The Springboard of Parody," *Wisconsin Studies in Contemporary Literature* VIII no. 2 (1967), pp. 219, 222, 236.

11. Norman Kiell, *Varieties of Sexual Experience: Psychosexuality in Literature* (New York: International Universities Press, 1976), chapter 11. [See also Lewis Carroll, *Alice's Adventures in Wonderland and Through the Looking Glass*, (Toronto: Bantam, 1981), pp. 64–65]. The Narcissus theme, connecting Carroll to Nabokov, is studied by Morris Fraser in *The Death of Narcissus* (London: Secker and Warbury, 1976), p. 178f.

12. Quoted in Bram Dijkstra, *Idols of Perversity: Fantasies of Feminine Evil in Fin-de-Siecle Culture* (New York: Oxford University Press, 1986), p. 189. Dijkstra shows how much exploitation of female innocence went on in the fantasy of late nineteenth-century European painters and writers. Images of loss of innocence are frequent, as in Edvard Munch's moving painting "Puberty." But Munch's compassionate realism is not the only rule, with many suggestively seductive pictures of children. Dijkstra writes that such images "represent the marketing of an aggression that dare not speak its name" (p. 191).

13. Alfred Appel, Jr., "An Interview with Vladimir Nabokov," *Wisconsin Studies in Contemporary Literature* VIII 2 (1967), pp. 142–43.

14. Vladimir Nabokov, *The Enchanter*, translated by Dmitri Nabokov (New York: G. P. Putnam's Sons, 1986), pp. 82–83. Could the reminiscence of his "Riviera love," Annabel, whose "juvenile breasts I had fondled one immortal day," be engaging feelings as far back as those for Olga (*Lolita*, p. 38)? Nabokov considered that the little girl in "The Magician" (and presumably also in *The Enchanter*) "wasn't alive. She hardly spoke. Little by little I managed to give her some semblance of reality." Alfred Appel, Jr., ed., *Vladimir Nabokov: The Annotated Lolita* (New York: McGraw Hill, 1970), p. lix.

15. Andrew Field, *The Life and Art of Vladimir Nabokov* (New York: Crown

Publications, 1986), p. 27. Boyd, however, says that Nabokov and his sisters were brought up "the old way, completely separately, and attention remained on young Vladimir," *Vladimir Nabokov: The Russian Years*, p. 44. Of his younger sister Olga, Boyd remarks that Nabokov "had never been close" to her (*Vladimir Nabokov: The American Years*, p. 388), lending no support to the possibility raised here of guilt-causing intimacy with his two sisters, as is suggested by the "fugitive flame" in *Ada*, pp. 279–82.

16. Images of monsters and beasts are frequent in the novel: see, for example, pp. 43, 78, 115, 129, 176, 235, 245, 250.

17. Boyd, *Vladimir Nabokov: The Russian Years*, p. 45.

18. Vladimir Nabokov, *Speak Memory* (New York: Wideview/ Perigree Books, 1966), p. 203. Interest in the sexuality of female preadolescents appears to trace Nabokov's childhood experiences more than it does his reading. Fascination with pedophila can certainly be found in Russian fiction Nabokov might have known, for instance in Fyodor Sologub's *The Petty Demon* (1905–7). While it may be that Nabokov's "final push in the the birth of *Lolita*'s central theme" was reading the anonymous Russian *Confessions of Victor X*, this lurid account of attraction to the sexuality of very young girls should not be taken as the novel's source. Donald Rayfield, ed., *The Confessions of Victor X* (London: Caliban Books, 1984), p. 141.

19. Vladimir Nabokov, *Ada or Ardor: A Family Chronicle* (New York: Vintage, 1990), p. 151. In *Vladimir Nabokov: The American Years*, Bryan Boyd asserts that Nabokov's powers of "choice" and "artistic control" in *Ada*'s "luxuriant fantasy" should not be questioned, pp. 553, 568. Because Nabokov used "code" (p. 544) for Van and Ada's incestuous relationship, it is assumed that he fully understood what was behind the "obvious obscurity"; Boyd does not consider that Nabokov was courageously discovering, and reconstructing, long repressed, intensely charged childhood memories of traumatic events.

20. Ibid., p. 281.

21. Nabokov, *Ada or Ardor: A Family Chronicle*, p. 588.

22. Ibid., p. 485.

23. See also p. 206 for dismembered store models; p. 215 for "Boschian cripples." Dolly is "crucified" (p. 346), her life "broken" (p. 254).

24. Nabokov, *Speak, Memory: An Autobiography Revisited*, p. 25. Boyd remarks that Nabokov's mother was "always . . . an eager accomplice in his artistic development" (*Nabokov: The Russian Years*, p. 52).

25. Ibid., p. 36.

26. Ibid., p. 257.

27. Field, *The Life and Art of Vladimir Nabokov*, p. 30.

28. Ibid., p. 26. His mother is said to have become physically ill when she went a week without a letter from Vladimir. This may reflect his having been brought up "on a mixture of coddling and starched-collar stiffness," *Vladimir Nabokov: The Russian Years*, p. 42.

29. "The Strong Opinions of Vladimir Nabokov—as imparted to Nicholas Garnham," *The Listener* 80 (10 October 1968), p. 463.

30. "Vladimir Nabokov on his Life and Work: A BBC television interview with Peter Duval Smith," *The Listener* 68 (22 November 1962, p. 857. He admits to reading newspaper accounts of "elderly gentlemen who seduced little girls," "but Lolita is a figment of my imagination."

31. Vladimir Nabokov, *Speak, Memory: An Autobiography Revisited*, pp. 25–26. In "On a Book Entitled *Lolita*," Nabokov noted that in about 1903 he acquired

English from his first governess in St. Petersburg, Miss Rachel Home. *Lolita*, p. 283.

32. Field, *The Life and Art of Vladimir Nabokov*, p. 29.

33. John Bowlby, *A Secure Base: Clinical Applications of Attachment Theory* (London: Routledge, 1988), p. 124.

34. "Vladimir Nabokov on his Life and Work," *The Listener* 68 (22 November 1962), p. 857. To Alain Robbe-Grillet Nabokov said that *Lolita* was "a certain problem" that he wanted to solve elegantly and economically. (Field, *The Life and Art of Vladimir Nabokov*, p. 319) Did Nabokov sense a pedophile interest in Robbe-Grillet's own work or vice versa? (See book review of *Ghosts in the Mirror* in *The Observer* 44 (20 November 1988). Nabokov told Alvin Toffler that a major difficulty in writing *Lolita* was that "I did not know any American 12-year-old girls, and I did not know America; I had to invent America and Lolita." (*Playboy* [January 1964], p. 38.

35. "A Blush of Colour—Nabokov in Montreux," "Robert Robinson interviewed Vladimir Nabokov for 'The Book Programme' (BBC2)," *The Listener* 97 (24 March 1977), p. 369.

36. Alvin Toffler, "Playboy Interview: Vladimir Nabokov," *Playboy* (January 1964), p. 37. For Nabokov art subsumed sex, rather than sublimating it. (See Boyd, *Vladimir Nabokov: The Russian Years*, p. 109). Yet in his youth, Don Juan sexuality was very much on Nabokov's mind, requiring art to contain it. Boyd alludes to "conquests" of many girls, but he denies any psychological implications. Ibid., p. 97. Nabokov is seen to be "normal," "committed to faithful love after a youth of energetic sexual adventure." "He had a fascination for human perversity, for the insane, the cruel, the sexually deviant," extrapolating bizarre characters such as Humbert "from his personality" (Ibid., pp. 4–5).

37. Kiell, *Varieties of Sexual Experience: Psychosexuality in Literature*, p. 510.

38. Field, *The Life and Art of Vladimir Nabokov*, pp. 326–27.

39. Ibid., p. 26. Both biographers Andrew Field and Brian Boyd were aware of a "Don Juan list" that Nabokov made of his early sexual conquests.

40. Ibid., p. 319

41. Martha Wolfenstein, "The Image of the Lost Parent," *The Psychoanalytic Study of the Child* 28 (1973). His mother committed suicide when Magritte was 13 (p. 445).

42. Stanislas Klossowski de Rola, *Balthus* (New York: Harper and Row, 1983), p. 7. Many of Balthus's nymphet paintings have a cat as a leering voyeur, suggestively standing in for the artist himself.

43. "Vladimir Nabokov on his Life and Work," *The Listener* 68 (22 November 1962), p. 858. In *Freud and Nabokov* (Lincoln: University of Nebraska Press, 1988) Geoffrey Green notes the possible inauthenticity of Nabokov's intention "to construct in the presence of my audience the semblance of what I hope is a plausible and not altogether displeasing personality" (p. 3).

44. See Sigmund Freud, *Introductory Lectures on Psycho-analysis (1916–17)*, part 3, lec. 20: The Sexual Life of Human Beings, *SE*, XVI, 303.

45. Robert J. Stoller, *Perversion: The Erotic Form of Hatred* (New York: Pantheon Books, 1975). See chapter 6, which takes issue with Freud's formulation above (especially pp. 101–2).

46. Vladimir Nabokov, *Speak, Memory: An Autobiography Revisited*, p. 123. Boyd points out that Nabokov's mother Elena was "always of a nervous disposition" and "she seems to have been deeply troubled . . . by her parents' ailing health

during the time she was pregnant with Sergy." (Boyd, *Vladimir Nabokov: The Russian Years*, p. 43.)

47. Field, *The Art and Life of Vladimir Nabokov*, p. 319. Dmitri Nabokov contests this claim in his comments on *The Enchanter* (New York: G. P. Putnam's Sons, 1986) pp. 107–8.

48. Nabokov, *Speak, Memory: An Autobiography Revisited*, p. 126.

49. Alfred Appel, Jr., "Nabokov: A Portrait," *Atlantic Monthly* (September 1971), p. 85. See *Lolita*, p. 284.

50. Ibid., p. 85. When Appel prompted Nabokov to speak of memory he said: "imagination is a form of memory. . . . An image depends on the power of association and association is supplied and prompted by memory." *Interview* (1967), p. 140.

51. "A Blush of Colour—Nabokov in Montreux," *The Listener* 97 (24 March 1977) p. 368. For butterfly hunting associated with an arousing young girl see *Speak, Memory: An Autobiography Revisited*, p. 210f.

52. Alfred Appel, "Nabokov: A Portrait," p. 88. (See *Speak, Memory: An Autobiography Revisited*, p. 65).

53. Field, *Life and Art of Vladimir Nabokov*, p. 323–24.

54. Appel, Jr., *Vladimir Nabokov: The Annotated Lolita*, pp. xxxvi–xxxvii.

55. Field, *Life and Art of Vladimir Nabokov*, p. 317.

56. Erica Jong, "Time Has Been Kind to the Nymphet: Lolita 30 Years Later," *The New York Times Book Review*, 5 June 1988, p. 3. Nabokov's Russian novel *Camera Obscura* (1932) translated by Nabokov as *Laughter in the Dark* (1938) and *Look at the Harlequins!* (1974) should also be considered in connection with interest in young girls. According to Boyd, Nabokov got the idea for "The Enchanter" from another author, "developing into a novella Boris Shchyogolev's idea for a novel about a man who marries in the hope of securing access to his stepdaughter-to-be." (*Nabokov: The Russian Years*, p. 520).

57. Nabokov, *Speak, Memory*, p. 87.

58. Ibid., p. 163. Attribution of nympholepsy to loss of Annabel is a cleverly placed false etiology, leaving the way open for such suggestions as this one.

59. Vladimir Nabokov, *Speak, Memory*, p. 178.

60. Ibid., p. 211.

61. Ibid., p. 240. The young girls are also aggregated and conflated as images of desire. See pages 212–13.

62. As a step in the fantasy analysis of *Lolita*, the use of love and death imagery has been briefly explored through the frequency of emotive word use.

Table 1

Conjunction of Love and Death Imagery in *Lolita*

	Times Word Mentioned	Percentage of Emotive Words/Phases
Love	115	21.9
Die	97	18.4
Beauty	61	11.6
Dark	55	10.5
Lovely	43	8.2

	Times Word Mentioned	Percentage of Emotive Words/Phases
Enchanted	35	6.7
Light	34	6.5
Perfect	33	6.3
Pretty	30	5.7
Mad	23	4.4
Total	526	100

"Love" and "die" are the most frequently used emotive words in the set shown in Table 1. They occur approximately twice as often as "beauty," "dark" and "lovely," and approximately three to five times as often as the remainder of the tabulated words. Thus, despite their simplicity, they must be considered powerful image-making tools for Nabokov. The words *love* and *die* form a positive-negative pair in terms of their common English usage and connotation: they each occur at approximately the same frequency in *Lolita*, 21.9 percent and 18.4 percent respectively. Likewise, "beauty" and "dark" form a positive-negative pair, and again their frequency of appearance is approximately the same at 11.6 percent and 10.5 percent respectively. It is possible that the 'union' of these opposites represents an unconscious emotional ambivalence in Nabokov revealed at the fundamental level of word usage. The imagery in this novel is consistently bizarre, contorted, and violent.

63. Alfred Appel, Jr., *Vladimir Nabokov: The Annotated Lolita*, (New York: McGraw-Hill, 1970), p. 438. See *Lolita*, pp. 282–83 for the caged ape.

64. Boyd, *Vladimir Nabokov: The Russian Years*, p. 44.

65. Ibid., p. 52.

66. Ibid., p. 69.

67. Charles W. Socarides, M.D., *The Preoedipal Origin and Psychoanalytic Therapy of Sexual Perversions* (Madison, Ct: International Universities Press, 1988), p. 449.

68. Ibid., p. 449.

69. Richard von Krafft-Ebing, *The Psychopathia Sexualis* (London: Panther, 1965), p. 99.

70. Kiell, *Varieties of Sexual Experience: Psychosexuality in Literature.*, p. 506. It should not be surprising that the child pornography trade uses the name "Lolita" to describe female children whose magazine and video images are offered for sale to addicts. The sordid story of pornography for pedophiles is told by Tim Tate in C. Itzin, ed., *Pornography: Women, Violence and Civil Liberties* (New York: Oxford University Press, 1993), p. 203f.

71. Beth Ann Bassien, *Women and Death: Linkages in Western Thought and Literature.* (Westport, Ct.: Greenwood Press, 1984), p. 40.

72. Simon Karlinsky ed., *The Nabokov-Wilson Letters, 1940–1971* (New York: Harper and Row, 1979), letter of 29 February 1956, p. 298.

Chapter 5. Female Sacrifice in the Novels of John Fowles

1. Fowles is acutely aware of shifts of values in our time: "We have in our own century lost all faith in the remembrance of God's praises. The profit now

is tallied in personal pleasure; but we remain puritan in our adamant pursuit of it. . . . It is all very well creating a permissive society. But we have not created the essential corollary of a pagan mind," he wrote in *Islands* (Boston: Little, Brown, 1978), pp. 105–6.

2. Heinz Kohut, *The Restoration of the Self* (New York: International Universities Press, 1977), pp. 206–7.

3. In *American Imago,* 29 no. 2 (Summer 1972), p. 169. As Fowles writes in "Hardy and the Hag," the artist tries to "recover . . . the early oneness with the mother that granted [his] ability to make the world mysteriously and deliciously change meaning and appearance. He was once a magician with a wand; and given the right other predisposing and environmental factors, he will one day devote his life to trying to regain the unity and the power by recreating adult versions of the experience . . . he will be an artist." Lance St. John Butler, ed., *Thomas Hardy After Fifty Years* (London: MacMillan, 1977), p. 31. Note how close Fowles's statement is to Hesse's in "Childhood of the Magician" (1923).

4. Fowles, *Islands,* p. 59. See also "Hardy and the Hag," p. 33. The theory of creative art as symbolic repair for early loss of a parent was set forth by Andrew Brink in *Loss and Symbolic Repair* (Hamilton, Ont.: Cromlech, 1977), just before Fowles's observation.

5. David North, "Interview with Author John Fowles," *Maclean's* 80 no. 23 (14 November 1977), p. 4.

6. Michael Millgate, *Thomas Hardy: A Biography* (New York: Oxford University Press, 1982), pp. 22–23. See also Fowles, "Hardy and the Hag," p. 39.

7. Fowles, "Hardy and the Hag," p. 29.

8. John Fowles, "Short Autobiography," in *World Authors,* John Wakeman, ed. (New York: The H. W. Wilson Co., 1975), p. 486.

9. Fowles, "Hardy and the Hag," p. 28.

10. Ibid., p. 30.

11. Ibid., p. 31.

12. Ibid., p. 33.

13. James R. Baker, "An Interview with John Fowles," *Michigan Quarterly Review* 25 no. 4 (1986), pp. 670–1. In a letter to me of 29 December 1977, Fowles commented "Those of us who understand the Loss-Repair mechanism begin secretly to enjoy it and most certainly *don't* want to be cured of it."

14. Lorna Sage, "Profile: John Fowles," *The New Review,* 1 no. 7 (October 1974), p. 33.

15. Ibid., p. 35.

16. Ibid., p. 37.

17. Richard Boston, "John Fowles, Alone But Not Lonely," *New York Times Book Review,* 9 November 1969, p. 2.

18. Raman K. Singh, "An Encounter with John Fowles," *Journal of Modern Literature* 8 no. 2 (1980), pp. 189–90. Speaking about free will and conditioning, Fowles observes "that ninety percent of human life is conditioned," adding, "All my novels are about how you achieve that possible—possibly nonexistent—freedom. The problem of seeing yourself" p. 185.

19. Sarah Benton, "Adam and Eve," *New Socialist* 11, (May/June), 1983, p. 18. Fowles adds that masculinity is an "appalling crust" that filters everything men hear and see. It is especially rigid for those who went through public school and military service. "The crude things in men should be educated out of them and jettisoned," but he is not optimistic that this will happen.

20. James Campbell, "An Interview with John Fowles," *Contemporary Litera-*

ture, XVII no. 4, (1976), p. 457. Presumably *The Collector* arose in one of the fantasies between sleeping and waking of which Fowles speaks.

21. Richard Boston, "John Fowles, Alone but Not Lonely," p. 52. See also Fowles's "The Blinded Eye": "First of all I was a collector. One of the reasons I wrote—and named—my novel *The Collector* was to express my hatred of this lethal perversion." Richard Mabey, ed., *Second Nature* (London: Jonathan Cape, 1984), p. 78.

22. Singh, "Encounter with John Fowles," p. 191.

23. John Fowles, *The Collector* (New York: Dell, 1963), p. 11. Further page references to the novels are given in the text. The novel's old French epigraph may be translated: "Except for them, nobody at all knew anything"—alluding to the deep privacy of male fantasy and there being no way out of captivity for Ferdinand and Miranda, islanded by their pain. By contrast, their prototypes in Shakespeare's *The Tempest,* may engender a healthier social order than the one which caused them to be marooned on Prospero's island.

24. Sadistic fantasy prevails in *The Collector.* Table 1 shows the most frequently found fantasy words: recurring images conveying authorial emotion as a function of group fantasy.

Table 1
Analysis of Fantasy Language in *The Collector*

	Times Word Mentioned	Percentage of Emotive Words/Phases
Die	97	16.9
Hate	93	16.2
Nice	84	14.7
Shocked	56	9.8
Beautiful	48	8.4
Kill	46	8.0
Silly	44	7.7
Nasty	39	6.8
Sick	35	6.1
Frightened	31	5.4
Total	573	100

25. John Fowles, *The Magus: A Revised Version* (New York: Laurel/Dell, 1978), p. 33. Alison's boyishness hints at bisexuality. On the Greek island Nicholas confesses "I had Gide-like moments, but they were not reciprocated. . . . Besides, I wasn't queer; I simply understood . . . how being queer might have its consolations" (p. 59).

26. Sage, "Profile of John Fowles," p. 33.

27. North, "Interview with John Fowles," p. 8.

28. "Many years ago I did read most of Jung," Fowles told James R. Baker in "An Interview with John Fowles," p. 673.

29. For eroticized mystical religion's being more ejaculatory than spiritual see

The Magus, pp. 244f. In "Why I Rewrote *The Magus*" Fowles observes: "I now know the generation whose mind it most attracts and that it must always substantially remain a novel of adolescence written by a retarded adolescent. My only plea is that all artists should range the full extent of their lives freely. The rest of the world can censor and bury their (sic) private past. We cannot, and so have to remain pretty green till the day we die—callow green in the hope of becoming fertile-green." Ellen Pifer, ed., *Critical Essays on John Fowles* (Boston: G. K. Hall, 1986), pp. 99.

Analysis of fantasy language in *The Magus* reveals a preoccupation with love and death, evidence of ambivalence toward sexuality and permancy in love relations. In the following table a sampling of emotive language is presented. Because of the considerable length of this novel, key passages in pivotal chapters only have been examined. These passages encompass the introductory five chapters, the meeting of Conchis, his story, the meeting of Lily, the hypnosis of Nicholas, seeing Alison, the German incident, Conchis's story continued, the trial, the affair of Lily de Seitas, and the conclusion. The analyzed passages cover 248 of a total of 668 pages or 37 percent of the whole text.

Table 2
Analysis of Fantasy Language of Selected Passages in *The Magus*

	Times Word Mentioned	Percentage of Emotive Words/Phrases
Love	64	21.3
Die	50	16.7
Kill	29	9.7
Shock	25	8.3
Hate	22	7.3
Pretty	21	7.0
Angry	21	7.0
Nice	18	6.0
Mad	18	6.0
Beautiful	16	5.3
Ashamed	16	5.3
Total	300	100

30. John Fowles, *Daniel Martin* (Toronto: Collins/Totem, 1977/8), p. 9. Freudian language of Oedipal splitting, ambivalence, and guilt pervades the novel.

31. Baker, "An Interview with John Fowles," p. 672. Earlier Fowles had told Mel Gussow that Daniel "was never concieved of as me," yet admitting "I don't think I'm hiding so much in this book. . . . In a way, it's a penance," "Talk with John Fowles," *New York Times Book Review,* 13 November 1977, pp. 84, 3.

32. Dan's sexual discontent is further analyzed in terms of preferring pleasurably compulsive conquests of women to homosexuality. He puzzles over the failure of Freudian psychology to explain why, as a boy who had lost his mother, he should need a succession of women as mirrors "before which he could make

himself naked." Dan's chronic sexual frustration and guilt are not attributed to possible Jocasta Mothering by Aunt Millie (pp. 253–54).

33. Dan's first love was Nancy Reed, a kind of victim; female loss through death, beginning with Dan's mother and reinforced by the dead woman floating in the reeds, acquires a sinister power in this novel. Jenny says of Dan "He has a mistress. Her name is Loss," and she fantasies a "strangler caressing a girl's neck and quietly weeping because he's going to kill her in a few minutes." She resists becoming another female sacrifice, "a vase and ashes on someone's mantelpiece" (p. 249).

34. John Fowles, *Mantissa* (Toronto: Collins, 1982), p. 85. An emotive word analysis is shown in the table that follows.

Table 3
Analysis of Emotive Language in *Mantissa*

	Times Word Mentioned	Percentage of Emotive Words/Phases
Anger	17	31.0
Shock	11	20.0
Horror	7	12.7
Violently	7	12.7
Disgusting	7	12.7
Embarrassment	6	11.0
Total	55	100

Other emotive words that occur less frequently are: obscure, desperate, lovely, kill, wicked, absurd, and despair. They each occur five times in the text, that is, at a frequency of approximately 11 percent.

35. Singh, "An Encounter with John Fowles," pp. 199–200. Fowles's idea of creative writing as regressive questing for lost wholeness is in keeping with radical therapies then current such as R. D. Laing's inner voyaging as "a natural way of healing our own appalling state of alienation called normality." *The Politics of Experience* (London: Penguin, 1967), p. 136. Fowles's retrieval of conflicted feelings about obsessive sexuality is therapeutic and adaptive for an entire psychoclass, as he had sensed.

36. Letter to me of 16 March 1982.

37. Heinz Kohut, *The Restoration of the Self*, pp. 243. Creative struggle against depressive Oedipal guilt holds Fowles's protagonists at the level of "Guilty Man," escaping the fragmented selves of "Tragic Man."

38. Bruce Woodcock, *Male Mythologies: John Fowles and Masculinity* (Sussex: Harvester, 1984). "Fowles recognized from the beginning that the crucial issue was male power and control—the power of men over women, and the control of patriarchal social forms over the identities of both. What Fowles presents and analyses through the male characters in his novels is the social legacy of patriarchal ideology and power as lived by the individual man" p. 8. But Fowles shows much more than this; in abuse of power by obsessional males he shows definable

gender effects. His communication to society concerns a broad subset, or psychoclass of males whose gender is precarious for the reasons advanced.

39. Fowles's view of nature is measured and sobering: "Nature was not born for death but to remind us of the continuity of life. It is a kind of brake, a sanctuary, a system of landmarks in time; a check on our craze for meaningless 'progress.'" "The Blinded Eye," *Second Nature*, p. 85.

40. John Fowles, "Glacier Men" in John Hoyland, ed., *Fathers and Sons* (London: Serpent's Tail, 1992), pp. 45–46.

41. Fowles, *Mantissa*, p. 187.

42. Fowles, *Daniel Martin*, p. 600.

43. Ibid., p. 562.

Chapter 6. Eros and Death in John Updike's Fiction

1. John Updike, *Self-Consciousness: Memoirs* (New York: Alfred A. Knopf, 1989), p. 135. From age six Updike was an habitué of the movies, whose sexual message "got through, to us adolescents out there, and eroticization of America is (in large part) a cinematic achievement." "On One's Own Oeuvre," *Hugging the Shore: Essays in Criticism* (New York: Knopf, 1983), p. 843. There is little doubt of the eroticizing of American society and culture; as Annette Lawson writes in *Adultery: An Analysis of Love and Betrayal*, "whereas almost no couples in this study sample marrying before 1960 discussed the possibility of extra-marital sexual relationships or their feelings about fidelity before they married, few did *not* do so if they married in or after 1970." For Lawson, the sexual revolution is a "talking revolution" in which partners discuss their needs and desires as never before (New York: Basic Books, 1988), p. 29.

2. Ibid., p. 229. That Updike has long been a serious religious seeker, reading many of the leading Christian thinkers of our time, appears in *Self-Consciousness*, pp. 98, 230. He speaks of a youthful passion for the visual arts not so much as a new secular religion "as a way of hanging on to my old one." (*Just Looking: Essays on Art.* New York: Knopf, 1989, p. 15.)

3. John Updike, "More Love in the Western World," *The New Yorker*, 24 August 1963, pp. 102, 103. It is interesting to find Updike giving thought to Don Juan's promiscuity as a principle expression of Western love: "As with a possessed artist, Don Juan is as much to be pitied as envied. It is his heroic fate to project into the treacherous realm of the actual the fantasies that most of us suffer in safety" (p. 103). This could be Piet Hanema, antihero of *Couples*.

4. Paul Streitz, "Art and Psychohistory," *Journal of Psychohistory* 10 no. 2 (Fall), 1982, p. 253. See Lloyd deMause, "Psychogenic Theory of History," *Foundations of Psychohistory* (New York: Creative Roots, 1982), p. 139.

5. Ibid., p. 254. There could, of course, be other nominees as leaders of Updike's psychoclass, Philip Roth author of *Portnoy's Complaint*, for instance. An interviewer elicited the following remark from Updike on Roth: "Well, we were born about the same time—he was born in Pennsylvania, not two hours' drive away. We were both cherished sons of nuclear families. . . . We both tried to first express that super-heated family experience we were born into." Robert Boyers *et al.*, "An Evening with John Updike," *Salmagundi* 57 (1982), p. 54.

6. In *Self-Consciousness* Updike takes a wry look at, but does not disown, the author of *Couples* as "a stag of sorts in our herd of housewife-does, flirtatious, malicious, greedy for my quota of life's pleasures, a distracted, mediocre father and worse husband" (p. 222).

7. David Updike, *Out of the Marsh* (New York: New American Library, 1988), p. 29. In "On One's Own Oeuvre," John Updike comments: "Both my parents were very encouraging by nature, and as an only child I reaped all the encouragement they had to give. . . . My mother was mentor number one in the matter of art, my father in the matter of life and reality." *Hugging the Shore: Essays in Criticism*, p. 840.

8. Updike, *Self-Consciousness*, pp. 208–9.

9. Ibid., p. 252.

10. John Updike, *Midpoint and Other Poems* (New York: Knopf, 1969), pp. 8–9. After the publishing success of *Couples*, Updike was surprised how little his readers were interested in *Midpoint*, "a long poem, all about myself," which "fell quietly into the void." "Why Rabbit Had to Go," *New York Times Book Review*, 5 August 1990, p. 24.

11. Ibid., p. 26. In "A Sandstone Farmhouse" Updike writes of his fictional hero Joey, "He knew he and his mother were regarded as having been unusually, perhaps unnaturally close; when in fact between themselves the fear was that they were not close enough." (*The New Yorker*, 11 June 1990, pp. 44–45.)

12. Updike, *Self-Consciousness*, p. 42.

13. *Midpoint*, pp. 26–27.

14. Ibid., pp. 27–28. Actual incest seems hardly a likelihood, judging by Joey's feelings about his mother in "A Sandstone Farmhouse"; although he felt her sexuality, he shunned it, avoiding her disappointment in marriage and outburst of anger (see p. 47).

15. Updike, *Self-Consciousness*, p. 75. Reflecting on the power of mothering, Updike comments: "Such a powerful personage must shoulder, like God, a lot of blame," adding that "Few things are harder, in this era so preoccupied with the monitoring of human relations, than to get to know one's mother as a person—to forgive her, in effect, for being one's mother." Updike writes movingly that at last in her old age he had learned to see his mother's best qualities which for decades were "muffled for me behind the giant mask of motherhood" ("Mother," *Odd Jobs* [New York: Knopf, 1991, pp. 67–69]).

16. Ibid., p. 28. In "Mother" Updike reminisces that one of his strongest early memories is of his mother "colouring at the same page of a coloring book," encouraging the creativity which in later life would enable him to deal with her influence in earliest childhood.

17. John Updike, *Just Looking: Essays on Art* (New York: Knopf, 1989), pp. 3–4. See also p. 94 for discussion of Claude Monet's "La Japonaise" in which a demonic male in the fabric of her dress appears to twist around the female figure—a visual trick Updike admires.

18. Ibid., p. 15.

19. Updike, *Self-Consciousness*, p. 151. For the changing status of fatherhood see, for example, Henry B. Biller, "Fatherhood: Implication for Child and Adult Development," *Handbook of Developmental Psychology*, (Englewood Cliffs, N.J.: Prentice Hall, 1982).

20. Ibid., p. 84. Updike was surprised as a child to discover that his mother had "an entire rival world," that of the writer which perhaps did not include him (p. 105). Later he remarks on often feeling "irate and frantic" as a child, "and have fought all my sensations of being smothered and confined, misunderstood and put-upon" (p. 256).

21. John Updike, *Of the Farm* (New York: Knopf, 1965), pp. 40, 134.

22. Ibid., p. 43.

23. Ibid., p. 107.

24. Ibid., p. 36. Discussing his story "The Happiest I've Been," a reworking of his own teen-age experiences in 1952/53, Updike shows that the writer articulates the unstated feelings of peer group, which forms part of a psychoclass. The writer finds words of "lively accuracy" for "experienced reality" to "extract hidden meanings" for a "responsive audience." "How Does the Writer Imagine?" *Odd Jobs* (New York: Knopf, 1991), pp. 135–36.

25. Ibid., p. 38.

26. "Interview with John Updike," *Paris Review* 45 (Winter 1968), p. 100. "The Female Body" (1991) brings out Updike's complex attitude to women's bodies, idealizing "a naked woman" as "the most beautiful thing [a man] will ever see," yet he also allows that men "see the female body as just a body, very much like their own." A nude woman is further qualified "as a kind of man, only smaller, lighter-framed, without a beard, but matching men tuft for tuft otherwise, and with bumps, soft swellings, unmale emphases stiffened with fat, softly swaying by gravity . . . a heap of wheat set about with lilies . . . those catenary curves, that curious, considerate absence . . . the moment of lucid vision vanishes." The assimilation of femaleness to a male standard is a provocative feature of this statement, reflecting sexual anxiety characteristic of this psychoclass. *Odd Jobs*, pp. 70–72.

27. Updike, *Self-Consciousness*, p. 123.

28. Ibid., p. 244.

29. John Romano, *Contemporary Literary Criticism*, (Detroit, Washington, D.C.: Gale Research, Inc., 1980) vol. 15, p. 545.

30. Updike, *Self-Consciousness*, p. 45. For body imagery in creativity see William G. Niederland, "Psychoanalytic Approaches to Artistic Creativity," *Psychoanalytic Quarterly*, XLV no. 2 (1976), 185.

31. John Updike, "Should Wizard Hit Mommy?" *Pigeon Feathers and Other Stories* (New York: Knopf, 1962), p. 74f.

32. Updike, *Self-Consciousness*, p. 47.

33. Ibid., p. 90. See also pp. 111, 215 for fears of entrapment; see *Midpoint*, p. 40 for mothering, violence, and war.

34. Ibid., p. 91. See also the fantasy of the sinking ship, p. 51.

35. Ibid., p. 93.

36. Ibid., pp. 98–99. See *Couples*, pp. 35–36 for imagery of walls closing in.

37. John Updike, *Too Far to Go: The Maples Stories* (New York: Fawcett Crest, 1979), p. 235.

38. Ibid., p. 253.

39. Ibid., p. 228.

40. John Halpern, "Mr. Updike's Birthday," *Observer*, 25 March 1979, Sunday Plus section. On completing *Sons and Lovers*, D. H. Lawrence remarked: "one sheds one's sickness in books, repeats and presents again one's emotions to be master of them" (Letters, II, p. 90).

41. John Updike, "Why Rabbit Had to Go," *New York Times Book Review*, 5 August 1990, p. 24.

42. Peter Gardella, *Innocent Ecstasy: How Christianity Gave America an Ethic of Sexual Pleasure* (New York: Oxford University Press, 1985), p. 3f. See also Lawrence Lipton, *The Erotic Revolution* (Los Angeles: Sherbourne Press, 1965), chapter 11.

43. Lewis Nichols, "Talk with John Updike," *New York Times Book Review*, 7

April 1968, 34. See *Couples*, p. 59 for Freddy Thorne's pornographic book collection.

44. John Updike, *Couples*, (New York: Fawcett Press, 1968), p. 462. Further page references to the novel are given in the text. See Charles Thomas Samuels, "John Updike: The Art of Fiction," *Paris Review*, 45 (Winter 1968) for Updike's statement: "when the church is burned, Piet is relieved of morality, and can choose Foxy . . . can move out of the paralysis of guilt into what after all is a kind of freedom. He divorces the supernatural to marry the natural" p. 101.

45. *Playboy*, January 1979, p. 81. See *Self-Consciousness*, p. 227 for love as an "invented" religion; for eroticism as a "humanizing" force see *Couples*, pp. 158, 178.

Protestant in upbringing, and later agnostic, Hugh Hefner became "one of the high priests of sex in this country," writes Frank Brady (p. 18). Hefner's intensely active sex life revolved around his famous Gatsbyesque parties, where heterosexual escapades were obligatory. It has been suggested that Hefner has made love to more beautiful women than any other man in history.

Born in 1926, Hefner was a child of the Depression. His upper middle-class family had much the same parental imbalance as is characteristic of the families of the writers under study. His father had to work long hours, leaving his mother in charge of the children:

> "I hardly ever saw my father as I was growing up," stated Hefner, and when his family did get together, Grace [his mother] was invariably the discussion leader. Conversation was not one of Glenn's [his father's] fortes.
>
> Most of Hugh's care, therefore, devolved to Grace, and she exerted a great influence on him in many ways. "It didn't help that my mother was the strong parent, and that I was brought up almost entirely under her supervision," he once said. As a boy, Hefner keenly felt the lack of a strong male figure with whom he could identify, but on another occasion he offered this account of his development: "The absence of the father figure inadvertently affected me in terms of my turning inward and developing my own fantasies and in many ways was responsible for the beginnings of my becoming a person and enabling me to do the things I've done."

Frank Brady, *Hefner* (New York: Ballantine, 1974) p. 23. According to Gay Talese, Hefner's religious background had been "fundamentalist Methodist" before his agnosticism, making his elevation to high priest of American sexuality the more dramatic. Gay Talese, *Thy Neighbour's Wife* (New York: Dell, 1980), p. 47.

In post-World War II film, the new priests of a sexually ambivalent psychoclass were the "rebel males": Montgomery Clift, Marlon Brando, and James Dean. As Graham McCann shows in *Rebel Males* (London: Hamish Hamilton, 1991), irregular parenting had much to do with the sullen menace and bisexual ambiguity of these stars and the roles they took. "All three were, in very profound ways, obsessed with their mothers: Clift's mother sought to enjoy success and high status vicariously through her son, and she dominated him until his premature death; Brando's mother encouraged him when he was a boy, but died an alcoholic as he was being acclaimed a star; Dean's mother died of cancer when he was only nine years of age, and the bitterness and regret over her absence never left him" (p. 2–3). They move Hefner's insistence on sexual freedom toward a violence of the self which has invaded popular imagery.

46. Ibid., p. 82.

47. John Ditsky, "Roth, Updike, and the High Expense of Spirit," *University of Windsor Review*, 5 (Fall 1969), p. 120. Updike felt himself a "kindred spirit" to Roth (see n. 5).

48. See Victor Strandberg, "Updike," *Contemporary Literary Criticism*, (Detroit, Washington, D.C.: Gale Research, Inc., 1980) vol. 13, p. 557, who sees Updike confronting a crisis of belief as did Tolstoy, Tennyson, and Hesse (see *Steppenwolf*, p. 25).

49. Foxy is no robust Whitmanesque sexualized being, an irony in the name.

50. Freddy jokes that he is homosexual, p. 388.

51. Piet forms an infantile dependency on Foxy, as her nursing him confirms; almost discovered, she becomes "A Christian slave stripped to be tortured" (p. 328). With Bea Guerin, "a nursing mammal," he becomes violent (p. 352).

Table 1
Analysis of Emotive Language in *Couples*

	Times Word Mentioned	Percentage of Emotive Words/Phases
Love	348	47.3
Death	180	24.5
Hate	63	8.6
Lovely	45	6.1
Frightened	44	6.0
Shock	29	3.9
Sadness	26	3.5
Total	735	100

These figures show a preoccupation with "love" in the novel, but "love" often meaning mere sexuality. "Death," "hate," "frightened" and "shock" make up 43 percent of the emotive words as against 53.5 percent for "love" and "lovely," revealing a surprizingly strong negative emotive undertow, while the level of depressive "sadness" from which reparative moral concern arises is very low.

52. That Piet is abusive comes out in his estranged wife Angela's comment, p. 425.

53. Robert Detweiler, "Updike's *Couples:* Eros Demythologized," in William R. Macnaughton, ed., *Critical Essays on John Updike* (Boston: G. K. Hall & Co., 1982), p. 133.

54. The old order passes; Mrs. Tarbox, last survivor of an old Ipswich clan was crushed to death—reversing the fear of women obsessive males like Piet have (pp. 34f, 41).

55. John Updike, *Rabbit Run* (New York: Fawcett Crest, 1962), p. 19. Updike was thinking about Jack Kerouac's *On the Road*, and "the price society pays for the unrestrained motion was on my mind," as he says in "On One's Own Oeuvre," *Hugging the Shore*, p. 850.

56. Ibid., p. 40. The homosexual solution to marital fatigue seldom appears in Updike's fiction; a rare instance is found in a story published in 1990, "A Sandstone Farmhouse." See p. 39.

57. John Updike, *Too Far to Go: The Maples Stories*, p. 10.

58. John Updike, *Marry Me* (New York: Fawcett Crest, 1977), p. 168.

59. John Updike, *The Witches of Eastwick* (New York: Fawcett Crest, 1984),

p. 248. Jonathan Yardley finds depiction of women in this novel "condescending," with "more than a suggestion of misogyny," in "Updike," *Contemporary Literary Criticism* , vol. 43, p. 433. Margaret Atwood sees the novel as another in the "long-running American serial called 'Blaming Mom,'" Ibid., p. 434.

60. John Updike, *A Month of Sundays* (New York: Fawcett Crest, 1975), p. 56.

61. John Updike, *Roger's Version* (New York: Fawcett Crest, 1986), p. 276.

62. Ibid., p. 277.

63. John Updike, "Why Rabbit Had To Go," *The New York Times Book Review,* 5 August 1990, p. 24.

64. John Updike, *Odd Jobs,* p. 872.

65. Ibid., p. 836.

Chapter 7. Obsession: The Driving Force of Culture

1. Patrick Carnes, *Don't Call It Love: Recovery From Sexual Addiction* (New York: Bantam, 1992), p. 148.

2. See Alvin Toffler, *Future Shock:* "Serial marriage—a pattern of successive temporary marriages—is cut to order for the Age of Transience in which all man's relationships, all his ties with the environment, shrink in duration." (Toronto: Bantam, 1971), p. 252.

In *Culture Against Man,* Jules Henry delineates the human meaning of American technological drivenness: "Urged on by drive, the American . . . may consume others by compelling them to yield to his drivenness. Values are merely ideas about good human relations, and though they do give people direction, they lack the compelling power of drives because they do not have institutional support" (New York: Vintage Books, 1965), p. 15.

3. Hermann Hesse, *Steppenwolf* (New York: Bantam, 1970), p. 24. Fiction provides many examples of overlap between Christian teaching of sexual restraint and breakaway male hypersexuality. See for instance, Paul Theroux, *My Secret History* (New York: Ivy Books, 1989).

4. Sigmund Freud, *Collected Papers,* vol. 2, (London: Hogarth, 1924), p. 81.

5. Ian Suttie, *The Origins of Love and Hate* (London: Pelican, 1960). Suttie was one of the earliest analytical writers to counteract Freud's "over-insistence upon the aggressive, selfish, and sensual aspects of *sexuality itself*" (p. 193).

6. Jessica Benjamin, *The Bonds of Love: Psychoanalysis, Feminism and the Problem of Domination* (New York: Pantheon, 1988), p. 171.

7. Cultural studies are beginning to recognize the psychogenic factors in the creativity of obsessional males. Bruce Bawer's *The Middle Generation. The Lives and Poetry of Delmore Schwartz, Randall Jarrell, John Berryman and Robert Lowell* contains the following statement: "Estrangement, insecurity, resentment, guilt. The parallels scar the early years of all four poets. All came from unstable environments; all, by one means or another, were separated from the father and out of the stress of abandonment grew a sense of unpardonable loss, the crippling absence seeming like an ineffable injustice; then arose the hate, and, in each of them, the illogical, disabling guilt only a child's pain can produce. In each of them, the problem of the absent father was compounded by the omnipresent mother" (Hamden, Ct.: The Shoe String Press, 1986), p. 16.

In *Gestures of Healing: Anxiety and the Modern Novel,* John J. Clayton studies the fiction of Henry James, Joseph Conrad, Ford Madox Ford, E. M. Forster, James Joyce, Virginia Woolf, D. H. Lawrence, F. Scott Fitzgerald, Ernest Hemingway, and William Faulkner. Clayton comments: "Each of the male writers has, in disguised or overt form, a painfully enlarged, distorted, grotesque image of woman. It is, of course, a *cultural* sickness, this picture of half the human race. But it seems even more intense in these writers than in the larger culture. I believe that the terror and hatred come from childhoods in which the father was not there to provide a foundation of strength for the self. [These fathers] provided no alternative to the desire to be re-engulfed by the mother. The mother became both intensely desired and intensely feared." Especially in the lives of Hemingway, Lawrence, and Forster, Clayton finds a desire to return to the mother's dark interior, "associated with the peace of death" (Amhurst: University of Massachusetts Press, 1991), pp. 86–87.

In *Rebel Males: Clift, Brando and Dean* (London: Hamish Hamilton, 1991) Graham McCann studies the film icons of a post-World War II rebel psychoclass: "All three were, in very profound ways, obsessed with their mothers" (p. 2). "They all felt themselves to be bisexual and therefore well suited to roles which expressed an erotic quality bereft of rigid gender identity" (p. 3). "They were fascinating neurotics, exuding a primeval sexuality" (p. 6). These film stars' eroticized menace, destructiveness and self-destructiveness caught the imagination of a far wider public than that which reads novels. James Dean's *Rebel Without a Cause* spoke to multitudes in the early 1950s—appealing "romantically to the 'hurt' children of post-war upheaval" (p. 26).

8. John Bowlby, *A Secure Base: Clinical Applications of Attachment Theory* (London: Routledge, 1988), p. 132.

The British psychotherapist Jeremy Holmes writes of "almost an epidemic of young psychotic men passing through our [psychiatric] unit. A common theme seems to be the pressure to achieve sexual maturity (at an emotional level rather than a physical level) and their failure to do so, with breakdowns in which fear of inadequacy, homosexual panic, a regressive demandingness and at times violence towards their mothers are prominent. Often brought up with weak or absent fathers, this constellation cannot be understood in classic Oedipal terms, but seems based on an infantile fear of the overwhelming power of the mother, reactivated in young adulthood when faced with the possibility of a real relationship with a woman and the lack of identification with a potent father" *Between Art and Science* (London: Tavistock/Routledge, 1993, p. 208).

Bibliography

General Sources

H. G. Wells

Wells, H. G. *Ann Veronica*. London: Virago, 1980.

———. *Experiment in Autobiography: Discoveries and Conclusions of a Very Ordinary Brain*. London: Victor Gollancz, 1966.

———. *H. G. Wells in Love: Postscript to an Experiment in Autobiography*. Edited by G. P. Wells. London: Faber, 1984

———. *The History of Mr. Polly (1910)*. Edited by Gordon N. Ray. Boston: Houghton Mifflin Co., 1960.

———. *In the Days of the Comet*. New York: Airmont, 1966.

———. Introduction to *The Book of Catherine Wells (1928)*. London: Chatto and Windus, 1928.

———. *The New Machiavelli*. Penguin Books, 1985.

Hermann Hesse

Hesse, Hermann. *Autobiographical Writings*. New York: Farrar, Straus and Giroux, 1972.

———. *Crisis, Pages from a Diary*. Translated by Ralph Manheim. New York: Farrar, Straus and Giroux, 1975.

———. *Demian*. London: Panther, 1969.

———. *Magister Ludi. The Glass Bead Game (1943)*. New York: Bantam, 1970.

———. *Klingsor's Last Summer*. New York: Harper and Row, 1971.

———. *My Belief*. London: Triad/Panther, 1978.

———. *Narcissus and Goldmund (1930)*. London: Penguin, 1971.

———. *Siddhartha*. New York: New Directions, 1951.

———. *Steppenwolf*. New York: Bantam, 1970.

Vladimir Nabokov

Nabokov, Vladimir. *Ada or Ardor: A Family Chronicle*. New York: Vintage, 1990.

———. *Lectures on Literature*. Edited by Fredson Bowers. New York: Harcourt Brace Jovanovich/ Bruccoli Clark, 1981.

———. *Laughter in the Dark*. Indianapolis: Bobbs-Merrill, 1938.

———. *Lolita*. New York: Berkeley Medallion Books, 1966.

———. *Look at the Harlequins!* New York: McGraw-Hill, 1974.

————. *Speak, Memory: An Autobiography Revisited.* New York: Wideview/Perigree Books, 1966.

————. *The Enchanter.* Translated by Dmitri Nabokov. New York: G. P. Putnam's Sons, 1986.

John Fowles

Fowles, John. *Daniel Martin.* Toronto: Collins/Totem, 1977/8.

————. "Glacier Men." In *Fathers and Sons,* Edited by John Hoyland. London: Serpent's Tail, 1992.

————. "Hardy and the Hag." In *Thomas Hardy After Fifty Years,* edited by Lance St. John Butler. London: Macmillan, 1977.

————. *Islands.* Boston: Little, Brown, 1978.

————. *Mantissa.* Toronto: Collins, 1982.

————. "Short Autobiography." In *World Authors,* edited by John Wakeman. New York: The H. W. Wilson Co., 1975.

————. *The Collector,* New York: Dell, 1963.

————. *The Magus: A Revised Version.* New York: Laurel/Dell, 1978.

————. "Why I Rewrote *The Magus.*" In *Critical Essays on John Fowles,* edited by Ellen Pifer. Boston: G. K. Hall, 1986.

John Updike

Updike, John Updike. *A Month of Sundays.* New York: Fawcett Crest, 1975.

————. "A Sandstone Farmhouse," *The New Yorker,* 11 June 1990, 44.

————. *Couples.* New York: Fawcett Press, 1968.

————. *Just Looking: Essays on Art.* New York: Knopf, 1989.

————. *Marry Me.* New York: Fawcett Crest, 1977.

————. *Midpoint and Other Poems.* New York: Knopf, 1969.

————. "More Love in the Western World," *The New Yorker,* 24 August 1963, 102.

————. *Odd Jobs.* New York: Knopf, 1991.

————. "On One's Own Oeuvre." In *Hugging the Shore: Essays in Criticism.* New York: Knopf, 1983.

————. *Of the Farm.* New York: Knopf, 1965.

————. *Pigeon Feathers and Other Stories.* New York: Knopf, 1962.

————. *Rabbit Run.* New York: Fawcett Crest, 1962.

————. *Roger's Version.* New York: Fawcett Crest, 1986.

————. *Self-Consciousness: Memoirs.* New York: Alfred A. Knopf, 1989.

————. *The Witches of Eastwick.* New York: Fawcett Crest, 1984.

————. *Too Far to Go: The Maples Stories.* New York: Fawcett Crest, 1979.

————. "Why Rabbit Had to Go," *New York Times Book Review,* 5 August 1990, 24.

Books

Introduction

Adams, Paul L. *Obsessive Children.* New York: Penguin, 1975.

Beech, H. R. and S. Perigault. "Towards a Theory of Obsessional Disorders." In *Obsessional States,* edited by H. R. Beech. London: Methuen, 1974.

Bowlby, John. *A Secure Base: Clinical Applications of Attachment Theory.* London: Routledge, 1988.

Burton, Robert. *The Anatomy of Melancholy.* Edited by Holbrook Jackson. London: J. M. Dent, 1961.

Bieber, Irving, *et al. Homosexuality: A Psychoanalytic Study of Male Homosexuals.* New York: Basic Books, 1962.

Carpenter, Edward. *Love's Coming of Age (1896).* London: Methuen and Co., 1962.

Carpineto, Jane F. *The Don Juan Dilemma.* New York: William Morrow, 1989.

Carroll, John. *Guilt: The Grey Eminence Behind Character, History, and Culture.* London: Routledge and Kegan Paul, 1985.

de Mause, Lloyd. *Foundations of Psychohistory.* New York: Creative Roots, 1982.

Diagnostic and Statistical Manual of Mental Disorders (DSM-III-R). Washington D.C.: American Psychiatric Association, 1987.

Dinnerstein, Dorothy. *The Mermaid and The Minotaur: Sexual Arrangements and Human Malaise.* New York: Harper and Row, 1977.

Donleavy, J. P. *The Ginger Man.* London: Penguin, 1955.

Donne, John. *Songs and Sonnets (1633).* In *The Complete English Poems,* edited by A. J. Smith. London: Penguin, 1971.

Ellenberger, Henri. *The Discovery of the Unconscious.* London: Allen Lane, Penguin Press, 1970.

Freud, Anna. *The Ego and the Mechanisms of Defence.* London: Hogarth, 1937.

Freud, Sigmund. *Standard Edition* [S.E]. translated and edited by James Strachey. London: Hogarth, 1953f.

Friedman, Richard C. *Male Homosexuality: A Contemporary Psychoanalytic Perspective.* New Haven: Yale University Press, 1988.

Gay, Peter. *Freud: A Life for Our Times.* New York: Doubleday, 1989.

Goodwin, Frederick K. and Kay Redfield Jamison. *Manic-Depressive Illness.* New York: Oxford University Press, 1990.

Horney, Karen. *Feminine Psychology.* New York: W. W. Norton, 1973.

Holbrook, David. *Where D. H. Lawrence Was Wrong about Woman.* Lewisburg, Pa.: Bucknell University Press; London and Toronto: Associated University Presses, 1992.

Kaplan, Harold I. and Benjamin J. Sadock. *Synopsis of Psychiatry.* Baltimore: Williams and Williams, 1988.

Jamison, Kay Redfield. *Touched With Fire: Manic-Depressive Illness and the Artistic Temperament.* New York: Free Press, 1993.

Jones, Ernest. *Hamlet and Oedipus.* New York: Doubleday Anchor, 1949.

Jung, C. G. *The Portable Jung.* Edited by Joseph Campbell. New York: Penguin, 1971.

Kundera, Milan. *The Unbearable Lightness of Being.* New York: Harper and Row, 1985.

Kohut, Heinz. *The Restoration of the Self.* New York: International Universities Press, 1977.

Laplanche, J., and J.-B. Pontalis. *The Language of Psychoanalysis.* New York: W. W. Norton, 1974.

Laughlin, Henry P. *The Neuroses.* Washington: Butterworth, 1967.

Lawrence, D.H. *Fantasia of the Unconscious* and *Psychoanalysis and the Unconscious.* London: Penguin, 1971.

Legman, G. *Love and Death: A Study on Censorship.* New York: Breaking Point, 1949.

Runyan, William McKinley. *Life Histories and Psychobiography: Explorations in Theory and Method.* (New York: Oxford University Press, 1984.

Miller, Alice. *Drama of the Gifted Child.* New York: Basic Books, 1981.

———. *Thou Shalt Not Be Aware: Society's Betrayal of the Child.* New York: Meridian, 1984.

Nagera, Humberto. *Obsessional Neuroses: Developmental Psychopathology,* New York: Jason Aronson, 1976.

Olivier, Christiane. *Jocasta's Children.* London: Routledge, 1989.

Rank, Otto. *The Don Juan Legend,* edited by David G. Winter. Princeton: Princeton University Press, 1975.

Rappoport, Judith L., M.D. *The Boy Who Couldn't Stop Washing: The Experience and Treatment of Obsessive-Compulsive Disorder.* New York: E. P. Dutton, 1989.

Russell, Bertrand. *Marriage and Morals.* London: Allen and Unwin, 1929.

Shaw, George Bernard. *Man and Superman.* London: Penguin, 1951.

Slater, Philip E. *The Glory of Hera: Greek Mythology and the Greek Family.* Boston: Beacon Press, 1968.

Stern, Karl. *The Flight from Women.* New York: Noonday, 1965.

Stoller, Robert J. *Perversion, the Erotic Form of Hatred.* New York: Pantheon, 1975.

Storr, Anthony. *The Dynamics of Creation.* London: Secker and Warburg, 1972.

Straus, Erwin W. *On Obsession: A Clinical and Methodological Study.* New York: Nervous and Mental Disease Monographs, 1948.

Swigart, Jane. *The Myth of the Bad Mother: The Emotional Realities of Mothering.* New York: Doubleday, 1991.

Trachtenberg, Peter. *The Casanova Complex: Compulsive Lovers and their Women.* New York: Poseidon, 1988.

von Franz, Marie-Louise. *Puer Aeternus.* Sigo Press, 1981.

Wegner, Daniel M. *White Bears and Other Unwanted Thoughts: Suppression, Obsession, and the Psychology of Mental Control.* New York: Penguin, 1989.

Weil, John Leopold. *Instinctual Stimulation of Children: From Common Practice to Child Abuse.* 2 vols. Madison, Ct.: International Universities Press, 1989.

Welldon, Estela V. *Mother, Madonna, Whore: The Idealization and Denigration of Motherhood.* London: Free Association, 1988.

Winter, David G. *The Power Motive.* New York: The Free Press, 1973.

H. G. Wells

Brome, Vincent. *H. G. Wells: A Biography.* London: Longmans, Green, 1951.

Dickson, Lovat. *H. G. Wells: His Turbulent Life and Times.* Toronto: Macmillan, 1969.

Freud, Sigmund. *The Interpretation of Dreams (1990). SE.,* V.

———. *Three Essays on the Theory of Sexuality (1905). S.E.,* VII.

Hammond, J. R. *An H. G. Wells Companion.* New York: Barnes and Noble, 1979.

Huxley, Juliette. *Leaves of the Tulip Tree* London: John Murray, 1986.

Kemp, Peter. *H. G. Wells and the Culminating Ape: Biological Themes and Imaginative Obsessions.* London: Macmillan, 1982.

Lawrence, D. H. *Sons and Lovers.* London: Penguin, 1961.

———. *Lady Chatterley's Lover.* New York: Grove Press, 1957.

MacKenzie, Norman and Jeanne. *The Time Traveller: The Life of H. G. Wells.* London: Weidenfeld and Nicolson, 1973.

Reik, Theodor. *The Compulsion to Confess: On the Psychoanalysis of Crime and Punishment.* New York: Farrar, Straus and Cudahy, 1959.

Smith, David C. *H. G. Wells: Desperately Mortal.* New Haven: Yale University Press, 1986.

St. Augustine. *The Confessions.* Translated by E. B. Pusey. London: Dent, 1957.

West, Anthony. *H. G. Wells: Aspects of a Life.* London: Hutchinson, 1984.

Hermann Hesse

Bachofen, Johann Jacob. *Myth, Religion, and Mother Right: Selected Writings.* Princeton: Princeton University Press, 1973.

Dijkstra, Bram. *Idols of Perversity: Fantasies of Feminine Evil in Fin-de-Siècle Culture.* New York: Oxford University Press, 1986.

Freedman, Ralph. *Hermann Hesse: Pilgrim of Crisis.* New York: Pantheon, 1978.

Green, Martin. *Mountain of Truth: The Counter Culture Begins, Ascona, 1900–1920.* Hanover and London: University Press of New England for Tufts University, 1986.

Hemingway, Ernest. *The Garden of Eden.* New York: Charles Scribner's Sons, 1986.

Hood, Thomas. *The Poetical Works.* London: Henry Frowde, n.d.

Jung, C. G. *Symbols of Transformation (1912/1952).* 2 vols. New York: Harper and Brothers, 1962.

Langevin, Ron. *Sexual Strands: Understanding and Treating Sexual Anomalies in Men.* Hillside, N.J.: Lawrence Erlbaum Associates, 1983.

Lawrence, D. H. *Women in Love (1920).* New York: Viking, 1960.

Leiris, Michel. *Manhood: A Journey From Childhood into the Fierce Order of Virility.* Translated by Richard Howard. San Francisco: North Point Press, 1984.

Mann, Thomas. *Death in Venice (1925).* New York: Bantam, 1971.

Michels, Volker. *Hermann Hesse: A Pictorial Biography.* New York: Farrar, Straus and Giroux, 1971.

Milech, Joseph. *Hermann Hesse: Life and Art.* Berkeley: University of California, 1978.

Miller, Alice. *Drama of the Gifted Child.* New York: Basic Books, 1981.

Mitscherlich, Alexander. *Society without the Father.* New York: Schocken, 1970.

Neumann, Erich. *The Great Mother: An Analysis of the Archetype.* Princeton: Princeton University Press, 1955.

Remys, Edmund. *Hermann Hesse's Das Glasperlenspiel: A Concealed Defense of the Mother World.* New York: Peter Lang, 1983.

Stelzig, Eugene L. *Hermann Hesse's Fiction of the Self: Autobiography and the Confessional Imagination*. Princeton: Princeton University Press, 1988.

Thweleit, Klaus. *Male Fantasies*. Minneapolis: University of Minneapolis Press, 1987.

Vladimir Nabokov

Appel, Alfred, Jr. ed. *Vladimir Nabokov: The Annotated Lolita*. New York: McGraw Hill, 1970.

Bassien, Beth Ann. *Women and Death: Linkages in Western Thought and Literature*. Westport, Ct.: Greenwood Press, 1984.

Berman, Jeffery. *The Talking Cure: Literary Representations of Psychoanalysis*. New York: New York University Press, 1987.

Bowlby, John. *A Secure Base: Clinical Applications of Attachment Theory*. London: Routledge, 1988.

Boyd, Brian. *Vladimir Nabokov: The Russian Years*. Princeton: Princeton University Press, 1990.

———. *Vladimir Nabokov: The American Years*. Princeton: Princeton University Press, 1991.

Carroll, Lewis. *Alice's Adventures in Wonderland and Through the Looking Glass*. Toronto: Bantam, 1981.

de Rola, Stanislas Klossowski. *Balthus*. New York: Harper and Row, 1983.

Eliade, Mircea. *Patterns in Comparative Religion*. Cleveland and New York: Meridian Books, 1963.

Field, Andrew. *The Life and Art of Vladimir Nabokov*. New York: Crown Publications, 1986.

Fraser, Morris. *The Death of Narcissus*. London: Secker and Warburg, 1976.

Freud, Sigmund. *Introductory Lectures on Psycho-analysis (1916–17)*. Pt. 3, Lec. 2. "The Sexual Life of Human Beings." *S.E.*, XVI, 303.

Green, Geoffery. *Freud and Nabokov*. Lincoln: University of Nebraska Press, 1988.

Itzin, C., ed. *Pornography: Women, Violence and Civil Liberties*. Oxford University Press, 1993.

Karlinsky, Simon, ed. *The Nabokov-Wilson Letters, 1940–1971*. New York: Harper and Row, 1979.

Kiell, Norman. *Varieties of Sexual Experience: Psychosexuality in Literature*. New York: International Universities Press, 1976.

Krafft-Ebing, Richard von. *The Psychopathia Sexualis*. London: Panther, 1965.

Miller, Alice. *Banished Knowledge: Facing Childhood Injuries*. New York: Doubleday, 1990.

———. *Breaking down the Wall of Silence: The Liberating Experience of Facing Painful Truth*. New York: Dutton, 1991.

———. *The Untouched Key: Tracing Childhood Trauma in Creativity and Destructiveness*. New York: Doubleday, 1990.

Rayfield, Donald, ed. *The Confessions of Victor X*. London: Caliban, 1984.

Socarides, Charles W. M.D. *The Preoedipal Origin and Psychoanalytic Therapy of Sexual Perversions*. Madison, Ct.: International Universities Press, 1988.

Sologub, Fyodor. *The Petty Demon* (1905–7). Translated by Ronald Wilks. (London: New English Library, 1962).

Stoller, Robert J. *Perversion: The Erotic Form of Hatred.* New York: Pantheon Books, 1975.

Ward, Elizabeth. *Father Daughter Rape.* London: The Women's Press, 1984.

John Fowles

Brink, Andrew. *Loss and Symbolic Repair.* Hamilton, Ont.: Cromlech, 1977.

Kohut, Heinz. *The Restoration of the Self.* New York: International Universities Press, 1977.

Laing, R. D. *The Politics of Experience.* London: Penguin Books, 1967.

Mabey, Richard, ed. *Second Nature.* London: Jonathan Cape, 1984.

Millgate, Michael. *Thomas Hardy: A Biography.* New York: Oxford University Press, 1982.

Pifer, Ellen, ed. *Critical Essays on John Fowles.* Boston: G. K. Hall, 1986.

Woodcock, Bruce. *Male Mythologies: John Fowles and Masculinity.* Sussex, Eng.: Harvester, 1984.

John Updike

Brady, Frank. *Hefner.* New York: Ballantine, 1974.

Gardella, Peter. *Innocent Ecstasy: How Christianity Gave America an Ethic of Sexual Pleasure.* New York: Oxford University Press, 1985.

Lawson, Annette. *Adultery: An Analysis of Love and Betrayal.* New York: Basic, 1988.

Lipton, Lawrence. *The Erotic Revolution.* Los Angeles: Sherbourne, 1965.

McCann, Graham. *Rebel Males.* London: Hamish Hamilton, 1991.

Romano, John. *Contemporary Literary Criticism,* (Detroit, Washington, D.C.: Gale Research, Inc., 1980) vol. 15, p. 545.

Talese, Gay. *Thy Neighbour's Wife.* New York: Dell, 1980.

Updike, David. *Out of the Marsh.* New York: New American Library, 1988.

Conclusion

Bawer, Bruce. *The Middle Generation: The Lives and Poetry of Delmore Schwartz, Randall Jarrell, John Berryman, and Robert Lowell.* Hamden, Ct.: The Shoe String Press, 1986.

Benjamin, Jessica. *The Bonds of Love: Psychoanalysis, Feminism and the Problem of Domination.* New York: Pantheon, 1988.

Carnes, Patrick. *Don't Call It Love: Recovery From Sexual Addiction.* New York: Bantam, 1992.

Clayton, John J. *Gestures of Healing: Anxiety and the Modern Novel.* Amhurst: University of Massachusetts Press, 1991.

Henry, Jules. *Culture Against Man.* New York: Vintage Books, 1965.

Holmes, Jeremy. *Between Art and Science: Essays in Psychotherapy and Psychiatry.* London: Tavistock/Routledge, 1993.

Theroux, Paul. *My Secret History.* New York: Ivy Books, 1989.

Toffler, Alvin. *Future Shock.* Toronto: Bantam Books, 1971.

Suttie, Ian. *The Origins of Love and Hate* (1935). London: Pelican, 1960.

Journal Articles

Introduction

Besdine, Matthew. "Cradles of Violence." *The Neurosis of our Time: Acting Out* (Springfield: Charles C. Thomas, 1973).

———. "The Jocasta Complex: Mothering and Genius." Parts 1 and 2. *Psychoanalytic Review* 55, (1968): 595.

———. "The Jocasta Complex, Mothering and Woman Geniuses." *Psychoanalytic Review,* 56 (1971/72): 574.

Crittenden, Patricia M., Mary F. Partridge, and Angelika H. Claussen. "Family Patterns of Relationship in Normative and Dysfunctional Families." *Development and Psychopathology* 4 (1992): 504.

Freud, Sigmund. "Further Remarks on the Neuropsychoses of Defence." (1896b), *S.E.,* III, 174.

———. "Inhibitions, Symptoms and Anxiety." (1926), *S.E.,* XX, 77.

———. "Notes upon a Case of Obsessional Neurosis." (1909), *S.E.,* X, 153.

———. "Obsessive Actions and Religious Practices." (1907), *S.E.,* IX, 115.

Glass, Leonard L. "Man's Man/Ladies' Man." *Psychiatry* 47 (August 1984): 274.

Holbrook, David. "The Symbolism of Woman" in *Images of Women in Literature* (New York University Press, 1989).

Holden, Constance. "Creativity and the Troubled Mind." *Psychology Today* (April 1987): 9.

Jung, C. G. "Marriage as a Psychological Relationship" (1925), in J. Campbell (ed.), *The Portable Jung* (New York: Penguin, 1971), 163.

Kernberg, Otto F. "Barriers to Falling and Remaining in Love." *Journal of the American Psychoanalytic Association* 22 (1974): 486.

Masud, M., R. Khan. "Infantile Neurosis as a False Self Organization." *Dynamische Psychiatrie* I, (1968): 92

———. "The Concept of Cumulative Trauma," in *The Privacy of Self* (London: Hogarth Press, 1974).

Martindale, Colin. "Father's Absence, Psychopathology, and Poetic Eminence." *Psychological Reports* 31 (1972): 843.

Monroe, Valerie. "The Erotic Image that Un-nerves Women Most." *Self,* September 1988, 110.

Pratt, Dallis. M.D., "The Don Juan Myth." *American Imago* 17 (1960): 330.

Ross, John Munder. "Oedipus Revisited: Laius and the 'Laius Complex.'" *Psychoanalytic Study of the Child* 37 (1982): 169.

Stewart, Harold. "Jocasta's Crimes." *International Journal of Psycho-Analysis* 42 (1961): 424.

Streitz, Paul. "Art and Psychohistory." *Journal of Psychohistory* 10 no. 2 (Fall 1982): 254.

Terr, Lenore C. "Childhood Trauma and the Creative Product: A Look at the

Early Lives and Later Works of Poe, Wharton, Magritte, Hitchcock, and Bergman." *Psychoanalytic Study of the Child* 42 (1987): 545.

Wolfenstein, Martha. "The Image of the Lost Parent." *The Psychoanalytic Study of the Child* 28 (1973): 444.

H. G. Wells

Besdine, Matthew. "The Jocasta Complex, Mothering and Genius." Parts 1 and 2, *Psychoanalytic Review* 55 (1968) 259–277; 574–600.

Glass, Leonard L. "Man's Man/Ladies' Man: Motifs of Hypermasculinity." *Psychiatry* 47 (1984): 260–278.

Hermann Hesse

Hesse, Hermann. "Artist and Psychoanalyst." *Psychoanalytic Review* 50 no. 3 (1963): 9.

Fleischer, Michael Lach. "Twin Fantasies, Bisexuality and Creativity in the Works of Ernest Hemingway." *International Review of Psycho-analysis* 17 (1990): 287.

Jung, C. G. "A Letter on Hesse's Inspiration" (March 24, 1950). *Psychoanalytic Review* 50 no. 3 (1963): 15.

Rado, Sandor. "A Critical Examination of the Concept of Bisexuality." *Psychosomatic Medicine* 2 no. 4, (October 1940): 459.

Reik, Miriam. "Translator's Introduction" to Hesse's" Artist and Psychoanalyst." *Psychoanalytic Review* 50 no. 3 (1963) 5.

Vladimir Nabokov

Appel, Alfred, Jr. "An Interview with Vladimir Nabokov." *Wisconsin Studies in Contemporary Literature* 8 no. 2 (1967): 142.

———. "Lolita: The Springboard of Parody." *Wisconsin Studies in Contemporary Literature* 8 no. 2 (1967) 219.

———. "Nabokov: A Portrait." *Atlantic Monthly,* September 1971, 85.

Garnham, Nicholas. "The Strong Opinions of Vladimir Nabokov—as imparted to Nicholas Garnham." *The Listener,* 80 (10 October 1968): 463.

Herman, Judith, M.D., Diana Russell, Ph.D., and Karen Trocki, Ph.D. "Long-term Effects of Incestuous Abuse in Children." *American Journal of Psychiatry* 143 no. 10 (October 1986): 1293.

Jong, Erica. "Time has been kind to the Nymphet: Lolita 30 Years Later." *The New York Times Book Review,* 5 June 1988, 3.

Shute, J. P. "Nabokov and Freud: The Play of Power." *Modern Fiction Studies* 30 no. 4 (1984): 637.

Smith, Peter Duval. "Vladimir Nabokov on his Life and Work: A BBC television interview with Peter Duval Smith." *The Listener* 68 (22 November 1962): 857.

Brookner, Anita. "The Everlasting Now." *The Observer* 44 (20 November 1988) 44.

Robinson, Robert. "A Blush of Colour—Nabokov in Montreux." "Robert Robinson interviewed Vladimir Nabokov for 'The Book Programme' (BBC2)." *The Listener* 97 (24 March 1977): 369.

Toffler, Alvin. "Playboy Interview: Vladimir Nabokov." *Playboy,* January 1964, 37.

Wolfenstein, Martha. "The Image of the Lost Parent." *The Psychoanalytic Study of the Child* 28 (1973): 445.

John Fowles

Baker, James R. "An Interview with John Fowles." *Michigan Quarterly Review* 25 no. 4 (1986): 670.

Benton, Sarah. "Adam and Eve." *New Socialist* 11 (May/June 1983): 18.

Boston, Richard. "John Fowles, Alone But Not Lonely." *New York Times Book Review,* 9 November 1969, 2.

Campbell, James. "An Interview with John Fowles." *Contemporary Literature* XVII no. 4 (1976): 457.

Gussow, Mel. "Talk with John Fowles." *New York Times Book Review,* 13 November 1977, 83.

North, David. "Interview with Author John Fowles." *Maclean's* 80 no. 23 (14 November 1977): 4.

Rose, Gilbert J. M.D. *"The French Lieutenant's Woman:* The Unconscious Significance of a Novel to its Author." American Imago 29 no. 2 (1972): 165

Sage, Lorna. "Profile: John Fowles." *The New Review* 1 no. 7 (October 1974): 33.

Singh, Raman K. "An Encounter with John Fowles." *Journal of Modern Literature* 8 no. 2 (1980): 189.

John Updike

Biller, Henry B. "Fatherhood: Implication for Child and Adult Development." In *Handbook of Developmental Psychology.* Englewood Cliffs, N.J.: Prentice Hall, 1982.

Boyers, Robert, *et al.* "An Evening with John Updike." *Salmagundi* 57 (1982): 54.

de Mause, Lloyd. "Psychogenic Theory of History." *Foundations of Psychohistory* (New York: Creative Roots, 1991), 139.

Detweiler, Robert. "Updike's *Couples:* Eros Demythologized." In *Critical Essays on John Updike,* edited by William R. Macnaughton, 133. Boston: G.K. Hall & Co., 1982).

Ditsky, John. "Roth, Updike, and the High Expense of Spirit." *University of Windsor Review* 5 (Fall 1969): 120.

Halpern, John. "Mr. Updike's Birthday." *Observer* Sunday Plus, 25 March 1979.

Hefner, Hugh. "The Playboy Philosophy." *Playboy,* January 1979, 81.

Nichols, Lewis. "Talk with John Updike." *New York Times Book Review,* 7 April 1968, 34.

Niederland, William G. "Psychoanalytic Approaches to Artistic Creativity." *Psychoanalytic Quarterly* 45 no. 2 (1976): 185.

Samuels, Charles Thomas. "John Updike: The Art of Fiction." *Paris Review* 45 (Winter 1968): 100.

Strandberg, Victor. "Updike." *Contemporary Literary Criticism* 13: 557.

Strietz, Paul. "Art and Psychohistory." *Journal of Psychohistory* 10 no. 2 (Fall 1982): 253.

Yardley, Jonathan. "Updike." *Contemporary Literary Criticism* 43: 433.

Index

241

suffocation imagery: asthma, emphysema, 180
Suttie, Ian, 18; *The Origins of Love and Hate*, 201
Swift, Jonathan: scatological obsessions in *Gulliver's Travels*, 27
symbolic repair, 196
symbols: and disclosure of feelings, 34

taboos, 169; examples of, 15; identification of male with mother, 39
technology: anxiety, 44, 45; drivenness and, 229 n.2
The Tempest (Shakespeare): prototypes for characters in *The Collector*, 221 n.23
Terr, Lenore C: "Childhood Trauma and the Creative Product," comments on Magritte's obsessive imagery, 27
The Time Machine (Wells), 57
"The Magician" (Nabokov): little girl in, 215 n.14
The Garden of Eden (Hemingway), 197
The Great Gatsby, (Fitzgerald), 197
theory, critical. *See* literary criticism.
Three Essays on the Theory of Sexuality (Freud), 83, 121
Through the Looking Glass (Carroll): sadism in, 103–4
Toffler, Alvin: 113; *Future Shock*, 200
toilet training, 32–33
Too Far to Go: The Maples Stories (Updike), 168
Trachtenberg, Peter, 49; *The Casanova Complex: Compulsive Lovers and their Women*, 47
trauma: in artistic output of Magritte, Bergman, Hitchcock, Poe, and Wharton, 27; birth, 31; brain and obsessions, 22; childhood and creativity, 214 n.1, chronic repetitions, and, 22; cumulative, 32, 33; early and self-healing, 23; implicit in wish fulfillment, 18; sexual, mother-inflicted, 20; weaning, 125
trauma theory: Dinnerstein and, 45; mothering and, 32
Tree The (Fowles), 163
Trocki, Karen: "Long Term Effects of Incestuous Abuse in Children," 98

Unbearable Lightness of Being The, (Kundera), 31
Updike, John, 12, 30, 47; adolescence, 177–78; "Aperto E Cuiuso" (1991), death obsession of male character in, 192–93; attitudes toward psychiatry, 181; autobiography, 168; childhood, 169, 225 n.20; *The Centaur*, 170; chicken-neck imagery, 172–73; 180, 187; chronicler of social change, 166–67; cruelty to dog, 180; *Couples*, 168–69; David, son of John, 170; on de Rougemont, 170; Dutch origins of, 166; "The Fairy Godfather," 181; father of, 169; first marriage, 178; grandparents, 171; inherited psoriasis, 173; *Marry Me*, 190; *Midpoint*, 172; *A Month of Sundays*, 188; mother, 225 n.15; parenting of, 171, 174–76, 225 n.7; *Odd Jobs*, 193; *Of the Farm*, 176–77; the *Rabbit* series, 168, 189, 200; on Philip Roth, 224 n.5; *Rabbit at Rest*, 193; *Roger's Version*, 188; "A Sandstone Farmhouse," mother in, 171; *Self Consciousness*, 166–69; self-perception and confessional writing, 171; serious religious seeker, 224 n.2; *Too Far to Go: The Maples Stories*, 168; *The Witches of Eastwick*, 191
utopia, 96

violence: impulses, reality of, 213 n.34; male, and fantasy in *Lolita* (Nabokov), 132, 137–38; nihilistic, 46
visual arts: Dadaism and surrealism, 46
Vladimir Nabokov: The Russian Years (Boyd), 98–99

"At War with my Skin" (Updike): in *Self Consciousness*, 173
Ward, Elizabeth: *Father Daughter Rape*, 98
Wegner, Daniel, 22–23: thoughts on early trauma, 22
Weil, John Leopold: abuse in boys, and behavior, 46; drivenness and, 46; *Instinctual Stimulation of Children*, 45; maternal attachment and, 45
The Well-Beloved (Hardy), 144, 146